Learning PHP and MySQL

Other resources from O'Reilly

Learning PHP and MySQL

Michele E. Davis and Jon A. Phillips

O'REILLY®

Beijing · Cambridge · Farnham · Köln · Paris · Sebastopol · Taipei · Tokyo

Learning PHP and MySQL
by Michele E. Davis and Jon A. Phillips

Published by O'Reilly Media, Inc., 1005 Gravenstein Highway North, Sebastopol, CA 95472.

O'Reilly books may be purchased for educational, business, or sales promotional use. Online editions are also available for most titles (*safari.oreilly.com*). For more information, contact our corporate/institutional sales department: (800) 998-9938 or *corporate@oreilly.com*.

Editor: Simon St.Laurent	**Indexer:** Johnna Van Hoose Dinse
Production Editor: Mary Brady	**Cover Designer:** Karen Montgomery
Copyeditor: Linley Dolby	**Interior Designer:** David Futato
Proofreader: Mary Brady	**Illustrators:** Robert Romano and Jessamyn Read

Printing History:

June 2006:	First Edition.

 This book uses RepKover,™ a durable and flexible lay-flat binding.

ISBN: 0-596-10110-4

[M]

Table of Contents

Preface

PHP and MySQL are a powerful combination that together make it easy to create web applications. If you've been creating web pages but want to build more sophisticated sites that can grow and interact with users, PHP and MySQL let you build your foundations quickly, and subsequently build on them to meet your needs.

Our goal is to help you learn the ins and outs of PHP and MySQL and save you some of the "Why doesn't that work?" moments that we've already been through. We'll show you what to watch for and how to fix these issues without pulling out your hair.

Audience

This book is for people who want to know how to create dynamic web sites. That could include graphic designers who are already working in an IT firm or advertising firm creating static web sites, who may need to move forward with coding database-driven web sites. It might also include people who already know, say, Flash development and HTML markup, but need to expand their repertoire of skills to database and open source programming environments.

Assumptions This Book Makes

This book assumes you understand how web browsers work and have a basic understanding of HTML. Some understanding of JavaScript may be useful (for Chapter 15) but isn't generally required.

You might also be over-qualified. If you already know how to create pages using MySQL and PHP, then you'd probably be better off with a book that is more a reference than a Learning book, such as one from the Nutshell series.

Organization of This Book

This book starts out with an overview of how all of the pieces you'll be working with fit together. Because there are multiple languages and technologies that interact to form the dynamic web pages, it's best to start with a solid foundation of how the pieces work together. The PHP that you'll learn works as a sort of a total integration package for dynamic web sites.

Next, we'll walk through installing the core software packages on your local computer. This book focuses on PHP and MySQL, but making this work also usually requires the Apache web server. The PHP interpreter works with the web server when processing dynamic content. Finally, you'll install the MySQL database. Installation is covered on the PC, Mac, and Linux systems. You can also use a hosted ISP account to develop your pages, if you don't want to install everything locally.

Since PHP plays an important role in pulling everything together, we take the time to explain the basics of working with the PHP language. This includes language essentials such as data types, program flow logic, and variables. Functions, arrays, and forms each get their own chapter to fully explore them.

Since you may be new to databases in general, we ease into MySQL by first explaining concepts that apply to designing and using any relational database. Then we give specific examples of using MySQL to interact with your data. Once you can get data in and out of the database, you'll need to work with PHP to integrate that data into your dynamic content.

Security and access control to your web pages each get their own chapter. While security may sound like a dull subject, it's still a huge issue if you store any information that's private on your web page. There are several common security pitfalls that we'll guide you around.

Finally, we close with sample applications that demonstrate how the technologies work together to rapidly build workable, fast web sites. You'll also learn where to look for additional information on the topics covered in the book.

Supporting Books

Even if you feel you are ready for this book, you may want to explore some of the XML technologies in greater depth than is possible here. The following list offers some good places to start:

- *Run Your Own Web Server Using Linux & Apache*, by Tony Steidler-Dennison (SitePoint, 2005).
- *PHP in a Nutshell*, First Edition, by Paul Hudson (O'Reilly, 2005).
- *MySQL in a Nutshell*, First Edition, by Russell Dyer (O'Reilly, 2005).
- *CSS Cookbook*, First Edition, by Christopher Schmitt (O'Reilly, 2004).

There are also several good online resources for dynamic web development, including onlamp.com, part of the O'Reilly Network. LAMP stands for Linux, Apache, MySQL, PHP. LAMP is the de facto standard for serving dynamic web pages.

Conventions Used in This Book

The following font conventions are used in this book:

Italic
> Indicates pathnames, filenames, and program names; Internet addresses, such as domain names and URLs; and new items where they are defined

`Constant width`
> Indicates command lines and options that should be typed verbatim; names and keywords in programs, including method names, variable names, and class names; and HTML element tags

`Constant width bold`
> Indicates emphasis in program code lines

`Constant width italic`
> Indicates text that should be replaced with user-supplied values

 This icon signifies a tip, suggestion, or general note.

 This icon indicates a warning or caution.

Using Code Examples

This book is here to help you get your job done. In general, you may use the code in this book in your programs and documentation. You do not need to contact us for permission unless you're reproducing a significant portion of the code. For example, writing a program that uses several chunks of code from this book does not require permission. Selling or distributing a CD-ROM of examples from O'Reilly books *does* require permission. Answering a question by citing this book and quoting example code does not require permission. Incorporating a significant amount of example code from this book into your product's documentation *does* require permission.

We appreciate, but do not require, attribution. An attribution usually includes the title, author, publisher, and ISBN. For example: "*Learning PHP and MySQL* by Michele E. Davis and Jon A. Phillips. Copyright 2006 O'Reilly Media, Inc., 0-596-10110-4."

If you feel your use of code examples falls outside fair use or the permission given above, feel free to contact us at *permissions@oreilly.com*.

Safari® Enabled

 When you see a Safari® Enabled icon on the cover of your favorite technology book, that means the book is available online through the O'Reilly Network Safari Bookshelf.

Safari offers a solution that's better than e-books. It's a virtual library that lets you easily search thousands of top tech books, cut and paste code samples, download chapters, and find quick answers when you need the most accurate, current information. Try it for free at *http://safari.oreilly.com*.

How to Contact Us

We have tested and verified the information in this book to the best of our ability, but you may find that features have changed (or even that we have made a few mistakes!) Please let us know about any errors you find, as well as your suggestions for future editions, by writing to:

O'Reilly Media, Inc.
1005 Gravenstein Highway North
Sebastopol, CA 95472
800-998-9938 (in the U.S. or Canada)
707-829-0515 (international/local)
707-829-0104 (fax)

We have a web page for this book, where we list errata, examples, and any additional information. You can access this page at:

http://www.oreilly.com/catalog/learnphpmysql/

To comment or ask technical questions about this book, send email to:

bookquestions@oreilly.com

For more information about our books, conferences, Resource Centers, and the O'Reilly Network, see our web site at:

http://www.oreilly.com

Acknowledgments

First, we'd like to thank our wonderful agent, Matt Wagner of Fresh Books, for bringing such a fabulous opportunity to the table for us. The opportunity to write for O'Reilly Media was a great honor. As technologists, our bookcase is already well populated with animals from the Nutshell series.

Thanks to our O'Reilly developmental editors, Brett McLaughlin and Simon St. Laurent. This book wouldn't be what it is without both of their help working with us. Second, profuse thanks to our technical editors, especially Jereme Allen and Christopher Finke, whom we met through our local Minneapolis/St. Paul PHP community: *http://www.tcphp.org*. Technical edit thanks also go to our last technical editor, Patrick Krekelberg.

Dynamic Content and the Web

There are two types of web pages: static and dynamic. A static site provides hyper-linked text and perhaps a login screen, but beyond that, it doesn't require additional participation from the user. *http://www.startribune.com* is an example of a static site, except that you do have to register to view articles. *http://www.amazon.com* is an example of a dynamic web site, because your ordering data is logged, and Amazon offers recommendations based on your purchasing history when you access their page. In other words, *dynamic* means that the user interacts more with the web site, beyond just reading pages, and the web site responds accordingly.

Creating dynamic web pages—even a few years ago—meant writing a lot of code in the C or Perl languages, and then calling and executing those programs through a process called a Common Gateway Interface (CGI). Having to create executable files doesn't sound like much fun, and neither does learning a whole new complicated language. Well, thankfully, PHP and MySQL make creating dynamic web sites simpler, easier, and faster.

PHP and MySQL's Place in Web Development

PHP is a programming language designed to generate web pages interactively on the computer serving them, called a *web server*. Unlike HTML, where the web browser uses tags and markup to generate a page, PHP code runs between the requested page and the web server, adding to and changing the basic HTML output. For example, PHP code could be used to display a counter of visitors to a site.

PHP, in less than 20 lines of code, can store the IP address from which a page request comes in a separate file, and then display the number of unique IP addresses that visited a particular site. The person requesting the web page doesn't know that PHP generated the page, because the counter text is part of the standard HTML markup language that the PHP code generated.

PHP makes web development easy, because all the code you need is contained within the PHP framework. This means that there's no reason for you to reinvent the wheel each time you sit down to develop a PHP program; that would be something you'd have to do if you were using a compiled language like C.

While PHP is great for developing web functionality, it is not a database. The database of choice for PHP developers is MySQL, which acts like a filing clerk for PHP-processed user information. MySQL automates the most common tasks related to storing and retrieving specific user information based on your supplied criteria.

 Take our Amazon example; the recommendations Amazon offers you can be stored in a MySQL database, along with your prior order information.

MySQL is easily accessed from PHP, and they're commonly used together as they work well hand in hand. An added benefit is that PHP and MySQL run on various computer types and operating systems, including Mac OS X, Windows-based PCs, and Linux.

Advantages of Using PHP with MySQL

There are several factors that make using PHP and MySQL together a natural choice:

PHP and MySQL work well together
> PHP and MySQL have been developed with each other in mind, so they are easy to use together. The programming interfaces between them are logically paired up. Working together wasn't an afterthought when the developers created the PHP and MySQL interfaces.

PHP and MySQL have open source power
> As they are both open source projects, PHP and MySQL can both be used for free. MySQL client libraries are no longer bundled with PHP. Advanced users have the ability to make changes to the source code, and therefore, change the way the language and programs work.

PHP and MySQL have community support
> There are active communities on the Web in which you can participate and they'll answer your questions. You can also purchase professional support for MySQL if you need it.

PHP and MySQL are fast
> Their simplicity and efficient design enables faster processing.

PHP and MySQL don't bog you down with unnecessary details.
> You don't need to know all of the low-level details of how the PHP language interfaces with the MySQL database, as there is a standard interface for calling MySQL procedures from PHP. Online APIs at *http://www.php.net* offer an unlimited resource.

The Value of Open Source

As we mentioned above, both PHP and MySQL are open source projects, so there's no need to worry about user licenses for every computer in your office or home. In open source projects and technologies, programmers have access to the source code; this enables individual or group analysis to identify potentially problematic code, test, debug, and offer changes as well as additions to that code. For example, Unix—the forerunner in the open source software community—was freely shared with university software researchers. Linux, the free alternative to Unix, is a direct result of their efforts and the open source licensing paradigm.

As Tim O'Reilly puts it, "Open source licensing began as an attempt to preserve a culture of sharing, and only later led to an expanded awareness of the value of that sharing." Today, open source programmers share their code changes on the Web via *php.net*, listservs, and web sites. If you're caught in a coding nightmare and can't wake up, the resources mentioned above can and will help you.

 We'll arm you with open source user forums later in this book so you can check them out yourself. We'll include listservs and web sites so that you have numerous resources if you run into a snafu.

The Components of a PHP Application

In order to process and develop dynamic web pages, you'll need to use and understand several technologies. There are three main components to creating dynamic web pages: a web server, a server-side programming language, and a database. It's a good idea to have an understanding of the three basic components for web development using PHP. Start with some rudimentary understanding of the history and purpose of Apache (your web server), PHP (your server-side programming language), and MySQL (your database). This can help you understand how they fit into the web development picture.

Remember that dynamic web pages pull information from several sources simultaneously, including Apache, PHP, MySQL, and Cascading Style Sheets (CSS), which we'll talk about later.

Birth of PHP

PHP grew out of a need for people to develop and maintain web sites containing dynamic client-server functionality. In 1994, Rasmus Lerdorf created a collection of open source Perl scripts for his personal use, and these eventually were rewritten in C and turned into what PHP is today. By 1998, PHP was released in its third version, turning it into a web development tool that could compete with similar products such as Microsoft's Active Server Pages (ASP) or Sun's Java Server Pages (JSP).

The real beauty of PHP is its simplicity coupled with its power, as well as it being an interpreted language, rather than a compiled one.

 Compiled languages create a binary *.exe* file, while interpreted languages work directly with the source code when executing as opposed to creating a standalone file.

PHP is ubiquitous and compatible with all major operating systems. It is also easy to learn, making it an ideal tool for web-programming beginners. Additionally, you get to take advantage of a community's effort to make web development easier for everyone. The creators of PHP developed an infrastructure that allows experienced C programmers to extend PHP's abilities. As a result, PHP now integrates with advanced technologies like XML, XSL, and Microsoft's COM. At this juncture, PHP 5.0 is being used.

Birth of Apache

Apache is a web server that turns browser requests into resulting web pages and knows how to process PHP code. PHP is only a programming language, so without the power of a web server like Apache behind it, there would be no way for web users to reach your pages that contain the PHP language code.

Apache is not the only web server available. Another popular web server is Microsoft's Internet Information Services (IIS), which is supplied with Windows 2000 and all later versions. For the most part, the differences between Apache and IIS come down to personal preference, although Apache has the decided advantages of being free, providing full source code, and using an unrestricted license. Apache 2.0 is the current version you'll be using. IIS is easier to integrate with Active Directory, Microsoft's latest authentication system, but this applies mostly to internal company web sites.

 According to the Netcraft web server survey, Apache has been the most popular web server on the Internet since April 1996.

Because web servers like Apache and IIS are made to serve up pages from HTML files, they need a way to know how to process PHP language code. Apache uses a system called modules to load extensions into its functionality. IIS uses a similar concept called ISAPI. These both allow for faster processing of the PHP code than the old school process of calling PHP as a separate executable each time the web server had a request for a page containing PHP. We'll discuss how the Apache module is set up in Chapter 2.

Apache Versions

Apache has only two major versions in use today. They are 1.3 and 2. Apache 2 is a major rewrite and supports *threading*. Threads are a way for a single process to manage more than one thing at a time. The benefit is an increase in speed and a reduction in the resources needed. Unfortunately, PHP isn't totally compatible with threading yet. Apache 2 has been out long enough to be considered stable for development and production use. Apache 2 also supports more powerful modules. Some additional modules can be found at *http://www.cri.ensmp.fr/~coelho/mod_macro/*. However, shared module DLLs that don't come with the official Apache source files, such as *mod_php4*, *mod_ssl*, *mod_auth_mysql*, and *mod_auth_ntsec*, can be found on the Web.

Birth of MySQL

MySQL was developed in the 1990s to fill the ever-growing need for computers to manage information intelligently. The original core MySQL developers were trying to solve their needs for a database by using mSQL, a small and simple database. It become clear that mSQL couldn't solve all the problems they wanted it to, so they created a more robust database that turned into MySQL

MySQL supports several different *database engines*. The database engine determines how MySQL handles the actual storage and querying of the data. Because of that, each storage engine has its own set of abilities and strengths. Over time, the database engines available are becoming more advanced and faster. Table 1-1 lists when various features have been added to MySQL.

Table 1-1. Major MySQL releases

Version	Features
3.23	The MyISAM database engine is added and is the default engine. It handles large amounts of data efficiently.
	The InnoDB database engine debuts for transaction safe database processing and support for *foreign keys*. Foreign keys allow the relationships between tables to be explicitly designated in the database.
4.0	Queries support *unions*. Unions allow merging the results of two queries into one result. Configuration changes can be made without restarting the database.
4.01	A help command is included for the database client. There is support for *unnamed views*, also known as *subqueries*. Unnamed views allow you to treat a query like a separate table within a query.
5.0	Database *triggers*, *stored procedures*, and *cursors* are added. A trigger allows code to run in the database when a triggering event occurs, such as inserting data into a table. Stored procedures allow programs to be defined and executed within the database. Cursors allow code in the database to be run for each row that matches a query.
5.1	*Constraints* and *partitioning* are added. Constraints are used to define rules for when rows can be added or modified in the database. Partitioning is used to split up the physical storage of large tables based on a defined rule. It is commonly used to increase the performance of large tables such as historical data.

The current production release of MySQL is the latest available 5.0x version. MySQL 5.0 provides performance that is comparable to any of the much more expensive enterprise databases such as Oracle, Informix, DB2 (IBM), and SQL Server (Microsoft). The developers have achieved this level of performance by leveraging the talents of many open source developers, along with community testing. For general web-driven database tasks, the default MyISAM database engine works perfectly fine.

> The newest advanced features of MySQL 5.1 are not as stable as features introduced in prior releases. MySQL 5.0 is the current stable general release. Download the latest minor release (the largest of the third portion of the version number) for whichever major version you choose. It has the most bug fixes for that version included.

Apache also has the advantage of being able to run on operating systems other than Windows, which now brings us to the subject of compatibility.

Compatibility

Web browsers like Firefox, Netscape, and Internet Explorer are made to process HTML, so it doesn't matter what operating system a web server runs on. Apache, PHP, and MySQL support a wide range of operating systems, so you aren't restricted to a specific OS on either the server or the client. While you don't have to worry much about software compatibility, the sheer variety of file formats and different languages that all come together does take some getting used to.

Integrating Many Sources of Information

In the early days of the Web, life was simple. There were files that contained HTML and binary files such as images. Several technologies have since been developed to organize the look of web pages. For example, *Cascading Style Sheets* (CSS) pull presentation information out of your HTML and into a single spot so that you can make formatting changes across an entire set of pages all at once; you don't have to manually change your HTML markup one HTML page at a time.

You can potentially have information coming from HTML files that reference CSS, PHP templates, and a MySQL database all at once. PHP templates make it easier to change the HTML in a page when it contains fields populated by a database query. We'll briefly discuss each of these information sources.

MySQL Database

MySQL is a relational database management system that stores data in separate tables rather than putting all the data in one spot. This adds flexibility, as well as speed. The SQL part of MySQL stands for *Structured Query Language*, which is the most common language used to access every type of database in existence. Just to give you a taste of what your code will look like, Example 1-1 is an example of MySQL code called from PHP for deleting a user from the MySQL database.

Example 1-1. A PHP function to delete a user from the user_name database table

```php
<?php

// A function to delete a user from the site_user table based on
//the $user_name parameter.
// An open database connection is assumed

function remove_user($user_name){
    // Remove a User
    // This is the SQL command
    $sql_delete = "DELETE FROM `site_user` WHERE `User`='$user'";
    $success = mysql_query($sql_delete) or die(mysql_error());

    // print the page header
    print('
        <html>
            <head>
                <title>Remove User</title>
                <link rel="stylesheet" type="text/css" href="user_admin.css" />
            </head>
            <body>
                <div class="user_admin">');

    // Check to see if the deletion was sucessful
    if ($success){
        // Tell the user it was sucessful
        print("The account for $user_name was deleted successfully.");
    }
    else {
        // Tell the user it was not sucessful
        print("User $user could not be deleted. Please try again later.");
    }

    // Print the page footer
    print('</div></body></html>');
}

?>
```

Don't worry about understanding precisely what's happening in Example 1-1. The idea is simply to realize that there's PHP code, database code, and a link to a stylesheet.

PHP Templates

To simplify the maintenance of sites that have many different pages, but that all have a common look, the header and footer of each page can be placed in a separate file and included in each PHP page. This allows changes to the header or footer to be made in one location, but not to change the look of every page automatically, which frees the developer from having to modify every single page on the web site.

PHP developers have learned that separating the PHP code from HTML can make life easier for both developers and business users who know how to modify HTML but don't understand PHP very well. By creating separate PHP template files that have placeholders for dynamic data, you can separate the HTML markup from the PHP code.

Example 1-2 shows an example template file.

Example 1-2. A PHP template

```
<html>
    <head>
        <title>My Books</title>
    </head>
    <body>
        <p>Favorite Books:</p>
        <p>
            Title: {$title}<br />
            Author: {$author}
        </p>
    </body>
</html>
```

When the page is processed by the PHP engine, the placeholders are replaced with their associated values, as shown in Example 1-3.

Example 1-3. The resulting HTML code after template substitution and processing

```
<html>
    <head>
        <title>My Books</title>
    </head>
    <body>
        <p>Favorite Books:</p>
        <p>
            Title: Java in a Nutshell<br />
            Author: Flanagan
        </p>
    </body>
</html>
```

The result is that while you've added another file to the mix, you've made the HTML markup easier to read, and the PHP code is less cluttered with extraneous HTML. A web developer who's not skilled in PHP can modify the look of the page without worrying about breaking the PHP code.

The last type of information we discuss also comes from a desire to separate the presentation styles such as colors and spacing from the core content.

Cascading Style Sheets

Cascading Style Sheets (CSS) are added to HTML to give web developers and users more control over the way their web pages display. Designers and users can create stylesheets that define how different elements, such as headers and links, appear on the web site. The term *cascading* derives from the fact that multiple stylesheets can be applied to the same web page. To apply CSS code, the example code shown is placed within the head of your HTML file.

```html
<html>
    <head>
        <title>CSS Example</title>
        <style type="text/css">
            h4, b {color: #80D92F; font-family: arial; }
            p { text-indent: 2cm; background: yellow; font-family: courier;}
        </style>
    </head>

    <body>
        <h3>Learn how to use CSS on your websites!</h3>
        <h4>It's cool, it's amazing, it even saves you time!</h4>
        <p>Isn't this <b>nifty</b>?</p>
    </body>
</html>
```

The code that begins with style is the CSS code. The document renders as shown in Figure 1-1.

Figure 1-1. CSS and HTML displayed in your browser

Although we include the CSS in the file in this example, it could come from a separate file as it did in Example 1-1 as *user_admin.css*.

Of course, we also have plain old HTML files in the mix, too.

 For more information on CSS, see Eric Meyer's *Cascading Stylesheets: The Definitive Guide*, Second Edition (O'Reilly, 2004).

HTML Markup

HTML markup applies *tags* to content to identify information that is of a particular type, or that needs special formatting. HTML tags are always enclosed in angle brackets (<>) and are case-insensitive; so it doesn't matter if you type in upper- or lowercase (though XHTML recommends all lowercase). Tags typically occur in begin-end pairs. These pairs are in the form

```
<tag>Isn't this nifty?</tag>
```

The first <tag> indicates the beginning of a tag-pair, and the last </tag> indicates the end. This complete pair of tags is called an element. Any content within an element has the rules of that element applied to it. In the earlier example, the text "Learn how to use CSS on your websites!" is contained by an h3 element.

```
<h3>Learn how to use CSS on your websites!</h3>
```

It's also good practice (and it's required by XHTML) that your tags nest cleanly to produce elements with clear boundaries. Always use end tags when you reach the end of an element, and avoid having pairs of tags that overlap. (Instead of bold <i>bold italic italic</i>, write bold <i>bold italic</i> <i>italic</i>, for example.)

Requesting Data from a Web Page

How all of these pieces integrate together can be tricky to understand. If a web server detects PHP code, it determines whether the file is a PHP file, and if so, turn over the processing of the page to the PHP interpreter without any additional participation by the web browser. But if you include an external CSS file, your browser issues a separate request for that file before viewing the page.

PHP Interpretation on the Server

This processing of the PHP on the server is called *server-side processing*. When you request a web page, you trigger a whole chain of events. Figure 1-2 illustrates this interaction between your computer and the web server (host of the web site).

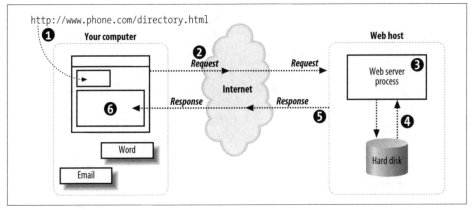

Figure 1-2. While the user only types in a URL and hits Enter, there are several steps that occur behind the scenes to handle that request

Here's the breakdown of Figure 1-2:

1. You enter a web page address in your browser's location bar.

2. Your browser breaks apart that address and sends the name of the page to the web server. For example, *http://www.phone.com/directory.html* would request the page *directory.html* from *www.phone.com*.

3. A program on the web server, called the web server process, takes the request for *directory.html* and looks for this specific file.

4. The web server reads the *directory.html* file from the web server's hard drive.

5. The web server returns the contents of *directory.html* to your browser.

6. Your web browser uses the HTML markup that was returned from the web server to build the rendition of the web page on your computer screen.

The HTML file called *directory.html* (requested in Figure 1-2) is called a *static web page*. It is static because everyone who requests the *directory.html* page gets exactly the same page.

For the web server to customize the returned page, PHP and MySQL are added to the mix. Figure 1-3 illustrates the extra steps that occur in the chain of events on the web host.

Each step in the chain is listed here:

1. You enter a web page address in your browser's location bar.

2. Your browser breaks apart that address and sends the name of the page to the host. For example, *http://www.phone.com/login.php* requests the page *login.php* from *www.phone.com*.

3. The web server process on the host receives the request for *login.php*.

4. The web server reads the *login.php* file from the host's hard drive.

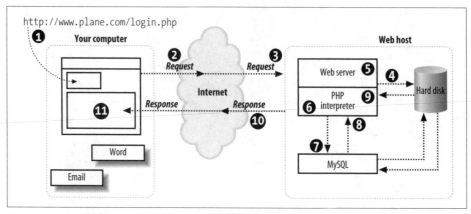

Figure 1-3. The PHP interpreter, MySQL, and the web server cooperate to return the page

5. The web server detects that the PHP file isn't just a plain HTML file, so it asks another process—the PHP interpreter—to process the file.

6. The PHP interpreter executes the PHP code that it finds in the text it received from the web server process. Included in that code are calls to the MySQL database.

7. PHP asks the MySQL database process to execute the database calls.

8. The MySQL database process returns the results of the database query.

9. The PHP interpreter completes execution of the PHP code with the data from the database and returns the results to the web server process.

10. The web server returns the results in the form of HTML text to your browser.

11. Your web browser uses the returned HTML text to build the web page on your screen.

This may seem like a lot of steps, but all of this processing happens automatically every time a web page with PHP code is requested.

When developing dynamic web pages, you work with a variety of variables and server components, which are all important to having an attractive, easy to navigate, and maintainable web site. Next, it's time to install the three major cogs needed to make this work: Apache, PHP, and MySQL.

Chapter 1 Questions

Question 1-1. What three components do you need to create a dynamic web page?

Question 1-2. What does Apache use to load extensions?

Question 1-3. What is the current stable release of PHP?

Question 1-4. What does the SQL part of MySQL stand for?

Question 1-5. What are angle brackets (< >) used for?

Question 1-6. What does the PHP Interpreter do?

See the Appendix for the answers to these questions.

Installation

Developers working with PHP and MySQL often find it convenient to work on a local computer rather than a web server. In general, it is also safer to create and test your applications on a local—preferably private—computer and then deploy them to a public server where others can enjoy your work. Typically, you need to install Apache, PHP, and MySQL on the local computer, while your ISP handles installation on the public server.

Developing Locally

Developing your construct on your local computer is the recommended way to learn, since you can interact with all of the components on your own machine and not risk causing problems on a production server. That way, if there are problems in the local environment, you can fix them immediately without exposing them to your site's visitors. Working with your files locally means that you don't have to FTP them to a server, you don't have to be connected to the Internet, and you know exactly what's installed since you did it yourself.

There are three components to install:

- Apache
- PHP
- MySQL

You will install the programs in that order. All our examples will be from the installation perspective of a PC with Windows installed, with notes for the Macintosh.

Installing Apache

First, Apache needs to be installed and operational before PHP and MySQL can be installed, or else they won't work correctly. Plus, there wouldn't be any use for the coding application and database without the Apache web server. A web server delivers web pages, has an IP address, and might have a domain name. For example, if you enter *http://www.oreilly.com/* in your browser, this sends a request to the server whose domain name is oreilly.com. The server fetches the page named *index.html* and sends it to your browser.

Any computer can be turned into a web server by installing server software and connecting the machine to the Internet, which is why you need to install Apache.

1. Download the Apache 2.0.5 Win32 binary. It's downloadable from *http://httpd. apache.or/download.cgi*. The file that you save to your desktop is called *apache2_ 0.55-win32-x86-no_ssl.msi*.

> If you are on Mac OS X, you already have Apache installed. Open up System Preferences, select the Sharing panel, and click to activate Personal Web Sharing (which is actually Apache). Mac OS X 10.2, 10.3, and 10.4 all come with different versions of Apache, but each works perfectly fine.

2. Install Apache using the Installation Wizard. Double-click the MSI installer file on your desktop, and you see the installer shown in Figure 2-1.

The Installation Wizard walks you through the installation process.

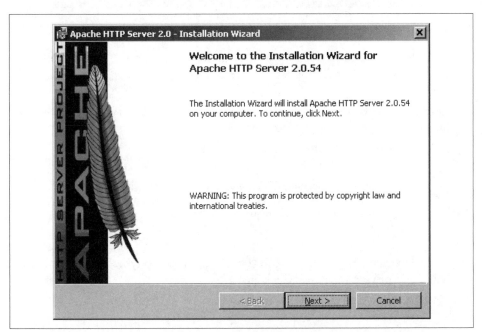

Figure 2-1. The Installation Wizard prompts you for basic configuration

3. Accept the license terms by clicking the radio button shown in Figure 2-2, and then click Next.

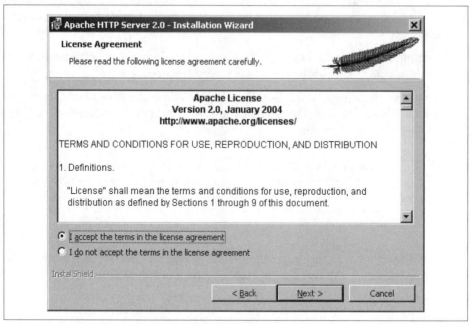

Figure 2-2. Apache license terms and conditions for use

4. You'll see a "Read This First" box, as shown in Figure 2-3. Additionally, this window offers a number of excellent resources related to the web server. Click Next.

5. In the blank dialog box shown in Figure 2-4, enter all pertinent network information.

A sample is provided in Figure 2-5. Then click Next.

 Port 80 is the default HTTP port. In other words, when you request *http://www.oreilly.com*, you're implicitly requesting port 80. By accepting this port, your web requests can be made without specifying a nondefault port.

6. In the next screen, shown in Figure 2-6, select the setup type. The Typical install will work for your purposes. Click Next.

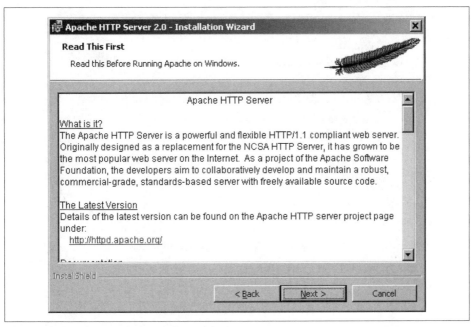

Figure 2-3. Apache HTTP Server information

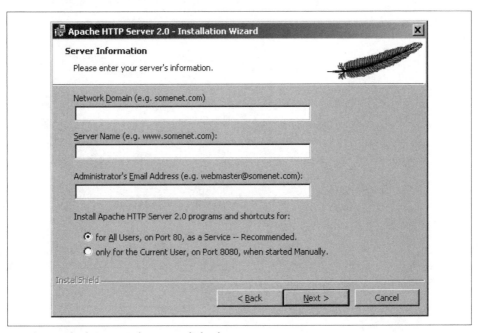

Figure 2-4. Blank Server Information dialog box

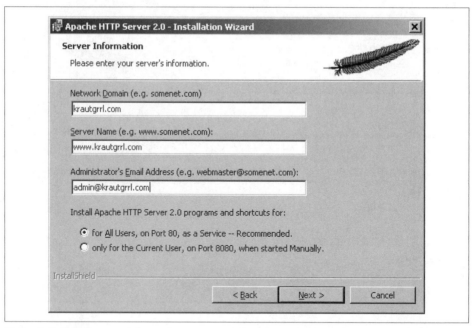

Figure 2-5. Sample server information

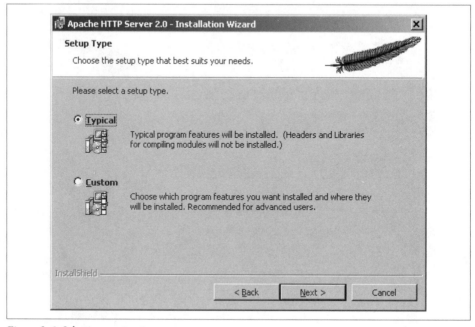

Figure 2-6. Selecting a setup type

7. Accept the default installation directory, as shown in Figure 2-7. Click Next.

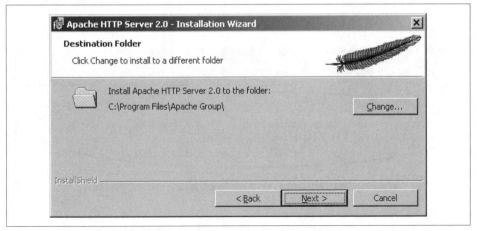

Figure 2-7. Destination Folder dialog box for the Apache installation files

 The default installation directory, *C:\Program Files\Apache Group*, is both standard and easy to find, especially when you need to make changes to your configuration.

8. As Figure 2-8 shows, it's time for the installation to begin. Click Install. The installer installs a variety of modules, and you will see some DOS windows appear and disappear. Click Finish when the installer is done.

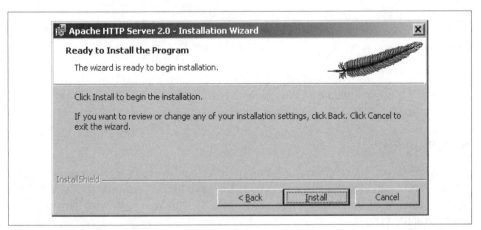

Figure 2-8. Ready to Install dialog box

9. Test your installation by entering `http://localhost/` in your browser's location field. The local host's IP address is 127.0.0.1.

10. After entering the URL in your browser, the default Apache page displays, which is similar to the one shown in Figure 2-9. Notice the circled part of the window where it indicates that the installation was successful.

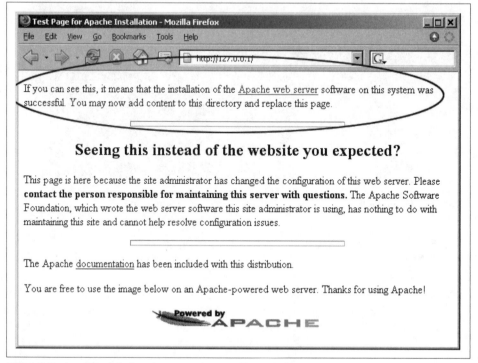

Figure 2-9. Apache's default index page after installation

Now that you can serve up web pages, you're ready to add PHP.

 Apache is installed along with Mac OS X on Macintoshes. To activate it, go to Sharing under System Preferences, and start Personal Web Sharing.

Installing PHP

Go to *http://www.php.net/downloads.php* to download the latest version of PHP; both binaries and source code can be found on this web site. You need to download the zip file rather than the Windows installer, because the Windows installer only configures the IIS web server.

Create a directory for PHP on your desktop. You don't need all the files provided in the archive, so unzip the PHP archive into another temporary location. (A temporary location could be on your desktop, which will be easier to find when you go looking for the files.)

1. Copy the following files into *C:\php*: *php.exe*, *php4ts.dll*, and *php2apache2.dll*. The *php2apache2.dll* file is located in the *sapi* directory.

Use *php2apache.dll* instead of *php2apache2.dll* if you are using Apache 1.3.*x*.

2. Load PHP extensions. If you plan to load PHP extensions, you need to copy the files in the *extensions* directory (or the *ext* directory, for PHP 5.*x*) to *C:\php*, or to a subfolder in *C:\php*—any subfolder—as long as the *PHP.ini* file is updated to reflect the appropriate directory.

MySQL support is now integrated into PHP and doesn't need an extension *.dll*. However, PHP 5 supports MySQL as a separate module for download. Follow the instructions below to make sure that your installation of PHP works before you start experimenting with installing extensions.

3. To configure PHP, copy *php.ini-dist* from the extracted files into your Windows directory—typically *C:\winnt* or *C:\Windows*—and rename it *php.ini*.

4. Set up PHP to load Apache as a module. To configure Apache to load PHP as a module to parse your PHP scripts, use a text editor to open the Apache configuration file, *httpd.conf*, typically found in *C:\Program Files\Apache Group\ Apache2\conf*. You can use Notepad, as shown in Figure 2-10.

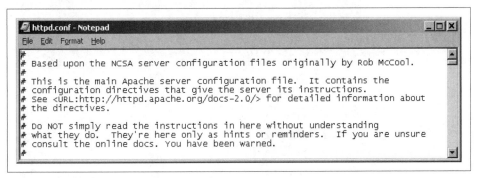

Figure 2-10. Viewing httpd.conf in Notepad

5. Load PHP as an Apache module. Open the *httpd.conf* file in Notepad or another text editor and search for the section that has a series of commented out `LoadModule` statements. You can find this around line 134, as shown in Figure 2-11. In Notepad, choose Edit → Go To… → 134.

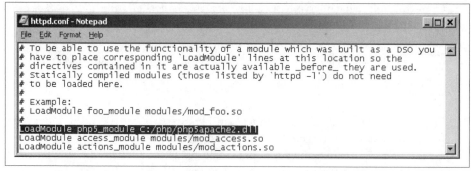

Figure 2-11. Notepad httpd.conf file with the LoadModule section highlighted

 Statements prefixed by the hash sign (#) in HTML and PHP are considered commented out and can be seen only by you, never your end
user in a browser window.

6. Restart the Apache server by selecting Start → Apache HTTP Server 2.0.x → Control Apache Server → Restart, so that it can read the new configuration directives
you placed into *httpd.conf*. Alternatively, in the system tray, double-click on the
Apache icon and click the Restart button.

7. Search for AddType in the file, around line 754 (shown in Figure 2-12), and add
the following line after the last AddType statement:

```
AddType application/x-httpd-php .php
```

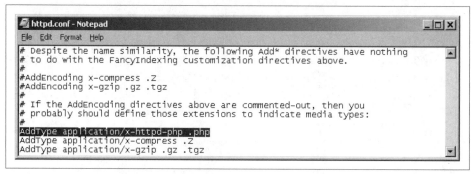

Figure 2-12. Notepad httpd.conf file with the AddType section highlighted

To test the installation, do the following:

1. Create a PHP file in any text editor, with the following line:

```
<?php phpinfo(); ?>
```

2. Save the file as *phpinfo.php*, and then save it under the Apache *htdocs* directory,
usually located at *C:\Program Files\Apache Group\Apache2\htdocs*.

3. Open your browser of choice.

4. Access the file you just created by typing `localhost/phpinfo.php` into your browser's location bar. You should see a page of information about your PHP setup, like Figure 2-13.

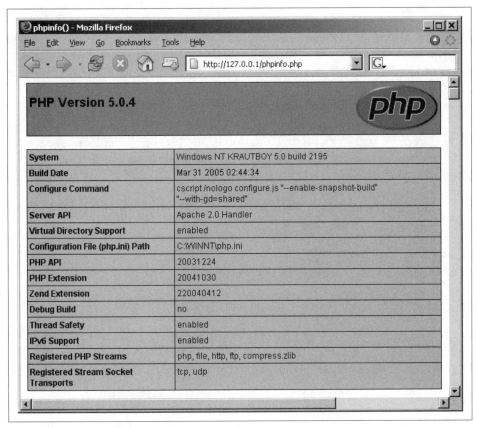

Figure 2-13. PHP introduction screen

If for some reason this doesn't work, check to see whether your PHP or Apache setup is causing the problem. Go to the command-line prompt and type `cd \php`. The prompt should change to `C:\php`. Then type in `php "C:\Program Files\Apache Group\Apache2\htdocs\phpinfo.php"`, since the file isn't in the *c:\php* directory.

If invoking PHP from the command line causes a large HTML file with all the PHP configuration information to be displayed, then your PHP setup is fine. The problem is probably your Apache configuration; go ahead and reread the procedure on how to install and configure Apache.

 If you are on Mac OS X, you have PHP preinstalled on your computer. You need to edit the Apache configuration file to enable PHP in much the same way you edited the PC text file.

Installing MySQL 4.1

The final component you need to develop and test pages on your local computer is MySQL. Now download the MySQL Installer.

1. Download the MySQL binaries. Both the binaries and the source code can be found at *http://dev.mysql.com/downloads/*. The link takes you to a page where you can enter personal info, or just click No Thanks to download the file. A number of download locations (or mirrors) are available; select one. Download the recommended version for the Windows Essentials (x86) MySQL 4.1 Installer. Save the installer file to your desktop.

2. Double-click the MSI installer file on your desktop. A setup wizard, shown in Figure 2-14, walks you through the installation process. (The install process for MySQL 5.0 is the same as it is for MySQL 4.1.) Click Next.

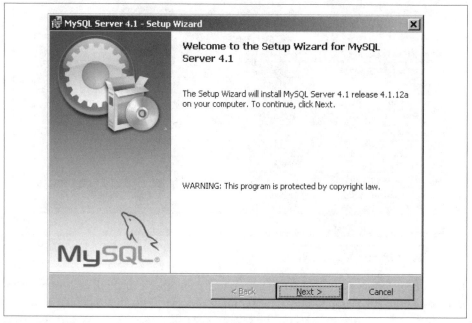

Figure 2-14. The Setup Wizard prompts you for configuration settings

3. Select Typical installation by clicking the Typical radio button shown in Figure 2-15, and then click Next.

4. Click Install on the Ready to Install the Program dialog box shown in Figure 2-16.

5. The setup program next will ask you to create a MySQL.com account, as shown in Figure 2-17. Select Skip Sign-Up and click Next, or sign up for an account, which provides access to a monthly newsletter as well as the ability to post bugs and comments on the online forums.

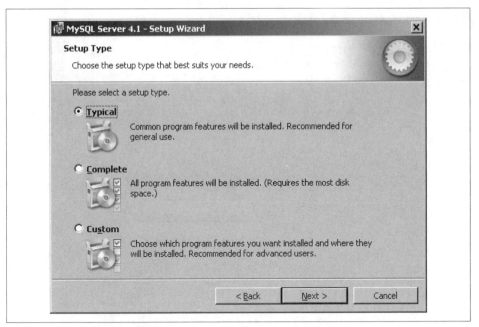

Figure 2-15. Select a setup type

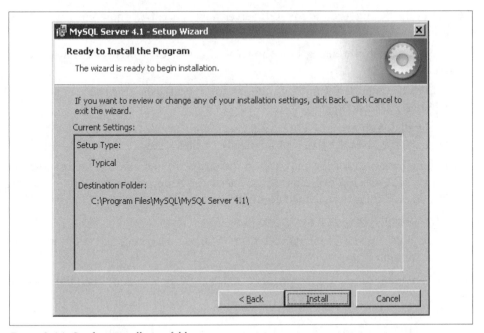

Figure 2-16. Confirm installation folder

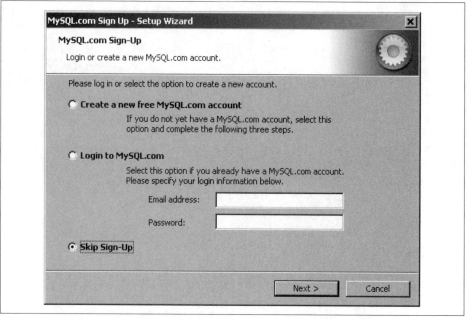

Figure 2-17. The MySQL.com account provides newsletters and bug reporting resources

6. Select the "Configure the MySQL Server now" checkbox shown in Figure 2-18, and then click Finish.

   This brings up the dialog box shown in Figure 2-19, where you can just click Next.

7. Select the Standard Configuration radio button from the dialog shown in Figure 2-20. Click Next.

8. In the dialog shown in Figure 2-21, check both Install As Window Service and "Launch the MySQL Server automatically." Click Next.

9. Enter a password for the root user in the password and confirm fields shown in Figure 2-22. Click Next. You do not need the Anonymous Account since you can do everything with named accounts.

10. Click Execute, as shown in Figure 2-23.

11. Click Finish, as shown in Figure 2-24. MySQL is now configured and running on your computer.

At this point, all critical components—Apache, PHP 5.0, and MySQL 4.1—are installed.

 The wizard will inform you of basic problems during installation, such as running out of free disk space or not having proper permissions on your system to install MySQL.

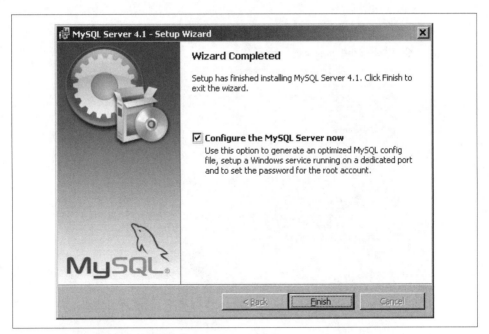

Figure 2-18. Configure the MySQL Server

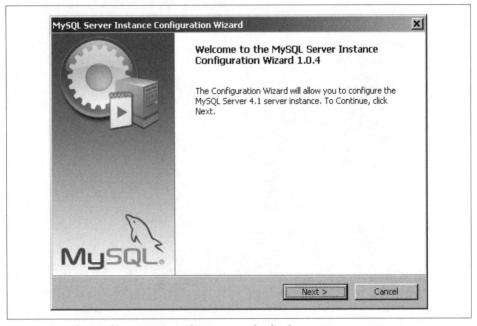

Figure 2-19. The Configuration Wizard customizes the database settings

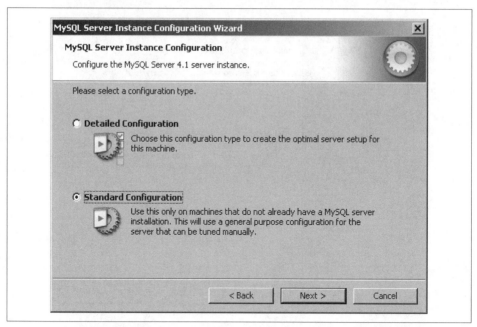

Figure 2-20. Choose the level of detail dialog box

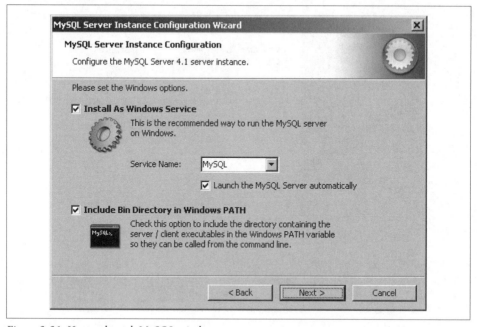

Figure 2-21. How to launch MySQL window

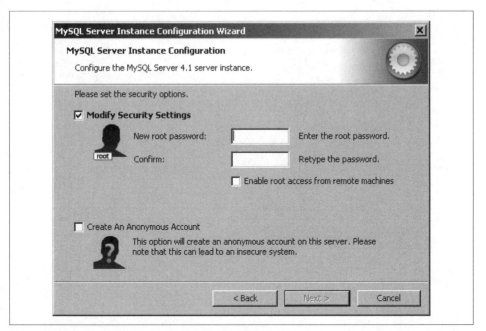

Figure 2-22. Security settings for the database window

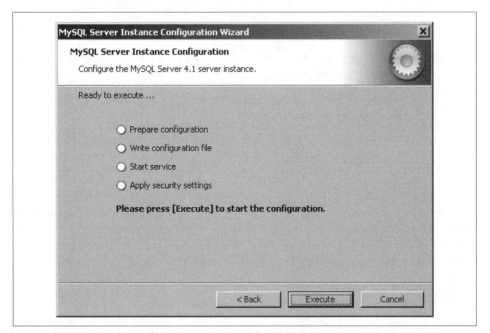

Figure 2-23. Commit the configuration settings window

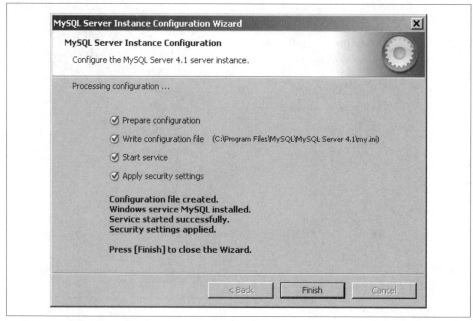

Figure 2-24. Installation is complete

Working Remotely

Although we recommend you start out working locally, you can use an ISP account as long as it supports PHP and MySQL.

You need login information to the remote server, and you may need to use your ISP's web-based tool to create your database.

To transfer your files and directories, you need to activate a File Transfer Protocol (FTP) account at your ISP, usually through your account control panel. Once you have an FTP login, you upload your HTML and PHP files using a FTP client.

While your computer likely has the command-line version of the FTP client available from the command prompt, it can be cryptic to use. Graphical FTP clients make using FTP much easier. FTP Voyager, available from *http://sourceforge.net/projects/ filezilla/*, is one FTP client you can use to upload files to your ISP. Your initial login screen looks similar to Figure 2-25. Fetch is a good FTP program for the Macintosh.

After connecting, you see a dialog similar to Figure 2-26, but you do not see the identical screen as this FTP Voyager screen. You can drag and drop the *.php* file you created. Remember, for your PHP file to run you need to save it with an extension of *.php* instead of *.html*; otherwise, it won't run, because the web server needs to know it's a PHP file in order to run the PHP interpreter.

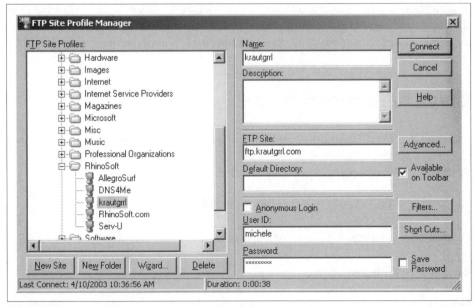

Figure 2-25. FTP Voyager initial screen

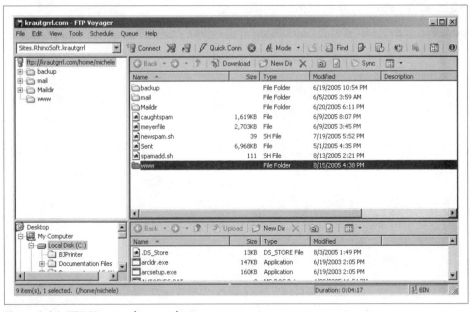

Figure 2-26. FTP Voyager directory listing

PHP files must be accessed through a web server since your web browser doesn't have the ability to interpret the PHP code. A PHP interpreter is used to process the PHP files.

You're ready to start learning all about basic facts, integration, and how to get your dynamic web page up and running as quickly and smoothly as possible. In the next chapter, we'll give you basic information about PHP and simple coding principles that apply to using PHP.

Chapter 2 Questions

Question 2-1. What three components must be installed to create a dynamic web site?

Question 2-2. What OS has Apache installed already?

Question 2-3. Where should you create a PHP directory for downloads?

Question 2-4. What does the hash (#) sign mean?

Question 2-5. How do you work remotely?

Question 2-6. How do you transfer files to your ISP?

Question 2-7. How must PHP files be accessed?

See the Appendix for the answers to these questions.

Exploring PHP

With PHP, MySQL, and Apache installed, you're ready to begin writing code. Unlike many languages, PHP doesn't require complex tools such as compilers and debuggers. In fact, you'll soon see that you can enter PHP directly into your existing HTML documents, and with just a few tweaks, you'll be off and running.

In this chapter, we'll start by showing you how PHP handles simple text, and then move on to basic decision making. Some really cool things you can do include showing an image based on the current user's browser, or perhaps printing a warning message if the user is browsing from an operating system that makes your web site look crummy. All this and more is possible with PHP, which makes these tricks easy and simple.

PHP and HTML Text

It's simple to output text using PHP; in fact, handling text is one of PHP's specialties. We'll begin with detailing where PHP is processed, some of the basic functions to output text, and from there go right into printing text based on a certain condition being true.

Text Output

You'll want to be able to spit out text easily and often. PHP will let you do that, though you'll need to use proper PHP syntax when creating the code. Otherwise, your browser assumes that everything is HTML and outputs the PHP code directly to the browser, and then everything looks like text and code mixed up. This will certainly confuse your users! You can use whatever text editor you like to write your PHP code, including Notepad or DevPHP (*http://sourceforge.net/projects/devphp/*).

Our examples will demonstrate how similar HTML markup and PHP code look and what you can do to start noticing the differences between them.

Example 3-1 is a simple HTML file that we'll use for an example.

Example 3-1. All you need to start with PHP is a simple HTML document

```
<html>
    <head>
        <title>Hello World</title>
    </head>
    <body>
        <p>I sure wish I had something to say.</p>
    </body>
</html>
```

Nothing is special here; just your plain vanilla HTML file. However, you can enter PHP right into this file; for example, let's use PHP's echo command to output some text in Example 3-2.

Example 3-2. Adding some PHP code to the HTML file

```
<html>
    <head>
        <title>Hello World</title>
    </head>
    <body>
        echo("<p>Now I have something to say.</p>");
    </body>
</html>
```

Separating PHP from HTML

This looks pretty simple, but there are some problems. There's no way to tell in this file which part is standard HTML and which part is PHP and therefore must be handled differently. To fix this, surround your PHP code in <?php and ?> tags.

When you start writing PHP code, you'll be working with plain vanilla text files that contain PHP and HTML code. HTML is a simple markup language that designates how your page looks in a browser, but it is simply that: *text only*. The server doesn't have to process HTML files before sending them to the user's browser. Unlike HTML code, PHP code must be interpreted before the resulting page is sent to the browser. Otherwise, it will be one big mess on the user's screen.

To set apart the PHP code to inform the web server what needs to be processed, the PHP code is placed between formal or informal tags mixed with HTML. Example 3-3 uses echo and print operators to achieve this.

Example 3-3. Calling echo and print

```
<html>
    <head>
        <title>Hello World</title>
    </head>
    <body>
        <?php
```

Example 3-3. Calling echo and print (continued)

```
    echo ("Hello world!<br />");
    print ('Goodbye.<br />');
    print 'Over and out.';

    ?>
  </body>
</html>
```

When a browser requests this file, PHP interprets it and produces HTML markup. Example 3-4 is the HTML that is produced from the code in Example 3-3.

Example 3-4. The HTML markup produced by the PHP code

```
<html>
<head>
    <title>Hello World</title>
  </head>
  <body>
    Hello world!<br />Goodbye.<br />Over and out.
  </body>
</html>
```

Save your HTML document to *C:\Program Files\Apache Group\Apache2\htdocs*, as we discussed in Chapter 2. Open the file in a web browser, and you see something like Figure 3-1. The code in Example 3-4 is the same code that you see if you select View → Page Source from your browser's menu.

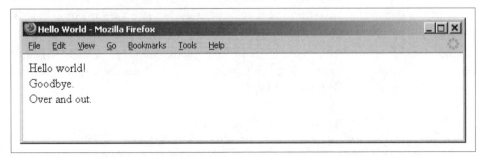

Figure 3-1. The output as it appears in the web browser

While writing PHP code, it's crucial to add comments so that your code is easier to read and support. Most people don't remember exactly what they were thinking when they look at the code a year or more later, so let comments permeate your code and you'll be a happier PHPer in the future. PHP supports two styles of comments. We suggest using single-line comments for quick notes about a tricky part while using multiple-line comments when you need to describe something in greater depth; both are shown in Example 3-5.

Comments are retained in the PHP file, but the interpreter doesn't output the PHP comments. The interpreter outputs only the HTML comments.

Example 3-5. Using comments to make your code easier to read

```
<html>
    <head>
        <title>Hello World</title>
    </head>
    <body>
        <?php

        // A single line comment could say that we are going to
        // print hello world.

        /* This is how to do a
            multi-line comment and could be used comment out a block
            of code */

        echo("Hello world!<br />");
        print('Goodbye.<br />');

        ?>
    </body>
</html>
```

In Example 3-5, two comment styles are used: // for single-line comments and /* ... */ for multiline comments. Keep in mind that if you want to place a comment in HTML markup, you need to use the open comment <!-- and close comment --> tags.

A semicolon (;) ends all code statements in PHP. (Because of this, semicolons can't be used in names.) It's good style as well as practical to also start a new line after your semicolon so the code is easier to read.

Since PHP files tend to switch back and forth between PHP code and HTML markup, using an HTML comment in the middle of PHP or a PHP comment in the middle of HTML makes a mess of your page, so be extra vigilant in not doing this!

The PHP files get to your web site just like any other file. To try the PHP code in Example 3-6, save the file in the document root that you selected when you installed Apache in Chapter 2. Once you have your PHP file—say, *example.php*—in your web accessible directory, you can view it by browsing to *http://yourdomain.com/your_directory/example.php*.

Now that you know how to include PHP code within your HTML markup and not let your user see a bunch of gobbledygook, we'll explore basic PHP programming.

Coding Building Blocks

To write programs in PHP that do something useful, you'll need to understand blocks of reusable code called *functions* or *methods*, and then how to temporarily store information that cannot be executed in *variables*. We talk about *evaluations*, which are basically things that allow your code to make intelligent decisions based on mathematical principles and user input.

Variables

Since you haven't done any programming, we understand that variables are a new concept. A *variable* stores a value, such as the text string "Hello World!" or the integer value 1. A variable can then be reused throughout your code, instead of having to type out the actual value over and over again for the entire life of the variable, which can be frustrating and tedious. Figure 3-2 shows a newly created variable that has been assigned a value of 30.

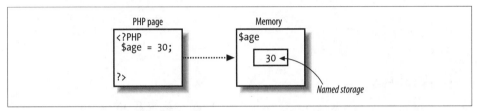

Figure 3-2. A variable holding a value

In PHP, you define a variable with the following form:

```
$variable_name = value;
```

Pay very close attention to some key elements in the form of variables. The dollar sign ($) must always fill the first space of your variable. The first character after the dollar sign must be a letter or underscore. It can't under any circumstances be a number; otherwise, your code will not execute, so watch those typos!

- PHP variables may only be composed of alphanumeric characters and underscores; for example, a–z, A–Z, 0–9, and _.
- Variables in PHP are case sensitive. This means that `$variable_name` and `$Variable_Name` are different.
- Variables with more than one word should be separated with underscores; for example, `$test_variable`.
- Variables can be assigned values by using the equals sign (=).
- Always end with a semicolon (;) to complete the assignment of the variable.

To create a simple PHP variable as in Figure 3-2, enter:

```
<?php
$age = 30;
?>
```

This code takes the variable named age and assigns it the number 30. You can use variables without worrying about the specific value assigned to them. (PHP is not strongly typed, if you have a background in Java or C.)

If you were to assign a new value to a variable with the same name, as happens in Example 3-6, the old name would be overwritten and you would have a potential logic error in your code.

Example 3-6. Reassigning a variable

```
<?php
 $age = 30;
 $age = 31;
 echo $age;
?>
```

The new value of $age replaces the old, and this is the output:

```
31
```

Reading a variable's value

To access the value of a variable that's already been assigned, simply specify the dollar sign ($) followed by the variable name, and use it as you would the value of the variable in your code. For example, Figure 3-3 displays the value of $age.

You don't necessarily have to clean up your variables when your program finishes. They're temporary, since PHP automatically cleans them up when you're done using them. Sort of like how Microsoft Word creates a temp file of your document, so when you close the document, the temp file deletes itself.

Variable types

Variables all store certain types of data. PHP automatically picks a data variable based on the value assigned. These data types include strings, numbers, and more complex types such as arrays. We'll discuss arrays later. What's important to know is that unless you have a reason to care about the data type, PHP handles all of the details, so you need not worry about that. However, it's good practice to learn about data types.

In situations where a specific type of data is required, such as the mathematical division operation, PHP attempts to convert the data types automatically. If you have a string with a single "2," it will be converted to an integer value of 2. This conversion is nearly always exactly what you want PHP to do and makes coding seamless for you.

Variable scope

PHP helps keep your code organized by making sure that, if you use code that some-one else wrote (and you very likely will), the names of the variables in your code don't clash with other previously written variable names. For example, if you're using a variable called $name that has a value of Bill, and you use someone else's code that also has a variable called $name but uses it to keep track of the filename *log. txt*, your value could get overwritten. Your code's value for $name of Bill will be replaced by log.txt, and your code will say "Hello log.txt" instead of "Hello Bill", which would be a big problem.

To solve this problem, PHP organizes code into *functions*. Functions allow you to group a chunk of code together and execute that code by its name. To keep variables in your code separate from variables in functions, PHP provides separate storage of vari-ables within each function. This separate storage space means that the *scope*, or where a variable's value can be accessed, is the local storage of the function. Figure 3-3 dem-onstrates how there are distinct storage areas for a function's variables.

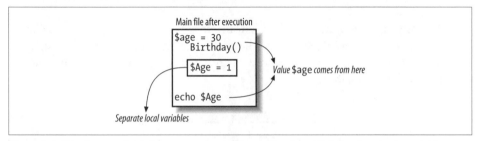

Figure 3-3. The $age variable has a separate value outside of the birthday function's variable storage area

Example 3-7 shows how the variable you use outside of the function isn't changed by the code within the function. Don't worry too much about understanding how the function works, as it has its own set of unique variables.

Example 3-7. The default handling of variable scope

```php
<?php

// define a function
function birthday(){
    // Set age to 1
    $age = 1;
}

// Set age to 30
$age = 30;
```

Example 3-7. The default handling of variable scope (continued)

```
// Call the function
birthday();

// Display the age
echo $age;

?>
```

This displays:

    30

Although calling the function `birthday` assigns 1 to the variable $age, it's not access-ing the same variable that was defined on the main level of the program. Therefore, when you print $age, you see the original value of 30. The bolded part of the code is what is seen when $age = is printed, because $age in `birthday` is a separate variable.

All of this is great, but if you really want to access or change the variable $age that was created outside the `birthday` function, you would use a global variable.

Global variables. *Global* variables allow you to cross the boundary between separate functions to access a variable's value. The `global` statement specifies that you want the variable to be the same variable everywhere, or globally. Figure 3-4 shows how a global variable is accessible to everything.

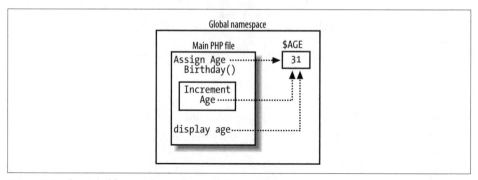

Figure 3-4. The global keyword creates one global variable called $age

Example 3-8 shows that use of a global variable can result in a change.

Example 3-8. Using a global variable changes the result

```
<?php

// Define a function
function birthday(){
    // Define age as a global variable
    global $age;
```

Example 3-8. Using a global variable changes the result (continued)

```
    // Add one to the age value
    $age = $age + 1;
}

// set age to 30
$age = 30;

// Call the function
birthday();

// Display the age
echo $age;

?>
```

This displays:

```
31
```

Global variables should be used sparingly, since it's easy to accidentally modify a variable by mistake. This kind of error can be very difficult to locate. Additionally, when we discuss functions in detail, you'll learn that you can send in values to functions when you call them and get values returned from them when they're done. That all boils down to the fact that you really don't have to use global variables.

If you want to use a variable in a specific function without losing the value each time the function ends, but you don't want to use a global variable, you would use a static variable.

Static variables. *Static* variables provide a variable that isn't destroyed when a function ends. You can use the static variable value again the next time you call the function.

 Call and *execute* mean the same thing.

The easiest way to think about this is to realize that the variable is a global to just that function. A static keyword is used to dictate that the variable you're working with is static, as illustrated in Figure 3-5.

In Example 3-9, we use the static keyword to define these function variables.

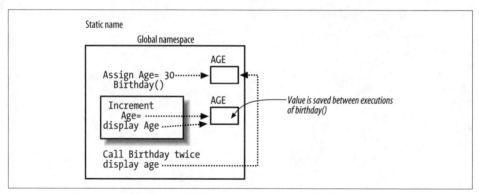

Figure 3-5. The static variable creates a persistent storage space for $age in birthday

Example 3-9. A static variable remembering its last value

```php
<?php

// Define the function

function birthday(){
    // Define age as a static variable
    static $age = 0;

    // Add one to the age value
    $age = $age + 1;

    // Print the static age variable
    echo "Birthday number $age<br />";
}

// Set age to 30
$age = 30;

// Call the function twice
birthday();
birthday();

// Display the age
echo "Age: $age<br />";

?>
```

This displays:

```
Birthday number 1
Birthday number 2
Age: 30
```

The XHTML markup <br /> command is turned into line breaks when your browser displays the results.

The value of $age is now retained each time the birthday function is called. The value will stay around until the program quits. We've discussed two types of variables, but there's one more to discuss: *super global*.

Super global variables. PHP uses special variables called *super globals* to provide information about the PHP script's environment. These variables don't need to be declared as global; they are automatically available and provide important information beyond the script's environment, such as values from a user input.

Since PHP 4.01, the super globals are defined in *arrays*. Arrays are special collections of values that we'll discuss in Chapter 7. The older super global variables such as those starting with $HTTP_* that were not in arrays still exist, but their use is not recommended as they are less secure. Table 3-1 shows the existing arrays since PHP 4.01.

Table 3-1. PHP super globals

Variable array name	Contents
$GLOBALS	Contains any global variables that are accessible for the local script. The variable names are used to select which part of the array to access.
$_SERVER	Contains information about the web server environment.
$_GET	Contains information from GET requests (a form submission).
$_POST	Contains information from POST requests (another type of form submission).
$_COOKIE	Contains inform from HTTP cookies.
$_FILES	Contains information from POST file uploads.
$_ENV	Contains information about the environment (Windows or Mac).
$_REQUEST	Contains information from user inputs. These values should not be trusted.
$_SESSION	Contains information from any variables registered in a session.

An example of a super global is PHP_SELF. This variable contains the name of the running script and is part of the $_SERVER array, as shown in Example 3-10.

Example 3-10. PHP_SELF being used with a file called test.php

```php
<?php
echo $_SERVER["PHP_SELF"];
?>
```

This outputs:

```
/test.php
```

This variable is especially useful, as it can be used to call the current script again when processing a form. Super global variables provide a convenient way to access information about a script's environment from server settings to user inputted data. Now that you've got a handle on variables and scope, we can talk about what types of information variables hold.

Strings

Variables can hold more than just numbers. They can hold characters and *strings*, or an ordered list of characters. Figure 3-6 demonstrates how an ordered list of characters becomes a string.

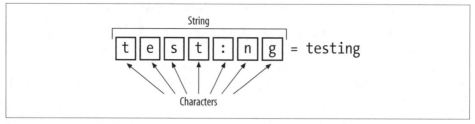

Figure 3-6. How individual characters form a string

A string can be used directly in a function call or it can be stored in a variable. In Example 3-11, we create the exact same string twice: first we store it in a variable, and then we place the string directly into a function.

Example 3-11. Working with strings

```
<?php
$my_string = "Margaritaville - Suntan Oil Application!";
echo "Margaritaville - Suntan Oil Application!";
?>
```

In Example 3-12, the first string is stored in the variable $my_string, while the second string is used in the echo function and *isn't* stored. Remember to save your strings into variables if you plan on using them more than once!

Strings are flexible. You can even insert variables into string definitions when using double quotes to start and end your string, as shown in Example 3-12. Using a single quote to start and end your string does not allow a variable to be placed in the string.

Example 3-12. Using a variable in a string definition

```
<?php
$my_string = "Margaritaville - Suntan Oil Application!";
echo "Time for $my_string";
?>
```

This example displays "Time for Margaritaville - Suntan Oil Application!" Double quotes are used in the above string, but single quotes or apostrophes can both be used as long as you won't be inserting variable values; see Example 3-13.

Example 3-13. Single quotes used in a string assignment

```php
<?php
$my_string = 'Margaritaville - Suntan Oil Application!';
echo $my_string;
?>
```

Remember, if you want to use a single quote within a string marked with single quotes, you have to *escape* the single quote with a backslash (\). Double quotes allow the use of many special escaped characters that you can't use with a single quote string, such as an apostrophe. If you had escaped an apostrophe with a backslash in a double-quoted string, the backslash would show up when you output the string.

Special characters in strings

Tab, newline, and carriage returns are all examples of extra, yet ignorable, whitespace (see Example 3-14). If you are writing to a file, a valuable tool is an escaped character. One downside of using the apostrophe to start and end a string is that you can't include a variable. This leads us to be careful about using HTML markup or any other string that includes quotes.

Example 3-14. Various special characters in string assignments

```php
<?php
$newline = "A newline is \n";
$return = "A carriage return is \r";
$tab = "A tab is \t";
$dollar = "A dollar sign is \$";
$doublequote = "A double-quote is \"";
?>
```

The echo function uses quotes to define the start and end of a string, so you must use one of the following tactics if your string contains quotations:

- Don't use quotes inside your string.
- Escape quotes within the string with a slash. To escape a quote, just place a slash directly before the quotation mark; i.e., \".
- Use single quotes (apostrophes) for quotes inside your string.
- Start and end your string with apostrophes.

In Examples 3-15 and 3-16, the wrong and right use of the echo function is demonstrated.

Example 3-15. Using echo with special characters

```php
<?php
// This won't work because of the quotes around specialH2!
echo "<h2 class="specialH2">Margaritaville!</h2>";
?>
specialH2
```

In the first echo example, we forgot to escape the double quotes that surround the specialH2, which is HTML text. Attempting to display this page produces the error:

> **Parse error:** parse error, unexpected T_STRING, expecting ','
> or ';' in **/home/www/html/oreilly/ch3/parse.php** on line **3**

If you see that error, start by checking your single and double quotes to make sure they all match up correctly, as in Example 3-16.

Example 3-16. Correct escaping of special characters

```php
<?php
// OK because we used single quotes
echo "<h2 class=\"specialH2\">Margaritaville!</h2>";
echo '<h2 class="specialH2">Margaritaville!</h2>';
?>
```

Example 3-16 *escapes* quotations by placing a slash in front of each one (\"). The slash tells PHP that you want the quotation to be used within the string and *not* ending echo's string. You can also use an apostrophe (') to mark the beginning and end of a string.

If you use an apostrophe or single quote to define your string, double quotes don't need to be escaped. However, you can't include variables when using single quotes.

You'll find that when you're working with strings, you'll want to combine them. This is actually like working with shorthand instead of writing out each and every word.

Comparing strings

PHP has functions to compare strings that aren't exactly alike. For example, you may want to consider "Bill" to be the same as "BILL," ignoring the case of the string.

Use strcmp (*string1, string2*) to compare two strings including the case. The return value is 0 if the two strings have the same text. Any nonzero value indicates they are not the same.

Use strcasecmp (*string1, string2*) to compare two strings without comparing the case. The return value is 0 if the two strings have the same text. Any nonzero value indicates they are not the same.

Example 3-17 compares "Bill" to "BILL" without considering the case.

Example 3-17. Using strcasecmp to compare two strings

```php
<?php

$name1 = "Bill";
$name2 = "BILL";

$result = strcasecmp($name1, $name2);

if (!$result){
    echo "They match.";
}

?>
```

This returns:

```
They match.
```

Concatenation

Concatenation combines one or more text strings and variables, as shown in Example 3-18. When performing this combination, you save yourself the hassle of creating numerous echo statements, or in other words, you build up a string and use it.

Example 3-18. Concatenating strings together

```php
<?php
$my_string = "Hello Max. My name is: ";
$newline = "<br />";
echo $my_string . "Paula" . $newline;
echo "Hi, I'm Max. Who are you? " . $my_string . $newline;
echo "Hi, I'm Max. Who are you? " . $my_string . "Paula";
//The last line is the same as echo "Hi, I'm max. Who are you? $my_string Paula";
?>
```

The output of your code looks like Figure 3-7 in your browser window.

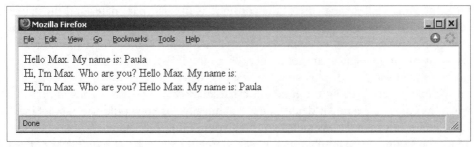

Figure 3-7. Concatenation output

Variables and text strings are joined together with a period (.). This can be done multiple times, as shown in Figure 3-8.

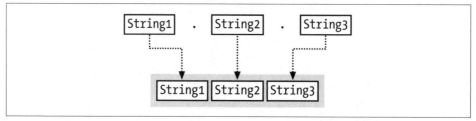

Figure 3-8. How strings come together with concatenation

Since your time is finite, tying strings and variables together helps you create dynamic web sites faster.

Combining strings with other types

If you combine a string with another data type, such as a number, the result is also a string, as shown in Example 3-19.

Example 3-19. Combining a string and a number

```
<?php
$str = "This is an example of ". 3 ." in the middle of a string.";
echo $str;
?>
```

This displays:

```
This is an example of 3 in the middle of a string.
```

$str contains a string even though a number was inserted into the middle.

Constants

You can define constants in your program. A constant, like its name implies, cannot change its value during the execution of your program. It's defined using the define function, which takes the name of the constant as the first parameter and the values as the second parameter. The definition of a constant is global and can be defined as any simple (scalar) data type such as a string or a number. You can get the value of a constant by simply specifying its name; see Example 3-20. Unlike how you handle variables, you should not put the dollar sign ($) before a constant. A cool thing you do with constants is using the function constant(*name*) to return a constant's value when the constant's name is determined dynamically. Or you could use get_defined_constants to return a list (as an array) of all your defined constants. If you're unsure about the arguments to a function, you can search the PHP site at *http://www.php.net* to find function parameters and return values.

These are the differences between constants and variables:

- Constants do not have a dollar sign ($) before them.
- Constants can only be defined using the `define` function, not by simple assignment.
- Constants are defined and accessed globally.
- Constants cannot be redefined or undefined once they have been set.
- Constants can only evaluate to scalar values.

Example 3-20 demonstrates how to use a constant in your program.

Example 3-20. Using a constant in your program

```php
<?php
define("HELLO", "Hello world!");
echo HELLO; // outputs "Hello world."
?>
```

This outputs:

```
Hello world!
```

Constants are useful for values that you need to make sure don't change, such as a configuration file location.

If you use an undefined constant, PHP assumes that you mean the name of the constant itself, just as if you called it as a string—for example, `CONSTANT` as opposed to `"CONSTANT"`. If the define line of Example 3-20 is commented out, the output becomes:

```
HELLO
```

Predefined constants

PHP provides a few constants that are predefined similar to the way we have some super globals. Examples of these include `__FILE__`, which returns the name of the PHP file that's being executed, and `__LINE__`, which returns the line number in that file. They can be handy for generating an error message as they tell you where in your code the error occurred, as shown in Example 3-21.

Example 3-21. Echoing the line and file predefined constants for a script called predefined_constants.php

```php
<?php
echo "Executing line ". __LINE__ . " of PHP script " . __FILE__ . '.';
?>
```

This returns:

```
Executing line 2 of PHP script /home/www/html/oreilly/ch3/predefined_constants.php.
```

The path to your script may be different than the example. On Windows, it's likely to be *C:\Program Files\Apache Group\htdocs\c3*.

Doing Math

Variables can hold numbers, too, and it's useful to perform mathematical operations on those numbers. All fundamental mathematical functions are available using PHP. You may feel like you're back in middle school algebra, but the basic functions are just like they were then: adding, subtracting, multiplying, and dividing. In Example 3-22, the divide (/) operator calculates the percentage from its operands sunny days and total days in a year to get a percentage of approximately 82 percent.

Example 3-22. PHP mathematical function usage

```
<?php
$sunny_days=300;
$Margaritaville_sunny_days_ratio=$sunny_days/365;
echo $Margaritaville_sunny_days_ratio;
?>
```

In Figure 3-9, the 82 percent outcome from our example code displays in your browser window.

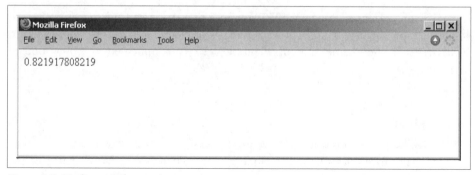

Figure 3-9. Mathematical operation output

PHP also supports the mathematical operations listed in Table 3-2.

Table 3-2. The basic mathematical operators

Mathematical operator	Name	Example	Result
+	Addition	2+2	4
−	Subtraction	2−1	1
*	Multiplication	2*2	4
/	Division	2/2	1
%	Modulo (remainder)	2%1	0

The operators can take whole numbers or decimal numbers as their input.

 Use caution when dividing to avoid dividing a number by zero, as this generates an infinite result and displays this PHP warning: "Warning: Division by zero."

Of course, you can do all sorts of complex mathematical operations such as trigonometry, and there is a specific order in which the math operators are applied, but we'll discuss those in the next chapter. You can also use *http://www.php.net* by entering Math into their search tool, which provides a link to *http://us3.php.net/manual/en/ref.math.php* that gives you a detailed listing and usage of all of the math functions.

Combined assignment

Combined assignment operators provide a shortcut for performing two common tasks at the same time. They combine reading a variable, performing an operation on it, and placing the result back in the same variable. The operations are mostly mathematical but can also include other operators like concatenation.

Combined assignment operators take the form the arithmetic operator directly followed by an equals sign (=). For example, the statement:

```
$counter=$counter+1;
```

is equivalent to:

```
$counter+=1;
```

Which is shorthand for taking the value in $counter, adding one to it, and then saving the result back in $counter.

Table 3-3 lists the most common combined assignment operators.

Table 3-3. Combined assignment operators

Combined operation	Operation	Produces
$num+=y	Addition	$num=$num+y
$num -=y	Subtraction	$num=$num-y
$num *=y	Multiplication	$num=$num*y
$num /=y	Division	$num=$num/y
$num.= "y"	Concatenation	$string=$string."y"

You'll find that these operators are very handy when creating your dynamic web pages. They'll also be used frequently in our examples. They have the added benefit of reducing the chance that you'll have a typo in your variable name, since you need to specify the variable name once only.

Along the same lines as combined operators comes a shorthand method for adding one or subtracting one from a variable.

Autoincrement and autodecrement

It's very common when writing your code to ether increment or decrement a variable by one. It's so common that PHP has a special shortcut for doing it. The autoincrement operator is ++ and is used like this:

```
$counter++;
```

What we did was:

```
$counter+=1;
```

Example 3-23 adds one to $counter.

Example 3-23. Using autoincrement to add to a variable

```
<?php
$counter=1;
$counter++;
echo $counter
?>
```

This produces:

```
2
```

The same concept applies to the automatic decrement operator, --.

Example 3-24 subtracts one from $counter.

Example 3-24. Using the autodecrement operator

```
<?php
$counter=1;
$counter--;
echo $counter
?>
```

This produces:

```
0
```

This notation is used frequently when doing repetitive tasks to keep track of how many times you've done them.

Pre-increment and -decrement

If you're incrementing or decrementing at the same time that you're also comparing the value of the variable, such as in a for or while loop, a pre-increment or -decrement can affect the value that's used for the comparison. When using the pre- operations, the value changes before the comparison, which is different than the de facto post-processing.

For example:

```
--$counter;
```

or:

```
++$counter;
```

Both of the operators still change the value of the counter variable, but they change the value sooner. If you are using that variable in a test, you'll see the current value before the change. We'll talk more about testing the values of variable executing blocks of code repetitively in the next chapter. Example 3-25 shows how these operators work.

Example 3-25. Using pre- and post-increment

```
<?php
$test=1;
echo "Preincrement: ".(++$test);
echo "<BR>";
echo "Value afterwords: ".$test;
echo "<BR>";
$test=1;
echo "Postincrement: ".($test++);
echo "<BR>";
echo "Value afterwords: ".$test;
?>
```

This produces:

```
Preincrement: 2
Value afterwords: 2
Postincrement: 1
Value afterwords: 2
```

Notice that in Example 3-25, the value after a post- or pre-increment is always 2. When using the pre-increment, the value is 2 in the echo statement that contains the combined operator.

In this chapter, you've learned about the basic concepts for writing PHP scripts. You've introduced variables that can remember information while our scripts execute. You know how to store values in variables and access those values. You don't have to worry about specifying data types, because PHP attempts to convert types automatically. You've also learned how to do basic mathematical operations and the shortcuts for the most common combined assignment operators.

These concepts will form the basis for the rest of what you learn about PHP programming, including building expressions.

The next chapter will introduce more complicated PHP code such as arrays, including looping and conditional logic. After that, we'll be able to jump into MySQL and how it operates as a database.

Chapter 3 Questions

Question 3-1. How does text output in your browser if you don't use PHP syntax?

Question 3-2. What do you combine with PHP code to create a dynamic web site?

Question 3-3. How do you add comments to your code?

Question 3-4. What are the two types of comments?

Question 3-5. How is a semicolon used in PHP?

Question 3-6. What does a variable store?

Question 3-7. How do you define a variable in PHP?

Question 3-8. Are variables in PHP case-sensitive?

Question 3-9. How are functions used with a chunk of PHP code?

Question 3-10. What is `PHP_SELF`?

Question 3-11. How do you escape a single quote?

Question 3-12. What does `strcmp` do?

Question 3-13. What combines one or more text strings as a variable?

Question 3-14. What is the result of combining a string with another data type?
See the Appendix for the answers to these questions.

PHP Decision Making

In the last chapter, you started to get a feel for programming with PHP and some code basics. Now it's time to expand your knowledge and ability with PHP. We'll start with expressions and statements. Concepts from Chapter 3 and this chapter lay the foundations for adding your database, MySQL, which will be explored in Chapter 5.

Expressions

There are several building blocks of coding that you need to understand: statements, expressions, and operators. A *statement* is code that performs a task. Statements themselves are made up of expressions and operators. An *expression* is a piece of code that evaluates to a value. A value is a number, a string of text, or a *Boolean*.

A Boolean is an expression that results in a value of either TRUE or FALSE. For example, the expression 10 > 5 (10 is greater than 5) is a Boolean expression because the result is TRUE. All expressions that contain *relational operators*, such as the less-than sign (<), are Boolean. The Boolean operators are AND, OR, XOR, NOR, and NOT.

An *operator* is a code element that acts on an expression in some way. For instance, a minus sign can be used to tell the computer to decrement the value of the expression after it from the expression before it. The most important thing to understand about expressions is how to combine them into compound expressions and statements using operators. So we're going to look at operators used to turn expressions into more complex expressions and statements.

The simplest form of expression is a literal or a variable. A *literal* evaluates to itself. Some examples of literals are numbers, strings, or constants. A *variable* evaluates to the value assigned to it. For instance, any of the expressions in Table 4-1 are valid.

Table 4-1. Valid expressions

Example	Type
1	A numeric value literal
"Becker Furniture"	A string literal
TRUE	A constant literal
$user_name	A variable with username as a string
1+1	A numeric value expression that evaluates to a literal

Although a literal or variable may be a valid expression, they aren't expressions that do anything. You get expressions to do things such as math or assignment by linking them together with operators.

 Assignment is a symbol that represents a specific action. For example, a plus sign (+) is an operator that represents addition.

An *operator* combines simple expressions into more complex expressions by creating relationships between simple expressions that can be evaluated. For instance, if the relation you want to establish is the cumulative joining of two numeric values together, you could write "3 + 4".

Figure 4-1 shows how the parts of an expression come together.

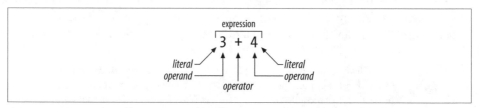

Figure 4-1. Operands and operators working together as an expression to form a value

The numbers 3 and 4 are each valid expressions. The equation 3 + 4 is also a valid expression, whose value, in this case, happens to be 7. The plus sign (+) is an operator. The numbers to either side of it are its arguments, or operands. An *argument* or *operand* is something an operator takes action on; for example, an argument or operand could be a directive from your housemate to empty the dishwasher, and the operator empties the dishwasher. Different operators have different types and numbers of operands. Operators can also be *overloaded*, which means that they do different things in different contexts.

You've probably guessed from this information that two or more expressions connected by operators are called an expression. You're right, as operators create complex expressions. The more subexpressions and operators, the longer and more complex the expression. But no matter what, as long as it equates to a value, it's still an expression.

When expressions and operators are assembled to produce a piece of code that actually does something, you have a statement. We discussed statements in Chapter 3. They end in semicolons, which is the programming equivalent of a complete sentence.

For instance, $Margaritaville + $Sun_Tan_Application is an expression. It equates to something, which is the sum of the values of $Margaritaville + $Sun_Tan_Application, but it doesn't do anything. While it's an expression, the output doesn't make any sense, but if you add the equals sign (=), $Fun_in_the_Sun = $Margaritaville + $Sun_Tan_Application;, you get a statement, because it does something. As Example 4-1 demonstrates, it assigns the sum of the values of $Margaritaville + $Sun_Tan_Application to $Fun_in_the_Sun.

Example 4-1. Sum of values

```php
<?php
$Margaritaville = 3; // Three margaritas
$Sun_Tan_Application = 2; // Two applications of sun tan
$Fun_in_the_Sun = $Margaritaville + $Sun_Tan_Application;
echo $Fun_in_the_Sun;
?>
```

Example 4-1 outputs:

    5

There really isn't much more to understand about expressions except for the assembly of them into compound expressions and statements using operators. Next, we're going to discuss operators that are used to turn expressions into more complex expressions and statements.

Operator Concepts

PHP has many types of operators. The categories are:

- Arithmetic operators
- Array operators
- Assignment operators
- Bitwise operators
- Comparison operators
- Execution operators
- Incrementing/decrementing operators
- Logical operators
- String operators

The operators are listed as found on *http://www.zend.com/manual/language. operators.php*. There are some operators we're not going to discuss in order for you to get up and running with PHP as quickly as possible. These include some of the casting operators that we'll just skim the surface of, for now. When working with operators, there are four aspects that are critical:

- Number of operands
- Type of operands
- Order of precedence
- Operator associativity

The easiest place to start is by talking about the operands.

Number of Operands

Depending on which operator you are using, it may take different numbers of operands. Many operators are used to combine two expressions into a more complex single expression; these are called *binary operators*. Binary operators include addition, subtraction, multiplication, and division.

Other operators take only one operand; these are called *unary operators*. Think of the negation operator (–) that multiplies a numeric value by –1. The auto-increment and -decrement operators described in Chapter 3 are also unary operators.

A *ternary operator* takes three operands. The shorthand for an if statement, which we'll talk about later when discussing conditionals, takes three operands.

Types of Operands

You need to be mindful of the type of operand an operator is meant to work on, because certain operators expect their operands to be particular data types. PHP attempts to make your life as easy as possible by automatically converting operands to the data type that an operator is expecting. But there are times that an automatic conversion isn't possible.

Mathematical operators are an example of where you need to be careful with your types. They take only numbers as operands. For example, when you try to multiply two strings, PHP can convert the strings to numbers. While "Becker" * "Furniture" is not a valid expression, it returns zero. Because the strings don't contain simple numbers, an expression that is converted without an error is "70" * "80". This outputs to 5600. Although 70 and 80 are strings, PHP is able to convert them to the number type required by the mathematical operator.

There will be times when you want to explicitly set or convert a variable's type. There are two ways to do this in PHP—first, by using settype to actually change the data type, or second, by casting, which temporarily converts the value. PHP uses *casting* to convert data types. When PHP does the casting for you automatically, it's called *implicit casting*. You can also specify data types explicitly, but it's not something that you'll likely need to do.

 PHP uses implicit casting to the type that the operator requires.

The cast types allowed are:

(int), (integer)
> Cast to integer

(bool), (boolean)
> Cast to Boolean

(float), (double), (real)
> Cast to float

(string)
> Cast to string

(array)
> Cast to array

(object)
> Cast to object

To use a cast, place it before the variable to cast, as in Example 4-2. The $test_ string variable contains the string "1234".

Example 4-2. Casting a variable

```
$test=1234;
$test_string=(string)$test;
```

Keep in mind that it may not always be obvious what will happen when casting between certain types. You might run into problems if you don't watch yourself when manipulating variable types.

Some binary operators such as the *assignment operators* have further restrictions on the lefthand operand. Because the assignment operator is assigning a value to the lefthand operator, it must be something that can take a value such as a variable. Example 4-3 demonstrates good and bad lefthand expressions.

Example 4-3. Lefthand expressions

```
3 = $locations; // bad - a value can not be assign to the literal 3
$a + $b = $c; //bad - the expression on the left isn't one variable
$c = $a + $b; //OK
$stores = "Becker"." "."Furniture"; // OK
```

There is a simpler way to remember this. The lefthand expression in assignment operations is known as an *L-value*. L-values in PHP are variables, elements of an array, and object properties. Don't worry about object properties.

Order of precedence

The *order of precedence* of an operator determines which operator processes first in an expression. For instance, the multiplication and division process before addition and subtraction. You can see a simplified table at *http://www.zend.com/manual/ language.operators.php#language.operators.precedence*.

If the operators have the same precedence, they are processed in the order they appear in the expression. For example, multiplication and division process in the order they appear in an expression, because they have the same precedence. Operators with the same precedence can occur in any order without affecting the result.

Most expressions do not have more than one operator of the same precedence level, or the order in which they process doesn't change the result. As shown in Example 4-4, when adding and subtracting, it doesn't matter whether you add or subtract first—the result is still 1.

Example 4-4. Order of precedence

```
2 + 4 - 5  == 1;
4 - 5 + 2 == 1;

4 * 5 / 2 == 10;
5 / 2 * 4 == 10;

2 + 4 - 5  == 1;
4 - 5 + 2 == 1;

4 * 5 / 2 == 10;
5 / 2 * 4 == 10;
```

When using expressions that contain operators of different precedence levels, the order can change the value of the expression. You can use parentheses, (and), to override the precedence levels or just to make the expression easier to read. Example 4-5 shows how to change the default precedence.

Example 4-5. The multiplication is done last because of the override

```
echo 2 * 3 + 4 + 1;
11
echo 2 * (3 + 4 + 1);
16
```

PHP has several levels of precedence, enough so that it's difficult to keep track of them without checking a reference. Table 4-2 is a list of operators in PHP sorted by order of precedence from highest to lowest. Operators with the same level number are all of the same precedence.

 The Association column lists operators that are right to left instead of left to right. We'll discuss associativity next.

Table 4-2. List of PHP operators

Operator	Description	Operands	Association	Level
NEW	Create new object	Constructor call	Right to left	1
.	Property access (dot notation)	Objects		2
[ ]	Array index	Array, integer, or string		2
( )	Function call	Function or argument		2
!	Logical NOT	Unary	Right to left	3
~	Bitwise NOT	Unary	Right to left	3
++, --	Increment and decrement operators	1value	Right to left	3
+, -	Unary plus, negation	Number	Right to left	3
(int)	Cast operators	Unary	Right to left	3
(double)	Cast operators	Unary	Right to left	3
(string)	Cast operators	Unary	Right to left	3
(array)	Cast operators	Unary	Right to left	3
(object)	Cast operators	Unary	Right to left	3
@	Inhibit errors	Unary	Right to left	3
*, /, %	Multiplication, division	Numbers		4
+, -	Addition, subtraction	Numbers		5
.	Concatenation	Strings		5
<<, >>	Bitwise shift left, bitwise shift right	Binary		6
<, <=, >, >=	Comparison operators	Numbers, strings		7
==, !=	Equality, inequality	Any		8
===, !==	Identity, non-identity	Any		8
&	Bitwise AND	Binary		9
^	Bitwise NOR	Binary		10
|	Bitwise OR	Binary		11
&&	Logical AND	Boolean		12
||	Logical OR	Boolean		13
? :	Conditional	Boolean	Right to left	14
=	Assignment	1value=any	Right to left	15

Table 4-2. List of PHP operators (continued)

Operator	Description	Operands	Association	Level
AND	Logical AND	Boolean		16
OR	Logical OR	Boolean		17
XOR	Logical XOR	Boolean		18

Associativity

All operators process their operators in a certain direction. This direction is called *associativity*, and it depends on the type of operator. Most operators are processed from left to right, which is called left associativity. For example, in the expression 3 + 5 – 2, 3 and 5 are added together, and then 2 is subtracted from the addition, resulting in 8. Left associativity means that the expression is evaluated from left to right. Right associativity means the opposite.

Since it has right associativity, the assignment operator is one of the exceptions, since it has right associativity. The expression $a=$b=$c processes by $b being assigned the value of $c, and then $a being assigned the value of $b. This assigns the same value to all of the variables. If the assignment operator is right associative, the variables might not have the same value.

If you're thinking that this is incredibly complicated, don't worry. These rules are only enforced if you fail to be explicit about your instructions. Keep in mind that you should always use brackets in your expressions to make your actual meaning very clear. This helps both PHP and also other people who may need to read your code.

Relational Operators

In Chapter 3, we discussed assignment and math operators. Relational operators provide the ability to compare two operands and return either TRUE or FALSE regarding the comparison. An expression that returns only TRUE or FALSE is called a Boolean expression, which we discussed earlier in this chapter. These comparisons include tests for equality and less than or greater than. These comparison operators allow you to tell PHP when to do something based on a comparison being true so decisions can be made in your code.

Equality

The equality operator, a double equals sign (==), is used frequently. Using the single = in its place is a common logical error in programs, since it assigns values rather than tests equality.

If the two operands are equal, TRUE is returned; otherwise, FALSE is returned. If you're echoing your results, TRUE is printed as 1 in your browser. FALSE is 0, which won't display in your browser.

It's a simple construct but it also allows you to test for conditions. If the operands are of different types, PHP attempts to convert them before comparing.

For example, '1' == 1 is true. Also, $a == 1 is true if the variable $a is assigned to 1.

If you don't want the equals operator to automatically convert types, you can use the *identity operator*, a triple equals sign ===, which checks that the values and types are the same. For example, '1' === 1 is false because they're different types, since a string doesn't equal an integer.

Sometimes you might want to check to see whether two things are different. The *inequality operator*, an exclamation mark before the equals sign (!=), checks for the opposite of equality, which means not equal to.

```
'1' != 'A'    // true
'1' != '1'    // false
```

Comparison operators

You may need to check for more than just equality. *Comparison operators* test the relationship between two values. You may be familiar with these from high school math. They include less than (<), less than or equal to (<=), greater than (>), and greater than or equal to (>=).

For example, 3<4 is TRUE, while 3<3 is FALSE but 3<=3 is TRUE.

Comparison operators are often used to check for something happening up until a set point. For example, a web store might offer free shipping if you purchase five or more items. So the code must compare the number of items to the number five before changing the shipping cost.

Logical operators

Logical operators work with the Boolean results of relational operators to build more complex logical expressions; there are four logical operators shown in Table 4-3.

Table 4-3. Logical operators

Logical operator	Meaning
AND	TRUE if both operands must be TRUE
OR	TRUE if at least one operand is TRUE
XOR	TRUE if only one operand is TRUE
NOT	TRUE if FALSE, FALSE if TRUE

To test whether both operands are true, use the AND operator, also represented as double ampersands (&&). TRUE is returned only if both operands are TRUE; otherwise, FALSE is returned. See Table 4-3 for more information.

To test whether one operand is TRUE, use the OR operator, which is also represented as double vertical bars (||). TRUE is returned only if either or both operands are TRUE.

> Using the OR operator can create tricky program logic problems. If PHP finds that the first operand is TRUE, it won't evaluate the second operand. While this saves execution time, you need to be careful that the second operator doesn't contain code that needs to be executed for your program to work properly.

To test whether either operand is TRUE *but not both*, use XOR. XOR returns TRUE if one and only one operand is TRUE.

To negate a Boolean value, use the NOT operator represented as an exclamation point (!). It returns TRUE if the operand has a value of FALSE. It returns FALSE if the operand is TRUE.

> If you accidentally use & instead of && or | instead of ||, you'll end up getting the wrong operator. They compare binary data bit by bit. PHP converts your operands into binary data and applies the binary operators.

Because they have different precedence levels, AND and OR have two representations. Table 4-4 displays logical statements and their results.

Table 4-4. Logical statements and their results

Example logical statement	Result
TRUE AND TRUE	TRUE
FALSE AND TRUE	FALSE
TRUE OR FALSE	TRUE
FALSE OR FALSE	FALSE
TRUE XOR TRUE	FALSE
!TRUE	FALSE

Conditionals

Since we've been talking about variables, we should also mention conditionals, which, like variables, form a building block in our foundation of PHP development. They alter a script's behavior according to the criteria set in the code. There are three primary elements of conditionals in PHP:

- if
- switch
- ? : : (shorthand for an if statement)

PHP also supports a conditional called a switch statement. The switch statement is useful when you need to take different action based on the contents of a variable that may be set to one of a list of values.

The if Statement

The if statement offers the ability to execute a block of code, if the supplied condition is TRUE; otherwise, the code block doesn't execute. The type of condition can be any expression, including tests for nonzero, null, equality, variables, and returned values from functions.

No matter what, every single conditional you create includes a conditional clause. If a condition is true, the code block in curly brackets ({}) is executed. If not, PHP ignores it and moves to the second condition and continues through as many clauses as you write until PHP hits an else, then it automatically executes that block.

Figure 4-2 demonstrates how an if statement works. The else block always needs to come last and be treated as if it's the default action. This is similar to the semicolon (;), which acts as the end of a sentence. Common true conditions are:

- $var, if $var has a value other than the empty set (0), an empty string, or NULL
- isset ($var), if $var has any value other than NULL, including the empty set or an empty string
- TRUE or any variation thereof

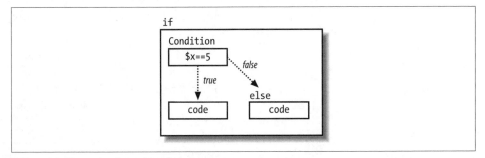

Figure 4-2. Execution branching based on an expression

We haven't talked about the second bullet point, isset, yet. isset() is a function that checks whether a variable is set. A set variable is one that has a value other than NULL. Table 4-2 shows comparative and logical operators, which can be used in conjunction with parentheses, (), to create more complicated expressions.

The syntax for the if statement is:

```
if (conditional expression)
  {
  block of code;
  }
```

If the expression in the conditional block evaluates to TRUE, the block of code after it executes. In this example, if the variable $username is set to Admin, a welcome message is printed. Otherwise, nothing happens.

```
if ($username=="Admin") {
  echo ('Welcome to the admin page.');
  }
```

The curly brackets aren't needed if you want to execute only one statement, but it's good practice to always use them, as it makes the code easier to read and more resilient to change.

The else statement

The else statement (see Example 4-6) provides for a default block of code that executes if the condition returned is FALSE. It must always be part of an if statement, as it doesn't take a conditional itself.

Example 4-6. else and if statements

```
if ($username == "Admin"){
    echo ('Welcome to the admin page.');
}
else {
    echo ('Welcome to the user page.');
}
```

Remember to close out the code block from the if conditional if you used brackets to start the block of code. Similar to the if block, the else block should also use curly brackets to begin and end the code.

The elseif statement

All of this is great except for when you want to test for several conditions at a time. To do this, you can use the elseif statement. It allows for testing of additional conditions until one is found to be true or you hit the else block. Each elseif has its own code block that comes directly after the elseif condition. The elseif must come after the if statement and before an else statement if one exists.

The elseif structure is a little complicated, but Example 4-7 should help you understand it.

Example 4-7. Checking multiple conditions

```
if ($username == "Admin"){
    echo ('Welcome to the admin page.');
}
elseif ($username == "Guest"){
    echo ('Please take a look around.');
}
```

Example 4-7. Checking multiple conditions (continued)

```
else {
    echo ("Welcome back, $username.");
}
```

Here you can check for and take different action based on two values for $username. Then you also have the option to do something else if the $user_name isn't one of the first two.

The next construct builds on the concepts of the if/else statement, but it allows you to efficiently check the results of an expression to many values without having a separate if/else for each value.

The ? Operator

The ? operator is a ternary operator, meaning it takes three operands. It works like an if statement but returns a value from one of the two expressions. The conditional expression determines the value of the expression. A colon (:) is used to separate the expressions:

```
{expression} ? return_when_expression_true : return_when_expression_false;
```

Example 4-8 tests a value and returns a different string based on it being TRUE or FALSE.

Example 4-8. Using the ? operator to create a message

```
<?php
$logged_in = TRUE;
$user = "Admin";
$banner = ($logged_in==TRUE)?"Welcome back $user!":"Please login.";
echo "$banner";
?>
```

Example 4-8 produces:

```
Welcome back Admin!
```

This can be pretty useful for checking errors. Now, let's look at a statement that lets you check an expression against a list of possible values to pick the executable code.

The switch Statement

The switch statement compares an expression to numerous values. It's very common to have an expression, such as a variable, for which you'll want to execute different code for each value stored in the variable. For example, you might have a variable called $action, which may have the values add, modify, and delete. The switch statement makes it easy to define a block of code to execute for each of those values.

To illustrate the difference between using the if statement and switch to test a variable for several values, we'll show you the code for the if statement (in Example 4-9), and then for the switch statement (in Example 4-10).

Example 4-9. Using if to test for multiple values

```
if ($action == "ADD") {
    echo "Perform actions for adding.";
    echo "As many statements as you like can be in each block.";
}
elseif ($action == "MODIFY") {
    echo "Perform actions for modifying.";
}
elseif ($action == "DELETE") {
    echo "Perform actions for deleting.";
}
```

Example 4-10. Using switch to test for multiple values

```
switch ($action) {
    case "ADD":
        echo "Perform actions for adding.";
        echo "As many statements as you like can be in each block.";
        break;
    case "MODIFY":
        echo "Perform actions for modifying.";
        break;
    case "DELETE":
        echo "Perform actions for deleting.";
        break;
}
```

The switch statement works by taking the value after the switch keyword and comparing it to the cases in the order they appear. If no case matches, no code is executed. Once a case matches, the code is executed. The code in subsequent cases also executes until the end of the switch statement or until a break keyword. This is useful for processes that have several sequential steps. If the user has already done some of the steps, he can jump into the process where he left off.

> The expression after the switch statement must evaluate to a simple type like a number, integer, or string. An array can be used only if a specific member of the array is referenced as a simple type.

There are numerous ways to tell PHP to not execute cases besides the matching case.

Breaking out

If you want only the code in the matching block to execute, you can place a break keyword at the end of that block. When PHP comes across the break keyword, processing jumps to the next line after the entire switch statement. Example 4-11 illustrates how processing works with no break statements.

Example 4-11. What happens when there are no break keywords

```
$action="ASSEMBLE ORDER";
switch ($action) {
    case "ASSEMBLE ORDER":
        echo "Perform actions for order assembly.<br>";
    case "PACKAGE":
        echo "Perform actions for packing.<br>";
    case "SHIP":
        echo "Perform actions for shipping.<br>";
}

    echo "Perform actions for shipping.<br>";
}
?>
```

If the value of $action is "ASSEMBLE ORDER", the result is:

```
Perform actions for order assembly.
Perform actions for packing.
Perform actions for shipping.
```

However, if a user had already assembled an order, a value of "PACKAGE" produces the following:

```
Perform actions for packing.
Perform actions for shipping.
```

Defaulting

The case statement also provides a way to do something if none of the other cases match, which is similar to the else statement in an if, elseif, else block.

Use DEFAULT: for the switches last case statement, as shown in Example 4-12.

Example 4-12. Using the DEFAULT: statement to generate an error

```
switch ($action) {
    case "ADD":
        echo "Perform actions for adding.";
        break;
    case "MODIFY":
        echo "Perform actions for modifying.";
        break;
    case "DELETE":
        echo "Perform actions for deleting.";
        break;
    default:
        echo "Error: Action must be either ADD, MODIFY, or DELETE.";
}
```

The switch statement also supports the alternate syntax in which the switch and endswitch keywords define the start and end of the switch instead of the curly braces {}, as shown in Example 4-13.

Example 4-13. Using endswitch to end the switch definition

```
switch ($action):
    case "ADD":
        echo "Perform actions for adding.";
        break;
    case "MODIFY":
        echo "Perform actions for modifying.";
        break;
    case "DELETE":
        echo "Perform actions for deleting.";
        break;
    default:
        echo "Error: Action must be either ADD, MODIFY, or DELETE.";
endswitch;
```

You've learned that you can have your programs execute different code based on conditions called expressions. The switch statement provides a convenient format for checking the value of an expression against many possible values.

Looping

Now change the flow of your PHP program based on comparisons, but if you want to repeat a task until a comparison is FALSE, you will need to use looping. Each time the code in the loop executes, it is called an *iteration*. It's useful for many common tasks such as displaying the results of a query by looping through the returned rows. PHP provides the while, for, and while...do constructs to perform loops.

Each of the loop constructs requires two basic pieces of information. First, when to stop looping is defined just like the comparison in an if statement. Second, the code to perform is also required and specified either on a single line or within curly braces. A logical error would be to omit the code in the loop, causing an infinite loop.

The code is executed as long as the expression evaluates to TRUE. To avoid an *infinite loop*, which would loop forever, your code should affect the expressions so that it becomes FALSE. When this happens, the loop stops, and execution continues with the next line of code, following the logical loop.

while Loops

The while loop takes the expression followed by the code to execute. Figure 4-3 illustrates how a while loop processes.

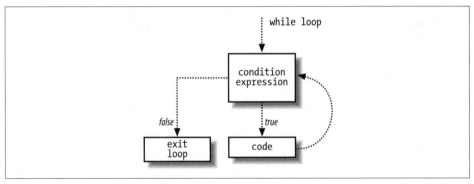

Figure 4-3. How a while loop executes

The syntax is for a while loop is:

```
while (expression)
{
    code to execute;
}
```

An example is shown in Example 4-14.

Example 4-14. A sample while loop that counts to 10

```php
<?php
$num = 1;

while ($num <= 10){
    print "Number is $num<br />\n";
    $num++;
}

print 'Done.';
?>
```

Example 4-14 produces:

```
Number is 1
Number is 2
Number is 3
Number is 4
Number is 5
Number is 6
Number is 7
Number is 8
Number is 9
Number is 10
Done.
```

Before the loop begins, the variable $num is set to 1. This is called initializing a counter variable. Each time the code block executes, it increases the value in $num by 1 with the statement $num++;. After 10 iterations, the evaluation $num <= 10 becomes FALSE and the loop stops, which then prints Done..

Be careful not to create an infinite loop. It has the undesirable effects of not returning your page and taking a lot of processing time on the web server.

do...while Loops

The do...while loop takes an expression such as a while statement but places it at the end. The syntax is:

```
do {
    code to execute;
} (expression);
```

This loop is useful when you want to execute the block of code once regardless of the value in the expression. For example, let's count to 10 with this loop, as in Example 4-15.

Example 4-15. Counting to 10 with do...while

```
<?php

$num = 1;

do {
    echo "Number  is ".$num."<br />";
    $num++;
} while ($num <= 10);

echo "Done.";

?>
```

Example 4-15 produces the same results as Example 4-14; if you change the value of $num to 11, the loop processes differently.

```
<?php

$num = 11;

do {
    echo $num;
    $num++;
} while ($num <= 10);

?>
```

This produces:

```
11
```

The code in the loop displays 11 because the loop always executes at least once. Following the pass, while evaluates to FALSE, causing execution to drop out of the do...while loop.

for Loops

for loops provide the same general functionality as while loops, but also provide for a predefined location for initializing and changing a counter value. Their syntax is:

```
for (initialization expression; test expression; modification expression){
    code that is executed;
}
```

Figure 4-4 shows a flowchart for a for loop.

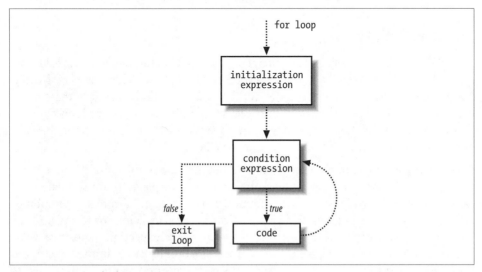

Figure 4-4. How a for loop executes

An example for loop is:

```
<?php
for ($num = 1; $num <= 10; $num++) {
    print "Number is $num<br />\n";
}
?>
```

This produces:

```
Number is 1
Number is 2
Number is 3
Number is 4
Number is 5
Number is 6
Number is 7
Number is 8
Number is 9
Number is 10
```

When your PHP program process the for loop, the initialization portion is evaluated. For each iteration of the portion that increments, the counter executes, followed by a check to see whether you're done. The result is a much more compact and easy-to-read statement.

 When specifying your for loop, if you don't want to include one of the expressions, such as the initialization expression, you may omit it, but you must still include the separating semicolons (;). Example 4-16 shows the usage of a for loop without the initialization expression.

Breaking Out of a Loop

PHP provides the equivalent of an emergency stop button for a loop: the break statement. Normally, the only way out of a loop is to satisfy the expression that determines when to stop the loop. If the code in the loop finds an error that makes continuing the loop pointless or impossible, you can break out of the loop by using the break statement. It's like getting your shoelace stuck in an escalator. It really doesn't make any sense for the escalator to keep going!

Possible problems you might encounter in a loop include running out of space when writing to a file or attempting to divide by zero. In Example 4-16, we simulate what can happen if you divide based on an unknown entry initialized from a form submission (that could be a user-supplied value). If your user is malicious or just plain careless, she might enter a negative value where you are expecting a positive value (although this should be caught in your form validation process). In the code that is executed as part of the loop, the code checks to make sure $counter is not equal to zero. If it is, the code calls break.

Example 4-16. Using break to avoid division by zero

```php
<?php

$counter = -3;

for (; $counter < 10; $counter++){
    // Check for division by zero
    if ($counter == 0){
        echo "Stopping to avoid division by zero.";
        break;
    }

    echo "100/$counter<br />";
}

?>
```

This displays:

```
100/-3
100/-2
100/-1
Stopping to avoid division by zero.
```

Of course, there may be times when you don't want to just skip one execution of the loop code. The continue statement performs this for you.

continue Statements

You can use the continue statement to stop processing the current block of code in a loop and jump to the next iteration of the loop. It's different from break; in that it doesn't stop processing the loop entirely. You're basically skipping ahead to the next iteration. Make sure you are modifying your test variable before the continue statement, or an infinite loop is possible.

Example 4-17 shows the preceding example using continue instead of break.

Example 4-17. Using continue instead of break

```php
<?php

$counter =- 3;

for (; $counter < 10; $counter++){
    // Check for division by zero
    if ($counter == 0){
        echo "Skipping to avoid division by zero.<br />";
        continue;
    }

    echo "100/$counter<br />";
}

?>
```

Example 4-17 displays:

```
100/-3
100/-2
100/-1
Skipping to avoid division by zero.
100/1
100/2
100/3
100/4
100/5
100/6
100/7
100/8
100/9
```

Notice that the loop skipped over the $counter value of zero but continued with the next value.

We've now covered all of the major program flow language constructs. We've discussed the building blocks for controlling program flow in your programs. Expressions can be as simple as TRUE or FALSE and as complex as relational comparison with logical operators. The expressions combined with program flow control constructs like the if statement and switch make decision making easy.

We also discussed while, while...do, and for loops. Loops are very useful for common dynamic web page tasks such as displaying the results from a query in an HTML table.

Chapter 4 Questions

Question 4-1. What is a statement?

Question 4-2. What is a code element that acts on an expression?

Question 4-3. What does an operator combine?

Question 4-4. What is the plus (+) sign?

Question 4-5. What is a binary operator?

Question 4-6. What is a ternary operator?

Question 4-7. Do mathematical operators take letters as operands?

Question 4-8. What type of operand is an Array Index?

Question 4-9. If you use two ampersands (&&) instead of one (&), will you get an error?

Question 4-10. What does isset() do?

Question 4-11. Write a switch statement that adds, subtracts, multiplies, or divides x using the action variable.

Question 4-12. What does the break keyword do?

Question 4-13. Write a for loop to count from 10 to 1.

See the Appendix for the answers to these questions.

Functions

To write programs in PHP that contain more than just a couple of pages of code and are still organized enough to be useful, you need to understand *functions*. Functions provide a way to eliminate repeating the same lines of code over and over in your programs. Functions work by assigning a name to a chunk of code, called a function name. Then you execute the code by calling that name.

There are hundreds of built-in functions in PHP. For example, print_r is a function that prints readable information about a variable in plain English rather than code.

If given a string, integer, or float, the value itself is printed with the print_r function. If given an array, values are shown as keys and elements. A similar format is used for objects. With the advent of PHP 5.0, print_r and var_export show protected and private properties of objects.

Functions run the gamut from aggregate_info to imap_ping through pdf_open_image. Since there are so many, we can only cover some basics in this chapter, but we'll give you enough information that you'll be using functions like a pro in no time at all. You can search *http://www.php.net* for an exhaustive list of functions.

Specifically, we'll go over the following:

- How to create a function, give it a name, and execute that function
- How to send values to a function and use them in the function
- How to return values from a function and use them in your code
- How to verify a function exists before you try using it

When to split out code into a function is a bit of a judgment call. Certainly, if you find yourself repeating several lines of code over and over, it makes sense to pull that code into its own function. That will make your code easier to read and also prevent you from having to make a lot of changes if you decide to do something different with that block of code, as it's then only in one spot, not numerous places where you'd have to search and replace to change it.

A function is a block of code that accepts values, processes them, and then performs an action. A function doesn't need to accept values, doesn't have to process anything, and doesn't have to perform an action, other than to return control at the end. Think of making cookies and baking them in oven as a function. You put the raw cookie dough into the oven, which makes the cookie dough the input. The oven bakes the cookie dough; this is the function. The result of the bake function is the edible, baked cookies. The bake function might even take other inputs, such as temperature and bake time. These various inputs are called *parameters*.

Parameters send information to a function, and then the function executes the code. Functions can use anywhere from zero parameters to a whole list of them. In this example, you'll use the echo function to display some text. echo displays text that you send to it as a parameter. Most functions require you to place their parameters inside of parentheses, but echo is an exception to this rule. Echoing of all variables is nearly foolproof!

Example 5-1 shows about as basic of a program as you can get.

Example 5-1. The ubiquitous Hello world!

```
<?php
echo ("Hello world!");
?>
```

Figure 5-1 shows how the output of the script appears in a browser.

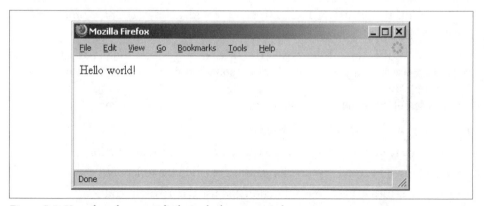

Figure 5-1. How the echo output looks in the browser window

The echo function simply passes on the "Hello world!" string to the browser once you load the PHP file.

echo is actually a PHP language construct. Practically, this translates to its ability to work without enclosing its parameters in parentheses. It's worthy to note that true functions always require parentheses.

You can use one of PHP's many built-in functions or define your own. We'll talk more about defining other functions later in this chapter.

Calling Functions

Functions that are built into PHP can be called from any PHP script. When you call functions, you are executing the code inside them, except the code is reusable and more maintainable. One built-in function, shown in Example 5-2, is phpinfo. It returns configuration and technical information about your PHP installation.

Example 5-2. Displaying information about the PHP environment

```
<?php
    phpinfo();
?>
```

The function helps you diagnose common problems and issues. You may find that this is one of the most helpful places to look when checking to see whether you meet the requirements of a PHP script. Figure 5-2 shows only part of the information contained on this page. If a function call doesn't work, this page helps diagnose whether PHP is compiled with the necessary modules.

To call a function, write the name of the function followed by an opening parenthesis (, the parameters, and then a closing parenthesis), followed by a semicolon (;). It would look like this: *function_name(parameters)*;. Function names aren't case sensitive, so calling phpinfo is the same as calling PhpInfo. As shown in Example 5-3, this is what calling a function looks like: md5($mystring);.

Most functions have return values that you'll either use in a comparison or store in a variable. A great place to start is the md5 function. md5 is a one-way hash function used to verify the integrity of a string, similar to a checksum. md5 converts a message into a fixed string of digits, called a message digest. You can then perform a hash-check, comparing the calculated message digest against a message digest decrypted with a public key to verify that the message was not tampered with. Example 5-3 creates a 128-bit long md5 signature of the string "mystring".

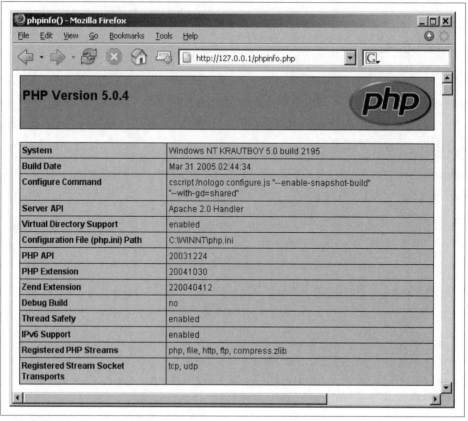

Figure 5-2. Information about PHP displayed in the browser

Example 5-3. Creating an md5 signature

```php
<?php
    $mystring = "mystring";
    $signature = md5($mystring);
    echo $signature;
?>
```

Example 5-3 displays:

```
169319501261c644a58610f967e8f9d0
```

The return value, which is discussed in detail in this chapter, is assigned to the variable $signature, which then displays the output.

> The optional raw_output parameter was added in PHP 5.0 and defaults to FALSE for the md5 function. There is no interpretation for raw_output.

A common use for md5 is to verify that a file didn't become corrupt while it was transferring. The file and its md5 signature are compared after they're received. If they match, you know that it's very unlikely that the file's contents were corrupted during transfer. If they're different, you know that the file is corrupt.

This example demonstrates how you can perform a complex process using a function without having to worry about how that process actually does it. This is the real power of functions.

Defining Functions

There are already many functions built into PHP. However, you can define your own and organize your code into functions. To define your own functions, start out with the function statement:

```
function some_function([arguments]) { code to execute }
```

The brackets ([ ]) mean optional. The code could also be written with *optional_ arguments* in place of [*arguments*]. The function keyword is followed by the name of the function. Function names abide by the same rules as other named objects such as variables in PHP. A pair of parentheses must come next. If your function has parameters, they're specified within the parentheses. Finally, the code to execute is listed between curly brackets, as seen in the code above.

You can define functions anywhere in your code and call them from virtually anywhere. Scope rules apply. The scope of a variable is the context within which it's defined. For the most part, all PHP variables have only a single scope. A single scope spans included and required files as well. The function is defined on the same page or included in an include file. Functions can have parameters and return values that allow you to reuse code.

To create your own function that simply displays a different hello message, you would write:

```php
<?php
function hi()
{
  echo ("Hello from function-land!");
}
//Call the function
hi();
?>
```

which displays:

```
Hello from function-land!
```

The hi function doesn't take any parameters, so you don't list anything between the parentheses. Now that you've defined a simple function, let's mix in some parameters.

Parameters

Parameters provide a convenient way to pass information to a function when you call it without having to worry about variable scope. In PHP, you don't have to define what type of data a parameter holds—only the name and number of parameters must be specified.

An example of a function is strtolower, which converts your string "Hello world!" to lowercase. It takes a parameter of the type string, which is a data type (described in a previous chapter). There's also another function strtoupper that converts all characters of your string into uppercase letters, as shown in Example 5-4.

Example 5-4. Using the string capitalization functions

```php
<?php
// Capitalize a string
function capitalize( $str )
{
  // First, convert all characters to lower case
  $str = strtolower($str);
  // Second, convert the first character to upper case
  $str{0} = strtoupper($str{0});
  echo $str;
}
capitalize("hEllo WoRld!" );

?>
```

Example 5-4 outputs:

```
Hello world!
```

The value of $str was echoed inside the function, because you didn't specify any way to get the value out of the function.

> PHP also doesn't require definition of whether a function actually returns a value, or what data type it returns.

Parameters can also contain default values. With a default value, you actually don't need to pass the function any input for it to set the default. Let's change your capitalize function to have a default value that allows you to capitalize the first letter of each word or just the sentence; see Example 5-5.

Example 5-5. Creating a capitalize function with a default parameter $each

```php
<?php
// Capitalize a string or the first letter of each word
function capitalize( $str, $each=TRUE )
{
  // First, convert all characters to lower case
```

Example 5-5. Creating a capitalize function with a default parameter $each (continued)

```
    $str = strtolower($str);
    if ($each === TRUE) {
        $str = ucwords ($str);
    } else {
        $str = strtoupper($str);
    }
    echo ("$str <br>");
}
capitalize("hEllo WoRld!");
echo ("Now do the same with the echo parameter set to FALSE.<br>");
capitalize("hEllo WoRld!",FALSE);
?>
```

Example 5-5 produces:

```
Hello World!
Now do the same with the echo parameter set to FALSE.
HELLO WORLD!
```

Example 5-5 shows that when you execute capitalize with just one parameter, hEllo WoRld!, $each takes on the default value of TRUE. Therefore, only the first letter of each word gets capitalized. When the second execution of capitalize sends in a value of FALSE from the parameter, $each becomes FALSE in the function and the output changes. Also, ucwords changes the first character of a string to uppercase.

Parameter References

When you pass an argument to the function, a local copy is made in the function to store the value. Any changes made to that value don't affect the source of the parameter. You can define parameters that modify the source variable by defining reference parameters.

Reference parameters define references by placing an ampersand (&) directly before the parameter in the functions definition.

Let's modify the capitalize function from Example 5-5 to take a reference variable for the string to capitalize (Example 5-6).

Example 5-6. Modifying capitalize to take a reference parameter

```
<?php
function capitalize( &$str, $each=true )
{
    // First, convert all characters to lower case
    $str = strtolower($str);
    if ($each === true) {
        $str = ucwords($str);
    } else {
        $str{0} = strtoupper($str{0});
    }
}
```

Example 5-6. Modifying capitalize to take a reference parameter (continued)

```
$str = "hEllo WoRld!";
capitalize( &$str );
echo $str;
?>
```

Example 5-6 returns:

```
Hello World!
```

Because capitalize defined the $str parameter as a reference parameter, a link to the source variable was sent to the function when it was executed. The function essentially accessed and modified the source variable. Had the variable not been declared as a reference, the original value of "hEllo WoRld!" would display.

Including and Requiring PHP Files

To make your code more readable, you can place your functions in a separate file. Many PHP add-ons that you download off the Internet contain functions already placed into files that you simply include in your PHP program. However, PHP provides four functions that enable you to insert code from other files.

- include
- require
- include_once
- require_once

All the include and require functions can take a local file or URL as input, but they cannot import a remote file. require and include functions are pretty similar in their functionality except for the way in which they handle an irretrievable resource. For example, include and include_once provide a warning if the resource cannot be retrieved and try to continue execution of the program. The require and require_once functions provide stop processing of the particular page if they can't retrieve the resource. Now we're going to get more specific about these four functions.

The include Statement

The include statement allows you to include and attach other PHP scripts to your own script. You can think of it as simply taking the included file and inserting them into your PHP file. Example 5-7 is called *add.php*.

Example 5-7. A sample include file called add.php

```
<?php
function add( $x, $y )
{
  return $x + $y;
}
?>
```

Example 5-8 assumes that *add.php* is in the same directory as the include function.

Example 5-8. Using the include function

```php
<?php
include('add.php');
echo add(2, 2);
?>
```

When executed, this produces:

4

As seen in Example 5-8, the include statement attaches other PHP scripts so that you can access other variables, functions, and classes.

 You can name your include files anything that you like, but you should always use the *.php* extension, because if you name them something else, such as *.inc*, it's possible that a user can request the *.inc* file and that the web server will return the code stored in it. This is a security risk, as it may reveal passwords or details about how your program works that can reveal weaknesses in your code. This is because PHP files are parsed by the PHP interpreter.

The include_once statement

A problem may arise when you include many nested PHP scripts, because the include statement doesn't check for scripts that have already been included.

For example, if you did this:

```php
<?php
include('add.php');
include('add.php');
echo add(2, 2);
?>
```

You'd get this error:

```
Fatal error: Cannot redeclare add() (previously declared in
/home/www/htmlkb/oreilly/ch5/add.php:2) in
/home/www/htmlkb/oreilly/ch5/add.php on line 2
```

The above directory may not be where your file is located; your file will go wherever you've designated a place for it. To avoid this type of error, you should use the include_once statement.

Example 5-9 shows the include_once statement.

Example 5-9. Using include_once to include a file

```php
<?php
include_once('add.php');
include_once('add.php');
```

Example 5-9. Using include_once to include a file (continued)

```
echo add(2, 2);
?>
```

This outputs the following when executed:

```
4
```

Obviously, you're not going to place the same `include` statements right next to each other, but it's far more likely that you may include a file, which includes another file you've already included. You should always use `include_once`, as there really isn't any drawback to using it instead of `include`.

There are a couple of problems to look out for when using `include` or `include_once` that can prevent the code from being included. If the file has been deleted, obviously, PHP can't include it. The other problem is if the `include` statement is accidentally deleted from the PHP page. This can happen if the `include` statement isn't obviously related to the code that uses it and nearby the code in the file. One way to prevent this problem is to place the code that uses the included code in a function that's defined next to the `include` statement. Then place a call to the function where you need to use the code in your main PHP code. Additionally, you could use `include_once` at the beginning of the function definition, making it very clear that the code needs the included file.

As demonstrated in the above two paragraphs, there are many potential solutions to numerous problems you may run into while creating functions and scripts. Keep in mind that coding is an iterative process, and, as we'll discuss in Chapter 15, you can use all the resources available on the Internet from other PHP programmers to help you work through any code issues and problems you may have while coding. The PHP community is available to help with all issues, and usually gets back to a posting board quicker than it might take you to sort out your problem!

require and require_once functions

To make sure that a file is included and to stop your program, immediately use `require` and its counter part, `require_once`. These are exactly the same as `include` and `include_once` except that they make sure that the file is present; otherwise, the PHP script's execution is halted, which wouldn't be a good thing! Examples of when you should use `require` instead of `include` are if the file you're including defines critical functions that your script won't be able to execute or variable definitions such as database connection details.

For example, if you attempt to require a file that doesn't exist:

```
<?php
require_once('add_wrong.php');
echo add(2, 2);
?>
```

you'd get this error:

```
Warning: main(add_wrong.php): failed to open stream: No such
file or directory in
/home/www/htmlkb/oreilly/ch5/require_once.php on line 2

Fatal error: main(): Failed opening required 'add_wrong.php'
(include_path='.:/usr/share/php:/usr/share/pear') in
/home/www/htmlkb/oreilly/ch5/require_once.php on line 2
```

All file paths are contingent on where your files are located. The last topic we'll cover with functions is how to test whether a function has been defined before attempting to use it.

Testing a Function

If compatibility with various PHP versions is especially important to your script, it's useful to be able to check for the existence of functions. The function function_exists does just what you'd expect. It takes a string with a function's name and returns TRUE or FALSE depending on whether the function has been defined. For example:

```php
<?php
$test=function_exists("test_this");
if ($test==TRUE)
{ echo "Function test_this exists.";
}
else
{
    echo "Function test_this does not exist.";
//call_different_function();
}
?>
```

displays:

```
Function test_this does not exist.
```

The "Function test_this does not exist" message displays because you haven't defined the function test_this, therefore the program code either displays an error message in plain English or attempts to use a different function.

You've learned how to define functions and their parameters, and how to pass information back and forth from them, plus we've given you some good examples of how to troubleshoot potential function problems.

Next, we'll introduce an alternate style of programming called Object-Orientated (OO) programming. PHP 4.1 had minimal support for OO programming, but with the introduction of 5.0, OO is fully developed. There is continuous debate about which type of coding is better, and really, neither is better or worse than the other; it's mostly a style issue and personal preference.

Object-Oriented Programming

Object-Oriented programming follows the same goals that we discussed when introducing functions, principally to make reusing code easier. It uses *classes* to group functions and variables together as an object. It may help to think of objects as little black boxes that can do work without you knowing exactly how it's done.

They still use functions, but they get a new name when defined in classes. They're called *methods*. The class works as a blue print for creating objects of that type. Variables can still be defined in methods, but they gain the new ability to be defined as part of the class itself.

When a new object is created from a class, it is called an *instance* of that class. Any variables that are defined in the class get separate storage space in each instance. The separate storage for variables provides the instance of an object with the ability to remember information between method executions. Figure 5-3 demonstrates the relationship between a class and its components.

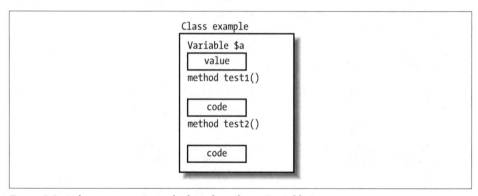

Figure 5-3. A class can contain methods and attributes (variables)

If you're new to the concepts of OO programming, don't worry about understanding everything right away. We'll work with a class in Chapter 7, so it's good enough just to know how to call the methods. In fact, anything that can be done with objects can be done with plain functions. It's just a matter of style and personal preference.

Creating a Class

Classes are typically stored in separate files for reuse. Although we show the class, it isn't required. Let's build an object called Cat that has three methods: meow, eat, and purr. The class construct defines a class. It takes the name of the class immediately after it. Class names follow the same naming rules as variables and functions. The code that makes up the class is placed between curly brackets. This example creates the Cat class without defining any methods or variables.

You can do a quick check to see whether the class has been defined, as Example 5-10 demonstrates.

Example 5-10. Creating an object from the Cat class

```php
<?php
class Cat {
}

$fluffy = new Cat();
echo "Fluffy is a new ".gettype($fluffy)."!";
?>
```

Example 5-10 displays:

```
Fluffy is a new object!
```

Creating an Instance

In Example 5-10, you not only defined the class but also created an instance of it. You used the new keyword to tell PHP to return a new instance of the Cat class. Although the class doesn't do anything, you can tell that it's defined as an object. The class is a blueprint for building instances. The class specifies what is included in each new instance of that class. Each instance can do everything the class defines, but does it independently of any other instance you've created.

Methods and Constructors

Methods are the functions defined within the class. They work within the environment of the class, including its variables. For classes, there is a special method called a *constructor* that's called when a new instance of a class is created to do any work that initializes the class, such as setting up the values of variables in the class. The constructor is defined by creating a method that has the same name as the class, as shown in Example 5-11.

Example 5-11. Creating the Cat constructor

```php
<?php
class Cat {
  // Constructor
  function Cat() {
  }
}
?>
```

PHP 5 supports a new syntax for creating a constructor method using __construct, as shown in Example 5-12. If a class in PHP 5 doesn't have this method, the old style of using the class name as the method name is used.

Example 5-12. Using the PHP 5 style constructor

```php
<?php
class Cat {
  // Constructor
  __construct(){
  }
}
?>
```

The constructor may also contain parameters like any other method. Additionally, classes can contain user-defined methods. For the Cat class, you can define meow, eat, and purr, as shown in Example 5-13.

Example 5-13. Defining three member functions for Cat

```php
<?php
Class Cat {
  // Constructor
  function Cat() {
  }

  // The cat meows
  function meow() {
    echo "Meow...";
  }

  // The cat eats
  function eat() {
    echo "*eats*";
  }

  // The cat purrs
  function purr() {
    echo "*Purr...*";
  }
}
?>
```

When you declare a new instance of a class, the user-defined constructor is always called, assuming that one exists. As you know, a class provides the blueprint for objects. You create an object from a class. If you see the phrase "instantiating a class," this means the same thing as creating an object; therefore, you can think of them as being synonymous. When you create an object, you are creating an instance of a class, which means you are instantiating a class.

The new operator instantiates a class by allocating memory for that new object, which means that it requires a single, postfix argument, which is a call to a constructor. The name of the constructor provides the name of the class to instantiate, and the constructor initializes the new object.

The new operator returns a reference to the object that was created. Most of the time, this reference is assigned to a variable of the appropriate type. However, if the reference is not assigned to a variable, the object is unreachable after the statement in which the new operator finishes executing. Example 5-14 shows how not to use new, and then how better to use it.

Example 5-14. Creating a new object without saving the reference, then creating an object to keep around

```php
<?php
new Cat;
//the Cat object cannot be accessed since its reference wasn't saved

$myCat=new Cat;
//this time we've kept the new Cat object available
?>
```

 When declaring new instances of a class, if the constructor does not contain any parameters, it's optional to use parenthesis (()) after the class name in the new statement.

Variable Scope Within Classes

Classes may contain variables that help define their structure and how they are used. Variables inside a class are declared with the var statement. The var statement declares a variable to have *class scope*. Class scope means they're visible with any methods of the class and can be referenced outside the class using a special construct. Example 5-15 adds the $age variable to the Cat class.

Example 5-15. Adding the $age variable to Cat

```php
<?php
class Cat {
  // How old the cat is
  var $age;
}
?>
```

When referring to methods and variables from within the class, you must use the syntax:

```
$this->variable or method name;
```

The special variable $this always points to the currently executing object.

In Example 5-16, the this-> operator is used to modify the value of $age. The arrow is similar to the dot (.) notation used in other languages to navigate objects.

Example 5-16. Accessing the $age variable using this->

```php
?php
class Cat {
  // How old the cat is
  var $age;

  // Constructor
  function Cat($new_age)
  {
    // Set the age of this cat to the new age
    $this->age = $new_age;
  }
  //The birthday method increments the age variable
  function Birthday()
  {
    $this->age++;
  }
}
// Create a new instance of the cat object that's one year old
$fluffy=new Cat(1);
echo "Age is $fluffy->age <br/>";
echo "Birthday<br/>";
// Increase fluffy's age
$fluffy->Birthday();
echo "Age is $fluffy->age <br/>";
?>
```

Example 5-16 produces:

```
Age is 1
Birthday
Age is 2
```

Notice that you can access the value of $age from outside of the class by using the name of the class instead of this with the -> operator.

Inheritance

When declaring classes, it is also possible to separate functionality into subclasses that automatically inherit the methods and variables of the class on which they are based. This can be useful if you're adding functionality to a class without modifying the original class. Example 5-17 demonstrates how properties and methods are inherited from the parent class for the Domestic_Cat class.

The extends operator

When a class inherits from another class, the class that it inherits from is called the *superclass*. When declaring a subclass, use the extends keyword to specify which class is being inherited from. Example 5-17 shows an example of this.

Example 5-17. Using the extends keyword to define a subclass

```php
<?php
class Cat {
  // How old the cat is
  var $age;

  function Cat($new_age)
  {
    // Set the age of this cat to the new age
    $this->age = $new_age;
  }
  function Birthday()
  {
    $this->age++;
  }
}
class Domestic_Cat extends Cat {
  // Constructor
  function Domestic_Cat() {
  }

  // Sleep like a domestic cat
  function sleep() {
  echo("Zzzzzz.<br/>");
  }
}
$fluffy=new Domestic_Cat();
$fluffy->Birthday();
$fluffy->sleep();
echo "Age is $fluffy->age <br/>";
?>
```

Example 5-17 outputs:

```
Zzzzzz.
Age is 1
```

Notice that you can access the Birthday function from the Cat class and the newly defined sleep method regardless of which level in the object defined the method.

The parent operator

A Domestic_Cat is a Cat in all respects. It still contains the base methods of a Cat. It's also possible to override existing functionality from the superclass to provide your own new code. When extending classes to override functions in your class that are already defined in the superclass, you can still execute the code from the parent class then add on your own functionality.

To call the parent class method before your code, use:

```
parent::method_from_parent
```

This calls the parent method in the superclass. You can then add to your code like in Example 5-18.

Example 5-18. Using the parent construct

```php
<?php
class Cat {
  // How old the cat is
  var $age;

  function Cat($new_age)
  {
    // Set the age of this cat to the new age
    $this->age = $new_age;
  }
  function Birthday()
  {
    $this->age++;
  }
  function Eat()
  {
    echo "Chomp chomp.";
  }
  function Meow()
  {
    echo "Meow.";
  }
}

class Domestic_Cat extends Cat {
  // Constructor
  function Domestic_Cat() {
  }

  // Eat like a Domestic_Cat
  function eat() {
    parent::eat();
    // After we're finished eating, let's meow
    $this->meow();
  }
}
?>
```

This calls the eat function from the superclass, and then adds the code for meowing.

When you extend a class and declare your own constructor, PHP won't automatically call the constructor of the parent class. You should always call the constructor of the parent class to be sure all initialization code gets executed, as shown in Example 5-19.

Example 5-19. Calling the constructor of the parent class

```php
<?php
  class Cat {
  // How old the cat is
  var $age;

  function Cat($new_age)
  {
    // Set the age of this cat to the new age
    $this->age = $new_age;
  }
  function Birthday()
  {
    $this->age++;
  }
  function Eat()
  {
    echo "Chomp chomp.";
  }
  function Meow()
  {
    echo "Meow.";
  }
}
class Domestic_Cat extends Cat {
  // Constructor
  function Domestic_Cat($new_age) {
    // This will call the constructor
    // in the parent class (the superclass)
    parent::Cat($new_age);
  }
}
?>
```

When a new instance of Domestic_Cat is created, the constructor from the Cat class is called.

Static Methods and Variables

Methods and variables can also be used and accessed as if they are static in a class. *Static* means the method or variable is accessible through the class definition and not just through objects. In PHP 4, there is no way to designate a variable to be static; however, in PHP 5.0, you can use the static modifier. We'll discuss the syntax that PHP provides to access static values in a class next.

The :: operator (scope resolution)

The :: operator allows you to refer to variables and methods on a class that doesn't yet have any instances or objects created for it. When you plan on using the scope resolution operator on a method, you can also detect inside the called function if the method was called using the scope resolution operator (::) or through an object (->) by the $this operator, as shown in Example 5-20.

Example 5-20. Using the -> operator to call hypnotize

```
class Hypnotic_Cat extends Cat {
  // Constructor
  function Hypnotic_Cat() {
  }

  // This is meant to be called statically
  function hypnotize() {
  //detects that the function is being called statically
  //since a static call doesn't have an object to point to
    if ($this == null)
      echo ("All cats are hypnotized.");
    else
    {
      echo ("The cat was hypnotized.");
      return;
    }
  }
}

// Hypnotize all cats
Hypnotic_Cat::hypnotize();

$hypnotic_cat = new Hypnotic_Cat();
// Does nothing
$hypnotic_cat->hypnotize();
```

When a method is called using the scope resolution operator (::), you can't use the $this object to refer to the object, since there is no object.

Variable References

In PHP, a variable name points to a location in memory that stores the data. There can be more than one variable name pointing to the same spot in memory. The ampersand operator (&) is used to indicate that you're interested in the location in memory that a variable points to instead of its value.

PHP references allow you to create two variables to refer to the same content. There-fore, changing the value of one variable can change the value of another. This can make it very difficult to find errors in your code, since changing one variable also changes the other.

The same syntax can be used with functions that return references—for example, using the new operator. Example 5-21 uses this to reference the $some variable.

Example 5-21. Referencing the $some_variable

```php
<?php
$some_variable = "Hello World!";
$some_reference = &$some_variable;
$some_reference = "Guten Tag World!";
echo $some_variable;
echo $some_reference;
?>
```

Example 5-21 outputs:

```
Gutentag World!Guten Tag World!
```

Example 5-21 shows that a reference is set using the & operator and precedes the $ in the existing variable. The variable $some_reference refers to $some_variable (the memory location where "Hello World!" resides) and any operation, with the exception of setting to another reference, operates on $some_variable.

As discussed earlier, variable references are useful for passing a variable by reference as a parameter to a function. This allows the function to modify the variable in your main code instead of modifying a local copy that's lost when the function completes.

Assigning a variable to another variable without using the reference operator results in a copy of the variable being placed into a new location in memory. The new variable can be changed without modifying the original variable. While this takes more memory, it's the way to go if you don't want to change the original variable's value.

Now that you've learned about functions and classes, you're ready to start working with more complex data, such as arrays. Arrays will be very useful when working with data from a database, since they can easily hold the data from a query.

Chapter 5 Questions

Question 5-1. What's wrong with this function call?

```php
<?php

// define a function
function Response {
echo "Have a good day!<br /><br />";
}

// driving to work
echo "Are you going to merge? <br />";
Response;

// at the office
echo "I need a status report on all your projects in the next 10 minutes for my
management meeting.<br />";
Response;
```

```
// at the pub after work
echo "Did Bill get everything he needed today? He was sure crabby!<br />";
Response;
?>
```

Question 5-2. Define a function called toast that takes minutes as a parameter. The function prints "done."

Question 5-3. Call the toast function with 5 as a parameter.

Question 5-4. What's the difference between using include() and require()?

Question 5-5. What is a function called when it is part of a class?

See the Appendix for the answers to these questions.

Arrays

Variables are great for storing a single piece of information, but what happens when you need to store data for a whole set of information, like the results of a query? For this, you use *arrays*. Arrays are a special kind of variable that store many pieces of data. Arrays allow you to access any of the values stored in them individually yet still copy and manipulate the array as a whole. Because they are so useful, you'll see arrays used frequently. PHP provides many functions for performing common array tasks such as counting, sorting, and looping through the data.

Array Fundamentals

When working with arrays, there are two new terms: elements and indexes. *Elements* are the values that are stored in the array. Each element in the array is referenced by an *index* that identifies the element by any other unique element in the array. The index value can be a number or a string, but it must be unique. You can think of an array like a spreadsheet or a database that has only two columns. The first column selects the row in the spreadsheet, while the second column contains a stored value.

Associative Versus Numeric Indexed Arrays

Numeric arrays use numbers as their indexes while *associative* arrays use stings. When using associative arrays, you must supply an index string each time you add an element. Numeric arrays allow you to just add the element, and PHP automatically assigns the first free number, starting at 0.

 Be careful, since most people tend to start counting at 1 not 0. If you're not careful, you might end up being off by one when accessing your array. This is called an off-by-one error! The last element in a numeric array is accessed as the length of the array minus 1.

A common symptom of starting to access the values of your array at 1 instead of 0 is attempting to access the last value and finding it's not there! For instance, if you use a numeric array to store four elements and let PHP pick the number index values, the last value is stored under the index value of 4. For example, Table 6-1 shows a numeric array with five elements. Attempting to access the fifth value at location 5 would miss it, getting the sixth instead. Table 6-1 displays numeric arrays, starting with the number 0.

Table 6-1. A numeric array containing colors, starting at zero

Key	Value
0	Black
1	Blue
2	Red
3	Green
4	Purple

Internally, PHP stores numeric arrays in the same way it stores associative arrays. Numeric arrays are provided because they make it easier to loop through a set of data, since you need only to perform an addition on the key to access the next value.

Creating an Array

To create an array, you must specify the elements and index values. In Table 6-2, we show a sample associative array that uses household objects and relates them to strings that describe their shapes.

Table 6-2. An associative array that relates objects to their shapes

Key	Value
Soda Can	Cylinder
Note Pad	Rectangle
Apple	Sphere
Orange	Sphere
Phone book	Rectangle

The elements of an array can be anything, including strings, numbers, and even other arrays! The key field must be a *scalar*. Scalar values are simple values such as a number or text, including true or false, not data that can have more than one value such as an array. The key field of an array must also be unique. Should you attempt to assign a value using a key you specified already, the new value simply replaces the old value.

Short yet meaningful values for your index keys make your programs run faster, which will make them easier to maintain.

Assignment via array identifiers

Now that you know what can go into an array, you'll need a way to get values into the array. PHP provides two ways of assigning values to arrays. We'll discuss *array identifiers* for assignment first.

Array identifiers look like normal variable assignments except a pair of brackets ([]) are added after the name of the array variable. You can optionally add an index value between the brackets. If you don't supply an index, PHP automatically picks the lowest empty numeric index value for the array. For example, to assign the first two days of the week to a numeric indexed array, you would use:

```php
<?php
$weekdays[]='Monday';
$weekdays[]='Tuesday';
?>
```

You could also specify the index values, which has the same end result as:

```php
<?php
$weekdays[0]='Monday';
$weekdays[1]='Tuesday';
?>
```

If you do specify the index yourself, be careful not to skip over numbers:

```php
<?php
$weekdays[0]='Monday';
$weekdays[1]='Tuesday';
$weekdays[3]='Wednesday';
?>
```

This code creates an array that doesn't have a value assigned for the index of 2. That might be OK, but if you're going through the array values sequentially and your code unexpectedly encounters a missing value, that'll cause problems, but not a PHP error.

Assignment using array

The other way to assign values to an array is to use the `array` function. The `array` function allows you to create your array and assign multiple elements all at once. The array takes pairs of index keys and values as parameters. It returns an array assigned to a variable. The elements to be assigned are separated by commas.

Example 6-1 creates a numeric array using `array`.

Example 6-1. Using the array function to create an array of weekdays

```php
<?php
$weekdays=array('Monday',
                'Tuesday',
                'Wednesday',
                'Thursday',
                'Friday',
```

Example 6-1. Using the array function to create an array of weekdays (continued)

```
                'Saturday',
                'Sunday');
?>
```

The whitespace you see in this code makes adding elements to the array easier. You can create as many elements in the array as you wish.

In Example 6-2, we create an associative array using the format *index => value*.

Example 6-2. Creating an associative array of shapes

```
<?php
  $shapes=array('Soda Can' => 'Cylinder',
                'Note Pad' => 'Rectangle',
                'Apple' => 'Sphere',
                'Orange' => 'Sphere',
                'Phonebook' => 'Rectangle');
?>
```

 When assigning array names, you need to be careful not to use the same name as another variable, since they share the same set of names. Assigning a variable to the same name as an existing array will overwrite the array without warning.

If you're not sure whether a variable is an array, you can use is_array. For example, you'd enter the code:

```
<?php
$yes = array('this', 'is', 'an array');
echo is_array($yes) ? 'Array' : 'not an Array';
echo "<br>";
$no = 'this is a string';
echo is_array($no) ? 'Array' : 'Not an Array';
?>
```

This outputs:

```
Array
Not an Array
```

Since you know how to assign values to an array and how to find out whether a variable is an array, it's time to discuss retrieving those values.

Looping through and referencing array values

Items in an array may be individually accessed by including the key to the array in brackets after the name of the variable in the form $*array*[*index*]. Arrays referenced in a string that have a key value with whitespaces or punctuation must be enclosed in curly braces ({}). For example, Example 6-3 displays the value of the $shapes array for 'Note Pad'.

Example 6-3. Displaying one value from an array

```php
<?php
  $shapes=array('Soda Can' => 'Cylinder',
                'Note Pad' => 'Rectangle',
                'Apple' => 'Sphere',
                'Orange' => 'Sphere',
                'Phonebook' => 'Rectangle');
  print "A note pad is a {$shapes['Note Pad']}.";
?>
```

Example 6-3 produces:

```
The Note Pad is a Rectangle.
```

In Example 6-4, a foreach loop displays all the values in an array. The foreach statement is handy, because it automatically advances and reads each value from an array until it reaches the last value *n* in the array. This eliminates having to remember 0-based arrays, and won't run beyond the length of an array, making it a very useful looping construct that avoids common logical errors. Example 6-4 shows an array's content using a loop.

Example 6-4. Display the contents of an array using a loop

```php
<?php
$shapes=array('Soda Can' => 'Cylinder',
              'Note Pad' => 'Rectangle',
              'Apple' => 'Sphere',
              'Orange' => 'Sphere',
              'Phonebook' => 'Rectangle');
foreach ($shapes as $key => $value) {
    print"The $key is a $value.<br>\n";
}
?>
```

Example 6-4 produces:

```
The Soda Can is a Cylinder.<br>
The Note Pad is a Rectangle.<br>
The Apple is a Sphere.<br>
The Orange is a Sphere.<br>
The Phonebook is a Rectangle.<br>
```

The breaks, <br>, won't show up in your browser as they are HTML markup, adding line breaks after each sentence. Each string in the array was processed, so the loop stopped automatically.

Adding values to an array

To add values to the end of an existing array, you can use the array identifier. For example, to add Thursday to the $weekdays array:

```php
<?php
$weekdays[] = "Thursday";
?>
```

To add another shape to your associative array, use a similar syntax:

```php
<?php
$shapes["Megaphone"]= "Cone";
?>
```

This works even though the array was created using the array function. This leads us to the opposite problem.

Counting how many elements are in an array

You can use the count function to find out how many elements are currently assigned to an array. The count function is identical to sizeof and can be used interchangeably. Example 6-5 counts the elements in the $shapes array.

Example 6-5. Counting the elements in an array

```php
<?php
$shapes=array('Soda Can' => 'Cylinder',
              'Note Pad' => 'Rectangle',
              'Apple' => 'Sphere',
              'Orange' => 'Sphere',
              'Phonebook' => 'Rectangle');
$numElements = count($shapes);
print"The array has $numElements elements.<br>\n";
?>
```

Example 6-5 displays:

```
The array has 5 elements.
```

The print command in Example 6-5 is identical to echo, for the purposes of arrays. It doesn't matter whether your array is associative or numeric when count sizes up your array. If you want the array to sort your data in alphabetical order, you'd use sort.

Sorting arrays

This function sorts an array. Elements are arranged from lowest to highest after this function is completed. Numbers are sorted numerically, while strings are sorted alphabetically. This function assigns new keys for the elements in an array. It removes any existing keys you may have assigned, rather than just reordering the keys.

 You need to be cautious when sorting arrays with mixed type values, because sort can produce unpredictable results.

Using the shapes example from Example 6-5, you can sort alphabetically. The code would look like Example 6-6.

Example 6-6. Using sort to alphabetize

```php
<?php
$shapes = array("rectangle", "cylinder", "sphere");
sort($shapes);
//The foreach loop selects each element from the array and assigns its value to $key
//before executing the code in the block.
foreach ($shapes as $key => $val) {
 echo "shapes[" . $key . "] = " . $val . "<br>";
}
?>
```

Example 6-6 outputs to:

```
shapes[0] = cylinder
shapes[1] = rectangle
shapes[2] = sphere
```

As you can see, the shapes have been sorted alphabetically. Table 6-3 shows an optional second parameter sort_flags that can be used to modify the sorting behavior using these values.

Table 6-3. sort_flags

sort_flag	Definition
sort_regular	Compares items normally, but doesn't change types
sort_numeric	Compares items numerically
sort_string	Compares items as strings
sort_locale_string	Compares items as strings, based on the current locale

You've learned a lot about arrays; now let's move on to multidimensional arrays that hold more elements instead of just simple values.

Multidimensional Arrays

While we've only shown arrays that hold simple values like strings so far, remember that an array can also store another array as an element. Multidimensional arrays exploit the fact that an array can have another array as an element. Each set of keys and values represents a *dimension*. Multidimensional arrays have a key and value set for each dimension. Don't worry if that sounds complicated; again, it's really just an array inside of an array, like those Russian dolls that open up to contain yet another smaller doll!

Expanding upon your shapes array, we create a new associative array called $objects with keys that are the names of the objects. Each element of the $objects array is another associative array containing the keys shape, color, and material with the associated values as the elements. Table 6-4 shows you what data is being stored.

Table 6-4. A multidimensional array that now stores shape, color, and material for each object

First key	Second key	Value
Soda can	Shape	Cylinder
	Color	Red
	Material	Metal
Note Pad	Shape	Rectangle
	Color	White
	Material	Paper
Apple	Shape	Sphere
	Color	Red
	Material	Fruit
Orange	Shape	Sphere
	Color	Orange
	Material	Fruit
Phonebook	Shape	Rectangle
	Color	Yellow
	Material	Paper

To create the array in Table 6-4, use the array function like that in Example 6-7.

Example 6-7. Creating a multidimensional array

```php
<?php
$objects=array('Soda Can' =>    array('Shape'    => 'Cylinder',
                                      'Color'    => 'Red',
                                      'Material' => 'Metal'),
               'Note Pad' =>    array('Shape'    => 'Rectangle',
                                      'Color'    => 'White',
                                      'Material' => 'Paper'),
               'Apple' =>       array('Shape'    => 'Sphere',
                                      'Color'    => 'Red',
                                      'Material' => 'Fruit'),
               'Orange' =>      array('Shape'    => 'Sphere',
                                      'Color'    => 'Orange',
                                      'Material' => 'Fruit'),
               'Phonebook' =>   array('Shape'    => 'Rectangle',
                                      'Color'    => 'Yellow',
                                      'Material' => 'Paper'));
echo $objects['Soda Can']['Shape'];
?>
```

Example 6-7 displays:

```
Cylinder
```

We're able to access the second dimension of the array by using a second set of brackets ([]) to specify the second key. If the array has more dimensions than just two, you must specify the key for each dimension. True to form, if you access $objects['Orange'], you would get an array.

Example 6-8 displays all of the elements of both arrays.

Example 6-8. Displaying a multidimensional array

```php
<?php
foreach ($objects as $obj_key => $obj)
{
  echo "$obj_key:<br>";
  while (list ($key,$value)=each ($obj))
  {
    echo "$key = $value ";
  }
 echo "<br>";
}
?>
```

The code displays something like Figure 6-1.

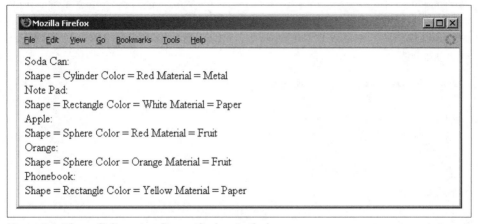

Figure 6-1. The multidimensional array displays in the browser

However, there's more than one way to display an array.

There's also a built-in function to display an array all in one step, called var_dump. If you specify your array from Example 6-7 like this:

```php
echo var_dump($ojbects);
```

you see:

```
array(5) { ["Soda Can"]=> array(3) { ["Shape"]=> string(8)
"Cylinder" ["Color"]=> string(3) "Red" ["Material"]=> string(5) "Metal" }
["Note Pad"]=> array(3) { ["Shape"]=> string(9) "Rectangle" ["Color"]=> string(5)
"White" ["Material"]=> string(5) "Paper" } ["Apple"]=> array(3) { ["Shape"]=>
string(6) "Sphere" ["Color"]=> string(3) "Red" ["Material"]=> string(5) "Fruit" }
["Orange"]=> array(3) { ["Shape"]=> string(6) "Sphere" ["Color"]=> string(6)
"Orange" ["Material"]=> string(5) "Fruit" } ["Phonebook"]=> array(3) {
["Shape"]=> string(9) "Rectangle" ["Color"]=> string(6) "Yellow"
["Material"]=> string(5) "Paper" } }
```

While it's not formatted as nicely as Example 6-8, it's less work and can take an array as its input. This is a great tool for debugging the values in an array. The numbers after the data types indicate how long each one is; for instance in this example, there are five elements in the first level of the array and each string has a different length based on its contents. There are general tools available for debugging your PHP code, and there are also PHP tools that can help you debug your code yourself, without the purchase of a separate program. Xdebug is a free debugger available from *http://xdebug.org/*. Zend Studio, available from *http://www.zend.com/store/products/zend-studio/*, includes a debugger as part of its Integrated Development Environment (IDE). An IDE includes editing, testing, and debugging in one application.

Extracting Variables from an Array

PHP provides a shortcut for placing elements in an array into variables, where the variables have the same names as the keys. This works for associative arrays only, unless of course, you specify a prefix that we'll talk about next. The extract function takes an array as a parameter and creates the local variables, as shown in Example 6-9.

Example 6-9. Using extract on an associative array

```php
<?php
$shapes=array('SodaCan' => 'Cylinder',
              'NotePad' => 'Rectangle',
              'Apple' => 'Sphere',
              'Orange' => 'Sphere',
              'PhoneBook' => 'Rectangle');

extract($shapes);
// $SodaCan, $NotePad, $Apple, $Orange, and $PhoneBook are now set
echo $Apple;
echo "<br>";
echo $NotePad;
?>
```

Example 6-9 produces browser output like that in Figure 6-2.

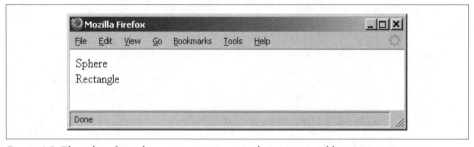

Figure 6-2. The values from the array now appear in their own variables

Notice that the spaces were removed from the key values in the $shapes array. Although they wouldn't have caused an error, they also wouldn't be accessible as variables, since variable names cannot have spaces. You need to use underscores instead of spaces in variable names. Also, if a variable already exists with the same name as a key in the array to expand, its value is overwritten by the value from the expanded array.

One way to prevent possibly overwriting a variable you're already using is to include a second set of parameters to expand that specify a prefix to be prepended to the name of each variable you extract from the array. It's specified using this syntax:

```
expand($array,EXTR_PREFIX_ALL,"the prefix");
```

Example 6-10 demonstrates the use of the EXTR_PREFIX_ALL option for extract.

Example 6-10. Using extract with the EXTR_PREFIX_ALL directive

```php
<?php
$Apple="Computer";
$shapes=array('SodaCan' => 'Cylinder',
              'NotePad' => 'Rectangle',
              'Apple' => 'Sphere',
              'Orange' => 'Sphere',
              'PhoneBook' => 'Rectangle');

extract($shapes,EXTR_PREFIX_ALL,"shapes");
// $shapes_SodaCan, $shapes_NotePad, $shapes_Apple, $shapes_Orange, and
//$shapes_PhoneBook are now set

echo "Apple is $Apple.<br>";
echo "Shapes_Apple is $shapes_Apple";
echo "<br>";
echo "Shapes_NotePad is $shapes_NotePad";
?>
```

Example 6-10 returns:

```
Apple is Computer.
Shapes_Apple is Sphere
Shapes_NotePad is Rectangle
```

The EXTR_PREFIX_ALL keyword allows you to use extract on a numeric array. Example 6-11 creates a numeric array, calls extract on it, and then accesses the variable for the zero position element.

Example 6-11. Using EXTR_PREFIX_ALL on a numeric array

```php
<?php
$shapes=array( 'Cylinder',
               'Rectangle');
extract($shapes,EXTR_PREFIX_ALL,"shapes");
echo "Shapes_0 is $shapes_0 <br>";
echo "Shapes_1 is $shapes_1";
?>
```

Example 6-11 displays:

```
Shapes_0 is Cylinder
Shapes_1 is Rectangle
```

PHP also gives you a function, called compact, that does the opposite of extract.

Using compact to build an array from variables

The compact function is the complement of extract. It takes the variables as parameters individually, as arrays, or a combination of both. The compact function creates an associative array whose keys are the variable names and whose values are the variable's values. Any names in the array that don't correspond to actual variables are skipped. Arrays of variables as parameters are automatically expanded. Here's an example of compact in action:

```php
<?php
$SodaCan='Cylinder';
$NotePad='Rectangle';
$Apple = 'Sphere';
$Orange = 'Sphere';
$PhoneBook = 'Rectangle';

$shapes=compact('SodaCan', 'Note Pad', 'Apple', 'Orange', 'PhoneBook');
echo var_dump($shapes);
?>
```

This produces something like Figure 6-3 in your browser.

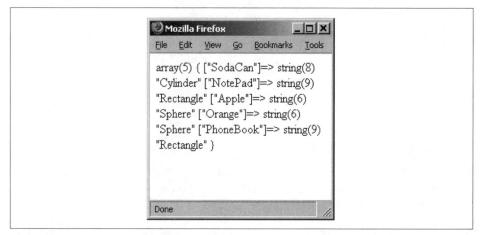

Figure 6-3. The browser displaying the variable dump for a compact created array

Array Functions in PHP

Although we've already discussed several array functions such as count, there are many more. Following are some of the most common ones that we haven't discussed yet; for a full listing, search *http://www.php.net*.

Reset(*array*)

Takes an array as its argument and resets the pointer to the beginning of the array. The *pointer* is how PHP keeps track of the current element in an array when working with functions that can move around in arrays.

Array_push(*array,elements*)

Adds one or more elements to the end of an existing array. For example, array_push($shapes,"rock","paper","scisors"); adds those three elements to an array called $shapes.

Array_pop(*array*)

Returns and removes the last element of an array. For example, $last_element=array_pop($shapes); removes the last element from $shapes and assigns it to $last_element.

Array_unshift(*array,elements*)

Adds one or more elements to the beginning of an existing array. For example, array_unshift($shapes,"rock","paper","scisors"); adds three elements to the beginning of an array called $shapes.

Array_shift(*array*)

Returns and removes the first element of an array. For example, $first_element=array_unshift($shapes); removes the first element from $shapes and assigns it to $first_element.

Array_merge(*array,array*)

Combines two arrays together and returns the new array. For example, $combined_array=array_merge($shapes,$sizes); combines the elements of both arrays and assigns the new array to $combined_array.

Array_keys(*array*)

Returns an array containing all of the keys from the supplied array. For example, $keys=array_keys($shapes); assigns an array to $keys that consists of only the keys like "Apple" and "Note Pad" from the array in Example 6-2.

Array_values(*array*)

Returns an array containing all of the values from the supplied array. For example, $values=array_values($shapes); assigns an array to $values that consists of only the element values like "Sphere" and "Rectangle" from the array in Example 6-2.

Shuffle(*array*)

Resorts the array in random order. The key values are lost when the array is shuffled because the returned array is a numeric array. For example, shuffle($shapes); could place the value "Rectangle" in $shapes[0] using the array from Example 6-2.

We've covered most everything you need to get going with PHP; it's now time to start introducing databases and MySQL in particular, then tackle how MySQL and PHP work synergistically.

Chapter 6 Questions

Question 6-1. Where is the first element in a numeric array?

Question 6-2. Create a numeric array called $months that contains the months of the year.

Question 6-3. Use array() to create an associative array of months and the number of days in the month.

Question 6-4. Display the $months array.

See the Appendix for the answers to these questions.

Database Basics

We're now going to introduce you to basic database structure so that you have an understanding of databases. Adding MySQL to PHP and combining the applications for your dynamic web site is a great start. But, it helps tremendously to structure your database right. We'll give you a solid understanding of both database design and the language that's used to communicate with the database, SQL. The first step in setting up your database is to design how you'll store your data. Then, you'll learn how to add, view, and change data.

Databases are a repository for information. They excel at managing and manipulating structured information. *Structured information* is a way to organize related pieces of information, which we discussed previously in our chapters on PHP. The basic types of structured information, which can also be called *data structures*, include:

- Files
- Lists
- Arrays
- Records
- Trees
- Tables

Each of these basic structures has many variations and allows for different operations to be performed on the data. An easy way to understand this concept is to think of the phone book. It's the most widespread database, and it contains several items of information—name, address, and phone number, as well as each phone subscriber in a particular area. Phone books have evolved, and some people may have bolded names, but for the most part, each entry in the phone book takes the same form.

If you think of the physical hardcopy phone book in similar terms as a database, the phone book is a *table,* which contains a *record* for each subscriber. Each subscriber record contains three *fields* (also known as *columns or attributes*): name, address, and phone number. These records are sorted alphabetically by the name field, which is called the *key field*. The phone book is alphabetized by last names first; look at Figure 7-1 for how typical record and fields display in your database based on the phone book analogy.

Name	Address	Phone Number
Davis, Michele	7505 N. Linksway FxPnt 53217	414-352-4818
Meyer, Simon	5802 Beard Avenue S 55419	612-925-6897
Phillips, Jon	4204 Zenith Avenue S 55416	612-924-8020
Phillips, Peter	6200 Bayard Avenue HgldPk 55411	651-668-2251

Figure 7-1. Phone book record and fields

If you took the same data from the phone book and put it into a database, you could build queries such as who has the phone number 651-668-2251 or everyone in a specific zip code who has the last name Davis. This type of database is like a big spreadsheet; it can be called a *flat-file* database, which means each database is self-contained in a single table. Since the 1970s, relational databases for managing data have replaced flat files.

The advantages of a fully relational RDBMS system are wide-ranging, including:

- Unbeatable performance
- Capability and power benefits
- Scalable and distributable systems
- Able to easily take advantage of new hardware technology
- Flexibility for evolution of users' data

Database Design

Designing your database properly is critical to your application performing well. Just like putting the printer all the way across your office, placing data in poor relationships makes work less efficient in that it can cause your database server to waste time looking for data. When thinking about you database, think about what kinds of questions will be asked when your database is used. For example, is this a valid username and password? Or, what are the details about a product for sale?

Relational Databases

MySQL is a *relational* database. An important feature of relational systems is that a single database can be spread across several tables as opposed to our flat-file phone book example. Related data is stored in separate tables and allows you to put them together by using a key common to both tables. The *key* is the relation between the tables. The selection of a *primary key* is one of the most critical decisions you'll make in designing a new database. The most important concept that you need to understand is that you must ensure the selected key is unique. If it's possible that two records (past, present, or future) share the same value for an attribute, don't use them as a primary key. Including key fields from another table to form a link between tables is called a *foreign key* relationship, like a boss to employees or a user to a purchase. The relational model is very useful because data is retrieved easier and faster.

 The name *relational databases* actually came from the original formal name for the tables, which was *relations*.

Now that you have separate tables that store related data, you need to think about the number of items in each table that relate to the number of items in another table. This is all about relationships and the type of relationships data falls into. Think of the relationship as a repository or bucket, and each bucket of data has a specific relationship.

Relationship Types

Databases relationships are quantified with the following categories:

- One-to-one relationships
- One-to-many relationships
- Many-to-many relationships

We'll discuss each of these relationships and provide an example. If you think of a family structure when thinking about relationships, you're ahead of the game. When you spend time alone with one parent, that's a specific type of relationship; when you spend time with both your parents, that's another one. If you bring in a significant partner and all of you—your parents, you, and your partner—all do something together, that's another relationship. This is identical to the bucket analogy. All those different types of relationships are like specific buckets that hold the dynamics of your relationships. In the database world, it's the data you've created.

One-to-one relationships

In a one-to-one relationship, each item is related to one and only one other item. Within the example of a bookstore. A one-to-one relationship exists between users and their shipping addresses. Each user must have exactly one shipping address. The key symbol in each figure represents the field that's the key for the table, as shown in Figure 7-2.

In Figure 7-3, you see that the user mdavis has one and only one address, as do the users jphillips and suzieq.

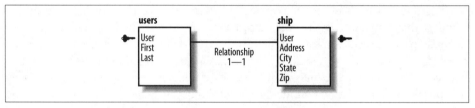

Figure 7-2. A one-to-one relationship between users and shipping addresses

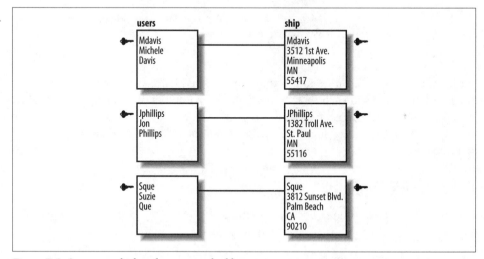

Figure 7-3. Some sample data for users and addresses

One-to-many relationships

A one-to-many relationship, shown in Figures 7-4 and 7-5, has keys from one table that appear multiple times in another table. This is the most common type of relationship. For example, the categories for books such as hardcover, soft cover, and audio books. Each book is in one of those three categories. However, they're never in more than one category.

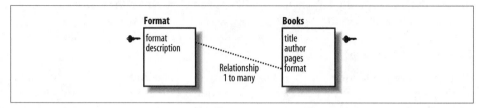

Figure 7-4. A one-to-many relationship between format and books

Many-to-many relationships

A many-to-many relationship means that two tables can each have multiple keys from the other table in them. For example, shoppers that use an online bookstore

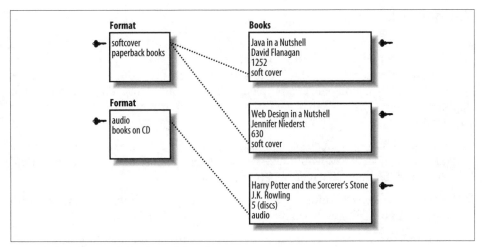

Figure 7-5. Some sample books and their formats

can purchase multiple books. Likewise, multiple users can purchase the same book title. Figure 7-6 shows a many-to-many relationship between users and books purchased.

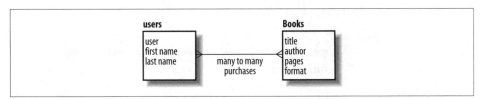

Figure 7-6. A many-to-many relationship between users and books purchased

The many-to-many relationship is converted to a mapping table with two one-to-many relationships in order for the database to represent the data. Figure 7-7 includes a mapping table for you to understand the connectivity between the relationships.

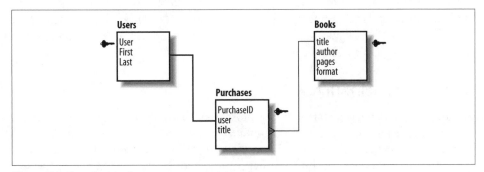

Figure 7-7. Sample data for many-to-many scenario

Notice that both columns have repeating keys.

Normalization

Thinking about how your data is related and the most efficient way to organize it is called *normalization*. Normalization of data is breaking it apart based on the logical relationships to minimize the duplication of data. Generally, duplicated data wastes space and makes maintenance a problem. Should you change information that is duplicated, there's the risk that you miss a portion and you risk inconsistencies in you database.

It's possible to have too much of a good thing though: databases placing each piece of data in their own tables would take too much processing time and queries would be convoluted. Finding a balance in between is the goal.

While the phone book example is very simple, the type of data that you process with a web page can benefit greatly from logically grouping related data.

Let's continue with the bookstore example. The site needs to keep track of the user's data, including login, address, and phone number, as well as information about the books, including the title, author, number of pages, and when each title was purchased.

Start by placing all of this information in one table, as shown in Table 7-1.

Table 7-1. Essentially, a flat file, as there is only one table

User ID	First name	Last name	Address	Phone	Title	Author1	Author2	Pages	When
Mdavis	Michele	Davis	7505 N. Linksway, Fx Pnt, MN, 55114	414-352-4818	Linux in a Nutshell	Ellen Siever	Aaron Weber	112	Sept 3rd, 2005
Mdavis	Michele	Davis	7505 N. Linksway, Fx Pnt, MN, 55114	414-352-4818	Classic Shell Scripting	Arnold Robbins	Nelson Beebe	576	Sept 3rd, 2005

While combining the data into one table may seem like a good idea, it wastes space in the database and makes updating the data tedious. All the user data is repeated for each purchase. Additionally, if the user moves, then her address changes and each of her entries in the table has to be updated.

Forms of Normalization

To normalize a database, start with the most basic rules of normalization and move forward step by step. The steps of normalization are in three stages, called *forms*. The first step, called First Normal Form (or FNF), must be done before the second normal form. Likewise, the third normal form cannot be completed before the second. The normalization process involves getting your data into conformity with the three progressive normal forms.

A higher level of normalization cannot be achieved until the previous levels have done so already.

First Normal Form

The First Normal Form involves removal of redundant data from horizontal rows. You want to ensure that there is no duplication of data in a given row, and that every column stores the least amount of information possible.

Put simply, in order for your database to be in first normal form, it must satisfy two requirements. Every table must not have repeating columns that contain the same kind of data, and all columns must contain only one value.

The table in Table 7-1 fails the repeating columns rule, because Author1 and Author2 store the same kind of information. This should be avoided, because you'll need to either add many author fields and waste space or you could potentially run out of fields to store the authors for a book that has many authors.

The solution is to break out the authors into a separate table that's linked to the books table.

Table 7-1 also violates the rule for a column having only one value. The Address field contains more than one value as it stores the street address, city, state, and zip code. This makes searching on a single portion of the address, such as the city, difficult.

Furthermore, because users and book aren't really related, you would split them apart into Tables 7-2, 7-3, 7-4, and 7-5.

Table 7-2. The user purchases table after any normalization

Purch-ase_ID (key)	User_ ID	First name	Last name	Address	City	State	Zip	Phone	Purchased	When
1	Mdavis	Michele	Davis	7505 N. Link-sway	FxPnt	MN	55114	414-352-4818	Linux in a Nutshell	Sept 3rd, 2005
2	Mdavis	Michele	Davis	7505 N. Link-sway	FxPnt	MN	55114	414-352-4818	Classic Shell Scripting	Sept 3rd, 2005

Table 7-3. The books table after first normal form application

Title_ID (key)	Title	Pages
1	Linux in a Nutshell	112
2	Classic Shell Scripting	576

Table 7-4. Authors now have their own table

Author_ID (key)	Author name
1	Ellen Siever
2	Aaron Weber
3	Arnold Robbins
4	Nelson Beebe

Table 7-5. The book_author table links authors to books

Title_ID (key)	Author_ID (key)
1	1
1	2
2	3
2	4

We've effectively reduced each field to holding a single value, split apart related chunks of data into separate tables, and eliminated the repeating columns.

Second Normal Form

As we stated above, the First Normal Form deals with redundancy of data across a horizontal row. The Second Normal Form (or 2NF) deals with redundancy of data in vertical columns. Normal forms are progressive. To achieve Second Normal Form, your tables must already be in First Normal Form. For a database table to be in Second Normal Form, you must identify any columns that repeat their values across multiple rows. Those columns need to be placed in their own table and referenced by a key value in the original table.

You may notice that Table 7-2 repeats the address information over multiple rows. In order to achieve Second Normal Form, you define a new addresses table to pull these out, creating Tables 7-6 and 7-7.

Table 7-6. The Users table after second normal form application

User ID	First name	Last name	Address	City	State	Zip	Phone
Mdavis	Michele	Davis	7505 N. Linksway	FxPnt	MN	55114	414-352-4818

Table 7-7. The Purchases table after second normal form application

User ID	Purchased	When
Mdavis	Linux in a Nutshell	Sept 3rd, 2005
Mdavis	Classic Shell Scripting	Sept 3rd, 2005

Your data is now in great shape. You have separate tables for Users, Books, Authors, and Purchases.

Third Normal Form

If you've followed the First and Second Normal Form process, you may not need to do anything with your database to satisfy the Third Normal Form (or 3NF) rules. In Third Normal Form, you're looking for data in your tables that's not fully dependent on the primary key, but dependent on another value in the table. Where this applies to your tables isn't immediately clear.

In Table 7-6, the components of the addresses can be thought of as not being directly related to the user. The street address relies on the zip code, the zip code on the city, and finally, the city on the state. Third Normal Form requires that each of these be split out into separate tables, as shown in Figure 7-8.

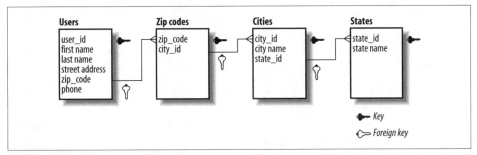

Figure 7-8. The address components broken out into separate tables

Figure 7-8 shows how the address can be split up. The lines with the webbed feet represent the foreign key relationships. On a practical level, you may find that following the Third Normal Form creates more tables than you'll want to manage in your database. It's up to you to know where to stop normalizing your data.

It's a good idea to make sure your data at least conforms to Second Normal Form. The goal is to avoid data redundancy to prevent corruption and make the best possible use of storage. You also need to make sure that the same value is not stored in more than one place. With data in multiple locations, you have to perform multiple updates when the data needs to be changed, which can lead to corruption in your database.

As you noticed, the Third Normal Form removed even more data redundancy, but at the cost of simplicity and performance. In our example just shown, do you really expect the city and street names to change very regularly? In this situation, the Third Normal Form still prevents misspelling of city and street names. Since it's your database, you decide on the level of balance between normalization and the speed or simplicity of your database.

Now that we've covered the basics of how to lay out your data, we can delve into the details of how columns are defined.

Column Data Types

Although databases store the same information that you collect and process in PHP, databases require fields to be set to specific types of data when they're created.

 Remember, PHP isn't strongly typed, but databases are!

A data type is classification of a particular type of information. When you read, you're used to conventions such as symbols, letters, and numbers. Therefore, it's easy to distinguish between different types of data because you use symbols along with numbers and letters. You can tell at a glance whether a number is a percentage, a time, or an amount of money. The symbols help you understand a percentage, time, or amount of money are that data's type. A database uses internal codes to keep track of the different types of data it processes.

Most programming languages require the programmer to declare the data type of every data object, and most database systems require the user to specify the type of each data field. The available data types vary from one programming language to another, and from one database application to another. But, the three main types of data—numbers, dates/times, and strings—exist in one form or another. Table 7-8 lists data types, with the values in brackets optional.

Table 7-8. Common MySQL data types

Field type	Description	Example
INT[(M)]	Integer number (max display size M)	997
FLOAT[(M,D)]	Decimal number (M places before the decimal D places after)	3.4156
CHAR(M)	Characters (M characters up to 255)	"test"
VARCHAR(M)	Text (M characters up to 256)	"testing 1, 2, 3"

TEXT or BLOB	Text up to 65,000 characters	"All work and no play makes Jack a dull boy. All
		  Work
		    And
		      No Play
		Makes Jack a dull boy."

DATE	Date YYYY-MM-DD	2003-12-25
TIME	Times HH:MM:SS	11:36:02

There are many more data types provided by MySQL; see *http://dev.mysql.com/doc/mysql/en/column-types.html* for a complete list.

To define tables like Tables 7-3 and 7-4, use the types in Tables 7-9 and 7-10.

Table 7-9. Books column data types

Field name	Database type
Title_ID	INT
Title	VARCHAR(150)
Pages	INT

Table 7-10. Authors column data types

Field name	Database type
Author_ID	INT
Title_ID	INT
Author	VARCHAR(100)

The numeric ID fields, combined with a source of unique numbers, provide a way of guaranteeing the key field is unique. Specifying the auto_increment keyword when creating a column is a great way to generate a unique ID for a column. For example, if there are two authors with the name John Smith, and you use their names as a key, you'd have a problem keeping track of which Smith you're using. Keeping keys unique is an important part of making sure you have the correct data in your database. Next, we're going to move on to modifying objects, and learn about the language used to modify objects like tables and work with data.

Structured Query Language

Now that you've defined a table, you can add data to it. MySQL will keep track of all the details. To manipulate data, use the Structured Query Language (SQL) commands. Because it's been designed to easily describe the relationship between tables and rows, the database uses SQL to modify data in tables.

SQL is a standard language used with any database such as MySQL, Oracle, or Microsoft SQL Server. It was developed specifically as a language used to retrieve, add, and manipulate data that resides in databases. We'll get into the nitty gritty of MySQL in Chapter 8, but we'll start with some easy-to-use commands. We're going to start with creating tables.

Each database adds on its own extensions to the standard SQL. These are usually more advanced capabilities, such as an outer join. An *outer join* is a special way of linking two tables so that data from one of the tables is included even if there isn't a match in the other table. The syntax for outer joins for tables in Oracle is a plus within parentheses (+), whereas MySQL uses the syntax left join on to perform an outer table join.

Creating Tables

Use the create table command to specify the structure of new database tables. When you create a database table, each column has a few options, in addition to the column names and data types. Values that must be supplied when adding data to a table use the NOT NULL keyword. The PRIMARY KEY keyword tells MySQL which column to use as a key field. Then, you have MySQL automatically assign key values by using the AUTO_INCREMENT keyword.

To create these tables, paste the code into the MySQL command-line client.

Example 7-1 creates the books table using the data types from Table 7-8.

Example 7-1. Creating the books and authors tables

```
CREATE TABLE books (
title_id INT NOT NULL AUTO_INCREMENT,
title VARCHAR (150),
pages INT,
PRIMARY KEY (title_id));
CREATE TABLE authors (
author_id INT NOT NULL AUTO_INCREMENT,
title_id INT NOT NULL,
author VARCHAR (125),
PRIMARY KEY (author_id));
```

If everything is OK, you'll see output that instructs MySQL to create a table called "books," and it'll look like this (the time the query takes to run may be different than 0.06 sec):

```
mysql> CREATE TABLE books (
    -> title_id INT NOT NULL AUTO_INCREMENT,
    -> title VARCHAR (150),
    -> pages INT,
    -> PRIMARY KEY (title_id));
Query OK, 0 rows affected (0.06 sec)
mysql> CREATE TABLE authors (
    -> author_id INT NOT NULL AUTO_INCREMENT,
    -> title_id INT,
    -> author VARCHAR (125),
    -> PRIMARY KEY (author_id));
Query OK, 0 rows affected (0.06 sec)
```

The code breaks down as follows:

- The first column, called title_id, is an integer. The auto_increment keyword is a unique value assigned to this field automatically during row insertion.
- The title column holds text up to 150 characters.
- The pages column is an integer.

- The PRIMARY KEY field tells MySQL which field is the key value. While this field isn't required, it allows MySQL to speed up access when you retrieve data from multiple tables or a specific row using the key value. MySQL does this by using a special data structure called an index. An *index* acts like a shortcut for finding a record, like a card catalog in a library. To verify your table columns, use DESCRIBE:

```
DESCRIBE books;
```

This returns:

```
+----------+--------------+------+-----+---------+----------------+
| Field    | Type         | Null | Key | Default | Extra          |
+----------+--------------+------+-----+---------+----------------+
| title_id | int(11)      |      | PRI | NULL    | auto_increment |
| title    | varchar(150) | YES  |     | NULL    |                |
| pages    | int(11)      | YES  |     | NULL    |                |
+----------+--------------+------+-----+---------+----------------+
3 rows in set (0.01 sec)
```

And the following:

```
describe authors;
```

returns:

```
+-----------+--------------+------+-----+---------+----------------+
| Field     | Type         | Null | Key | Default | Extra          |
+-----------+--------------+------+-----+---------+----------------+
| author_id | int(11)      |      | PRI | NULL    | auto_increment |
| title_id  | int(11)      |      |     | 0       |                |
| author    | varchar(125) | YES  |     | NULL    |                |
+-----------+--------------+------+-----+---------+----------------+
3 rows in set (0.01 sec)
```

Everything is as we specified in our description.

 Notice that because we didn't specify the size of the integer columns, MySQL used the default of 11 places.

Adding Data to a Table

The insert command is used to add data. Its syntax is INSERT INTO *table* VALUES ([*values*]);. This syntax displays which table data needs to be added to, and a list of the values. They should be in the same order they were defined when the table was created (as long as you don't skip any column values). There are specific rules for how you handle data to populate your database using SQL commands.

- Numeric values shouldn't be quoted.
- String values should always be quoted.
- Date and time values should always be quoted.
- Functions shouldn't be quoted.
- NULL should always be quoted.

Lastly, if a row isn't given a value, it automatically is considered NULL. However, if a column can't have NULL, even if it was set to NOT NULL; if you don't specify a value, an error is created.

For example:

```
INSERT INTO books VALUES (1,"Linux in a Nutshell",112);
INSERT INTO authors VALUES (1,1,"Ellen Siever");
INSERT INTO authors VALUES (2,1,"Aaron Weber");
```

As long as there were no errors, you should get:

```
mysql> INSERT INTO books VALUES (1,"Linux in a Nutshell",112);
Query OK, 1 row affected (0.00 sec)

mysql> INSERT INTO authors VALUES (NULL,1,"Ellen Siever");
ES (2,1Query OK, 1 row affected (0.00 sec)

,"Aaron Weber");
mysql> INSERT INTO authors VALUES (NULL,1,"Aaron Weber");
Query OK, 1 row affected (0.00 sec)
```

When adding data, you must specify all the columns even if you aren't supplying a value for each one. Even though we didn't supply the author_id field and we let MySQL assign it for us, we still had to leave a placeholder for it.

Likewise, we add the other book:

```
INSERT INTO books VALUES (2,"Classic Shell Scripting",256);
INSERT INTO authors VALUES (NULL,2,"Arnold Robbins");
INSERT INTO authors VALUES (NULL,2,"Nelson Beebe");
```

This gives us two rows in the books table. Now that you know how to create a table and enter data into it, you'll need to know how to view that information.

Querying the Database

Having data in tables doesn't do much good if you can't view what's in it. The SELECT command specifies which table(s) to query and which rows to view based on specific conditions. The syntax of SELECT is SELECT *columns* FROM *tables* [WHERE *CLAUSE*];.

Columns indicate a list of columns to display from the selected tables. The WHERE clause optionally restricts which rows are selected. WHERE provides limits to the results that are returned from a query. For example, rows can be rejected if a field doesn't equal a literal value or is less than or greater than a value. Fields from multiple tables can be forced to be equal. If multiple tables are included in a SELECT statement without a WHERE clause, the resultant set becomes the *Cartesian* product, in which every row in the first table is returned with all rows in the second table followed by the same thing for the second row in the first table. To put it another way, that's a lot of results!

The simplest query is to view all data in a table:

```
SELECT * FROM books;
```

This displays:

```
+----------+-----------------------+-------+
| title_id | title                 | pages |
+----------+-----------------------+-------+
|        1 | Linux in a Nutshell   |   112 |
|        2 | Classic Shell Scripting |  256 |
+----------+-----------------------+-------+
2 rows in set (0.01 sec)
```

And the following:

```
SELECT * FROM authors;
```

displays:

```
+-----------+----------+-------------------+
| author_id | title_id | author            |
+-----------+----------+-------------------+
|         1 |        1 | Ellen Siever      |
|         2 |        1 | Aaron Weber       |
|         3 |        2 | Arnold Robbins    |
|         4 |        2 | Nelson Beebe      |
+-----------+----------+-------------------+
5 rows in set (0.01 sec)
```

Limit results with WHERE

If you're only interested in the title Classic Shell Scripting, you can use a WHERE clause to restrict your query:

```
SELECT * FROM books WHERE title=('Classic Shell Scripting');
```

This returns:

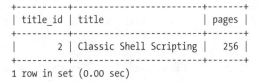

```
+----------+-----------------------+-------+
| title_id | title                 | pages |
+----------+-----------------------+-------+
|        2 | Classic Shell Scripting |  256 |
+----------+-----------------------+-------+
1 row in set (0.00 sec)
```

You can also list out just the columns you're interested in from a table by using:

```
SELECT pages FROM books WHERE title=('Classic Shell Scripting');
```

This returns:

```
+-------+
| pages |
+-------+
|   256 |
+-------+

1 row in set (0.00 sec)
```

Conditions come after the WHERE clause and should be enclosed by parentheses (()). This forces the condition to be evaluated. Additionally, parentheses are a good idea, since you'll need them when you have nested conditions in complex queries. Getting into the habit of doing this from the beginning is best. At some point, you might want to display data from multiple tables in a query. You should also get into the habit of using the full TABLE.COLUMN reference. This prevents confusion when selecting columns if both tables have a column with the same name. For example, if two tables include a description field, it may not be clear which description to include in the query unless the full reference is included.

Specifying the order

The ORDER BY keyword can be used to change the order of the results from a query. The default for ORDER BY is ascending, so if you want alphabetical order for the author column, you would just type in ORDER BY author. To select in reverse order, add the DESC keyword after author. For example, to select the authors in alphabetical order:

```
SELECT * FROM authors ORDER BY author;
```

This displays:

```
+-----------+----------+-------------------+
| author_id | title_id | author            |
+-----------+----------+-------------------+
|         2 |        1 | Aaron Weber       |
|         5 |        9 | Alex Martelli     |
|         3 |        2 | Arnold Robbins    |
|         1 |        1 | Ellen Siever      |
|         4 |        2 | Nelson Beebe      |
+-----------+----------+-------------------+
```

Next, we'll select from more than one table.

Joining tables together

The SELECT statement allows you to query more than one table at a time. Example 7-2 creates the purchases table and adds a couple of sample entries.

Example 7-2. The SQL to create and populate a purchases table that links user_ids and title_ids to a purchase_id

```
CREATE TABLE `purchases` (
purchase_id int(11) NOT NULL auto_increment,
user_id varchar(10) NOT NULL,
title_id int(11) NOT NULL,
purchased timestamp NOT NULL default CURRENT_TIMESTAMP,
PRIMARY KEY (purchase_id));
INSERT INTO `purchases` VALUES (1, 'mdavis', 2, '2005-11-26 17:04:29');
INSERT INTO `purchases` VALUES (2, 'mdavis', 1, '2005-11-26 17:05:58');
```

Example 7-2 returns:

```
SELECT * FROM purchases;
+-------------+---------+----------+---------------------+
| purchase_id | user_id | title_id | purchased           |
+-------------+---------+----------+---------------------+
|           1 | mdavis  |        2 | 2005-11-26 17:04:29 |
|           2 | mdavis  |        1 | 2005-11-26 17:05:58 |
+-------------+---------+----------+---------------------+
2 rows in set (0.00 sec)
```

To create a query that lists the purchases, author, and pages, enter the following SELECT statement:

```
SELECT books.*, author FROM books, authors WHERE books.title_id = authors.title_id;
```

which produces:

```
+----------+-----------------------+-------+---------------+
| title_id | title                 | pages | author        |
+----------+-----------------------+-------+---------------+
|        1 | Linux in a Nutshell   |   112 | Ellen Siever  |
|        1 | Linux in a Nutshell   |   112 | Aaron Weber   |
|        2 | Classic Shell Scripting |  256 | Arnold Robbins |
|        2 | Classic Shell Scripting |  256 | Nelson Beebe  |
+----------+-----------------------+-------+---------------+
4 rows in set (0.00 sec)
```

The books.*, author portion tells the database to select all of the fields from the books table but only the author from the authors table. The WHERE books.title_id = authors.title_id portion links the tables together by the title_id.

You could have selected *, which includes all the fields from both tables. But the title_id field would be included twice, since it's in both tables. There's no limit to how many tables and columns you can join together.

As you've noticed, SQL is a combination of alpha characters and symbols used in mathematics. The *structure* in SQL means it uses English phrases to define an action but uses math-like symbols to make comparisons. Remember this analogy, and it should make it easier to remember that you always need a math-like symbol in your context. Then it will be easier for you to catch your errors!

Natural joins

You can specify the NATURAL JOIN keyword to accomplish the same query as above with less typing. With natural joining, MySQL can take two tables and automatically join the fields that have the same name. In the case of the two tables you're working with, that's the title_id field. It also knows not to display title_id twice and not to display the author_id for author. The following:

```
SELECT * FROM books NATURAL JOIN authors;
```

produces:

```
+----------+----------------------+-------+-----------+-------------------+
| title_id | title                | pages | author_id | author            |
+----------+----------------------+-------+-----------+-------------------+
|        1 | Linux in a Nutshell  |   112 |         1 | Ellen Siever      |
|        1 | Linux in a Nutshell  |   112 |         2 | Aaron Weber       |
|        2 | Classic Shell Scripting |   256 |      3 | Arnold Robbins    |
|        2 | Classic Shell Scripting |   256 |      4 | Nelson Beebe      |
+----------+----------------------+-------+-----------+-------------------+
4 rows in set (0.00 sec)
```

Aliases

Use aliases when listing which tables to include in your query. The AS keyword comes after the full table name and before the alias. In this example, "books" is aliased to b and "purchases" to p:

```
SELECT * FROM books AS p,authors AS b WHERE b.title_id = p.title_id;
```

This results in:

```
+----------+----------------------+-------+-----------+----------+-------------+
| title_id | title                | pages | author_id | title_id | author      |
|          |                      |       |           |          |             |
+----------+----------------------+-------+-----------+----------+-------------+
|        1 | Linux in a Nutshell  |   112 |         1 |        1 | Ellen Siever |
|        1 | Linux in a Nutshell  |   112 |         2 |        1 | Aaron Weber  |
|        2 | Classic Shell Scripting |   256 |      3 |        2 | Arnold Robbins |
|        2 | Classic Shell Scripting |   256 |      4 |        2 | Nelson Beebe |
+----------+----------------------+-------+-----------+----------+-------------+
4 rows in set (0.00 sec)
```

Once you alias a table in a query, you must refer to the table as the alias everywhere in the query. Aliases are useful for replacing long table names with a short abbreviation. They also allow you to include the same table twice in a query and to be able to specify which instance of that table you're referencing.

Modifying Database Data

If you make a mistake, say, by entering the wrong number of pages for a book, you can change data by using the UPDATE command.

UPDATE uses the same WHERE clause as the SELECT statement but adds a SET command that specifies a new column value.

If you forget to include the WHERE clause for an update, it changes every record in the table.

For example, you'll update the books table:

```
UPDATE books SET pages = 476 WHERE title = "Linux in a Nutshell";
```

The example returns:

```
Query OK, 1 row affected (0.00 sec)
Rows matched: 1  Changed: 1  Warnings: 0
```

This changes any book with the title *Linux in a Nutshell* to 476 pages. Modifying the data cleans up any data errors you might have made.

```
SELECT * FROM books;
```

This returns:

```
+----------+------------------------+-------+
| title_id | title                  | pages |
+----------+------------------------+-------+
|        1 | Linux in a Nutshell    |   476 |
|        2 | Classic Shell Scripting |  256 |
+----------+------------------------+-------+
2 rows in set (0.00 sec)
```

Deleting Database Data

This command is used to delete rows or records in a table. The DELETE command takes the same WHERE clause as UPDATE but deletes any rows that match. Without the WHERE clause, you'd have an "oops!" moment, because all records in the table would be deleted.

```
DELETE FROM authors WHERE author= "Ellen Siever";
```

In this example, only Ellen Siever's book is deleted from the database.

Search Functions

As you have seen in the above examples, MySQL has the ability to find specific search data. However, we have not covered general search syntax. The % character in MySQL is the wildcard character and is used with the LIKE keyword. That is, it can literally represent anything. Sort of like searching in DOS, or even in the Windows Explorer Search field where *.doc means any document, regardless of the name before the *.doc* ending displays.

For example, to do a general search, you would use the following syntax:

```
SELECT * FROM authors WHERE author LIKE "%b%";
```

This returns:

```
+-----------+----------+-------------------+
| author_id | title_id | author            |
+-----------+----------+-------------------+
|         2 |        1 | Aaron Weber       |
|         3 |        2 | Arnold Robbins    |
|         4 |        2 | Nelson Beebe      |
+-----------+----------+-------------------+
3 rows in set (0.00 sec)
```

This results in finding anything with the letter b in the column. Notice that two %
signs were used. This checks for anything before or after that letter. You can use just
one if you like, but there is no hard and fast rule that one or two be used.

You can place the % sign anywhere within the query's LIKE string, as the search is
based upon the placement of this character.

Another wildcard character is the _ character. It will match exactly one character. To
use a literal wildcard character in your searches:

```
SELECT * FROM authors WHERE author like "Aaron Webe_"
```

This returns all the records containing an author name that starts with "Aaron
Webe" and can have any letter for the last character of the name.

Logical Operators

The same logical operators that we discussed with PHP's conditional logic can also
be used in the WHERE clause.

You can use AND, OR, and NOT in your query's WHERE clause.

```
SELECT * FROM authors WHERE NOT (author = "Ellen Siever" );
```

This returns all records without Ellen Siever as the author. The parentheses are
important, as they relate the NOT operator to the author comparison.

```
SELECT *
  FROM books, authors
 WHERE (title = "Linux in a Nutshell")
   AND (author = "Aaron Weber"
);
```

This query returns all records with author names of either Aaron Weber or Ellen
Siever.

```
SELECT *
  FROM books, authors
 WHERE (author = "Aaron Weber")
    OR (author = "Ellen Siever")
```

Now that all the basics have been covered, start getting excited. In our next chapter,
we'll walk through using PHP to connect and work with MySQL data. We're well on
our way to creating that blog at the end of the book.

Chapter 7 Questions

Question 7-1. Create a table called `months` that contains the month name and the number of days in the month.

Question 7-2. Write `insert` statements to populate the months and days.

Question 7-3. Write a `select` statement to display the months.

Question 7-4. Write a `select` statement to display only the months that have 28 days.

Question 7-5. Write a query to display only the months that end in "ber."

See the Appendix for the answers to these questions.

Using MySQL

Now that we've learned basic SQL information and the essentials of designing a database, it's time to learn how to connect to the MySQL database using the client tools that come with MySQL. We'll also cover how to use SQL to create databases, users, and tables, as well as to modify existing objects in the database.

MySQL Database

MySQL has its own client interface, allowing you to move data around and change database configuration. Note that you must use a password to log in. Assigning database *users* allows you to limit access to server tables that have multiple users. Each MySQL server, where tables are grouped together, can host many databases. Normally, a web application has its own proprietary database.

You may have installed MySQL yourself or have access through your ISP. Most ISPs that support PHP also provide a MySQL database for your use. Should you have difficulty, check their support pages or contact them to determine connection details. You'll need to know the following:

- The IP address of the database server
- The name of the database
- The username
- The password

If you've installed MySQL on your computer, you'll be able to use the defaults from the installation and the password you specified. This chapter looks at two ways to communicate with MySQL, the command line and phpMyAdmin, a web-based tool.

Accessing the Database with the Command Line

One way of communicating with MySQL is via the MySQL Command Line Client. Depending on which operating system you're using, you either need to open a command shell for Windows (type `cmd` from the Run dialog, as shown in Figure 8-1) or open a terminal session, in Mac OS X and Unix environments.

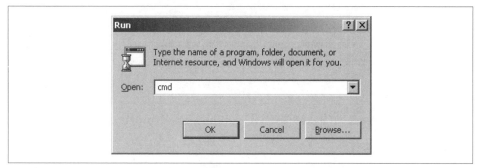

Figure 8-1. Windows Run dialog

Once you reach the command line, type `mysql` and press Enter. The syntax for the `mysql` command is:

```
mysql -h hostname -u user -p
```

If you've installed MySQL on your computer, the default username is root. You can omit the hostname flag and value. Enter your password when MySQL displays the "Enter password" prompt. If the password, username, and hostname are correct, you'll see a banner message like that in Figure 8-2.

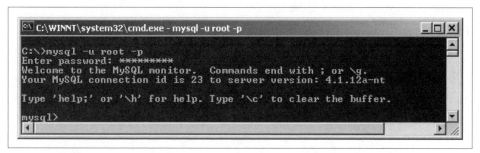

Figure 8-2. A successful login to MySQL

Don't let the MySQL command-line interface alarm you; it's not difficult to use.

Prompts

At the MySQL prompt, you can enter database commands followed by Enter. There is also a set of commands that MySQL itself interprets. For a list of these commands, type `help` or `\h` at the `mysql>` prompt. Table 8-1 shows some of the prompts you'll see and summarizes what they mean.

Table 8-1. Command prompt meanings

Prompt	Meaning
mysql>	Waiting for a command
->	Waiting for the next line of a command
'>	Waiting for the next line of a string that starts with a single quote
">	Waiting for the next line of a string that starts with a double quote

Commands

Table 8-2 lists commands that are available at the MySQL prompt.

Table 8-2. MySQL client commands

Command	Parameter	Meaning
quit		Exit the command-line utility
use	Database name	Use a specific database
show	tables or databases	Show lists such as tables or databases available
describe	Table name	Describe a table's columns
status		Display database version and status
source	Filename	Execute commands from a file as a script

These commands allow you to perform tasks such as executing SQL commands that are stored in a script file using the source.

To display the available databases, type:

```
mysql> SHOW DATABASES;
```

which returns:

```
+----------+
| Database |
+----------+
| mysql    |
+----------+
1 rows in set (0.00 sec)
```

 To scroll back though commands you've already entered in MySQL, use the up arrow key.

The default database that is present after an install is called mysql. The mysql database also stores the database user authentication information. Don't delete it! When you started mysql, you didn't specify connection to a particular database. The use command allows you to do this.

To connect to the mysql database, type the following at the MySQL prompt:

```
USE `mysql`;
```

This returns:

```
Database changed
```

If your ISP supplied a different database name, use that instead of mysql.

Managing the Database

Now that you're connected to the database, you can create users, databases, and tables. You may not need to create a database or user account if you're using a MySQL server in a hosted environment, and if they supplied you with a username and a database name.

Creating Users

To create users above and beyond the default privileged root user, issue the grant command. The grant command uses this syntax:

```
GRANT PRIVILEGES ON DATABASE.OBJECTS TO'USER'@'HOST' IDENTIFIED BY 'PASSWORD';
```

For example:

```
GRANT ALL PRIVILEGES ON *.* TO 'michele'@'localhost' IDENTIFIED BY 'secret';
```

This creates the user michele who can access anything locally. To change to the michele user, at the mysql command prompt, type:

```
exit
```

Then start MySQL from the command line with the new username and password. The syntax for specifying the username and password when starting MySQL is:

```
mysql -h hostname -u username -ppassword
```

If you don't want users to access tables other than their own, replace * with the name of the user's database, like this:

```
GRANT ALL PRIVILEGES ON `store`.* TO 'michele'@'localhost' IDENTIFIED BY 'secret';
```

You'll need to run the above line as root or as someone with permission. In the above code, the word store correlates to the database name to which privileges are assigned, which you'll create in the next section.

Creating a MySQL Database

You're going to create a database called store. The create database command works like this:

```
CREATE DATABASE `store`;
```

If this works, you'll get a result like this one:

```
Query OK, 1 row affected (0.03 sec)
```

 Database names cannot contain any spaces. On Unix servers, such as Linux and Mac OS X, database names are also case sensitive.

To start using this database, type:

```
USE `store`;
```

You will get the result:

```
Database changed.
```

Assuming you've done everything correctly, you'll be set up with new data and selected it for use. Creating tables is an important concept, so that's where we're headed!

Table Manipulation

Once you've created a table and started storing information in it, you may find that you need to make a change to the column types. For example, you may find a field you thought would need only 30 characters actually needs 100. You could start all over and redefine the table, but you'd lose all your data. Thankfully, MySQL allows you to modify column types without losing your data.

Renaming a table

To rename a table, use ALTER TABLE *table* RENAME *newtable*. In this example, we are renaming the table from books to publications.

```
ALTER TABLE `books` RENAME `publications`;
```

This would look like Figure 8-3.

Figure 8-3. Renaming a table

Changing a column's data type

To change a column data type, use ALTER TABLE *table* MODIFY *column datatype*. The following syntax modifies the author field so that the column can take 150 characters.

```
ALTER TABLE `authors` MODIFY `author` VARCHAR(150);
```

Changing a column's data type will look like Figure 8-4.

Figure 8-4. Changing column's data type

Adding a column

To add a column, use ALTER TABLE *table* ADD *column datatype*. Here, we're changing the publications table so a timestamp is automatically added to it.

    ALTER TABLE publications ADD time TIMESTAMP;

Figure 8-5 shows the result.

Figure 8-5. Adding a column

Remove a column

If you look at your database tables and decide you don't need a specific column, you can remove it. To remove a column, use ALTER TABLE *table* DROP *column*. Here, we're removing the pages column; therefore, we'll no longer know how many pages are in a book listed in the database.

    ALTER TABLE publications DROP COLUMN pages;

Figure 8-6 shows how it would look after you execute the command.

Figure 8-6. Removing a column

Deleting an entire table

Sometimes you may want to completely remove a table. Use the DROP command to permanently remove a table and its data.

    DROP TABLE `authors`;

Using phpMyAdmin

The tool phpMyAdmin, available from *http://www.phpmyadmin.net/*, allows you to administer a MySQL database through your web browser. All that's required is a web server with PHP installed and a MySQL database to administer.

To install phpMyAdmin, follow these steps:

1. Download the archive file, such as *phpMyAdmin-2.7.0-pl2.tar.gz* (Unix) or *phpMyAdmin-2.7.0-pl2.zip* (Windows).

2. Unpack the archive (including subdirectories) to a directory on your computer.

3. Transfer them to your ISP account where PHP files can be executed. Or, if you have a web server installed locally, transfer them to the document root.

4. Create the configuration file *config.inc.php* using a text editor. You can use the existing *config.default.php* file as an example. For versions of phpMyAdmin before 2.7, modify *config.inc.php* instead of creating a new file. You may modify this file before sending it to your web server to avoid having to use the editor that is native to the server.

5. You will need to set the value of $cfg['PmaAbsoluteUri'] to the URI location of where you are placing the files. For example, if you place the files in *www/phpmyadmin/* on your ISP, the URI value is *http://www.isp_domain_name/phpmyadmin/*.

6. You also need to set the hostname of your database, the MySQL username, and the password.

7. We recommend that you either limit access to this directory or set up a cookie or cookie authentication so that authorized users only can make changes to your database.

8. Browse to *http://www.yourhost.com/myadmin_dir/index.php*.

Once installed and connected to the database, phpMyAdmin's main page looks similar to Figure 8-7, except in the case that you're running the stable release of 2.7.0-pl2, instead of the 2.6.2-pl1 release.

You can select any configured databases from the drop-down list labeled Databases. The admin provides an easy way to see how your database is configured and what objects exist (such as tables), and you're even offered the option to add tables through the graphical interface. Using PHP admin, you can create new databases and tables, run queries, and display server statistics.

Figure 8-8 shows the tables that are in the test database. Click on the authors table on the left to get more details on that table.

In Figure 8-9, the table structure of the authors table is displayed. This screen provides an easy way to visualize the layout of a database, particularly if it's a database that you did not create yourself.

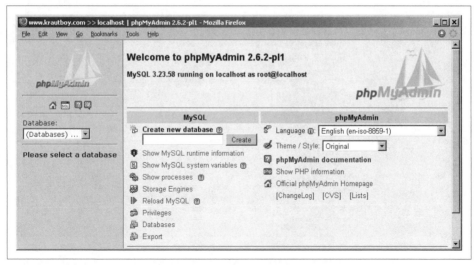

Figure 8-7. Selecting a database to administer in phpMyAdmin

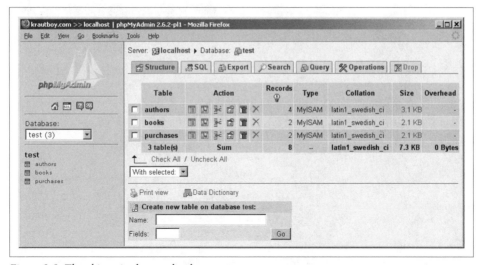

Figure 8-8. The objects in the test database

To view the contents of a table, click on the Browse tab. Figure 8-10 shows the Browse tab for the authors table.

The web-based administration tool provides an easy-to-use interface for both exploring your database and creating new objects or modifying data. You may find the graphical interface to be a refreshing change from the text-based command line of the mysql client.

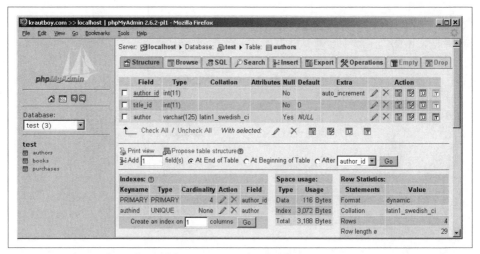

Figure 8-9. Viewing the authors table structure in phpMyAdmin

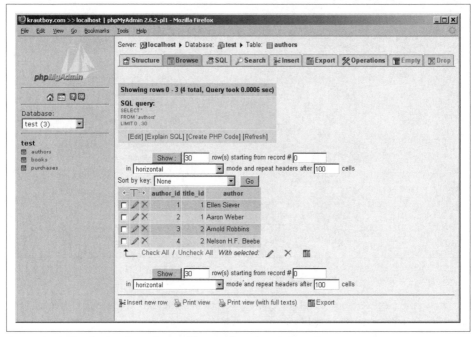

Figure 8-10. The data in the authors table as well as the query used to generate it

Since you have MySQL up and running and have created a database, let's talk about backing up your databases. As you know, backing up your data is important. Between security, data integrity, and backups, you have the most crucial pieces of a database. We'll discuss security later in the book.

Backing Up and Restoring Data

Even the best maintained databases occasionally develop problems. Hardware failures, in particular, can really throw a monkey wrench into your web pages. Now that you're using a database, just backing up the files (HTML, PHP, and images) on your web server isn't enough. There's nothing worse than informing your web users that they have to reenter information, such as their accounts, or have to recreate your catalog items. Having a complete backup can make the difference between an hour of down time and having to recreate the wheel. There are a couple of tactics that we'll discuss for backing up your database data.

Copying Database Files

You can also do a simple file backup of your MySQL database's datafiles, in the same way that you can back up your HTML and PHP files. If you can back up files, you can back up the MySQL database files.

We don't recommend this tactic for moving a database from one machine to another server, since different versions of MySQL may expect these files to be in a different format. MySQL stores its datafiles in a special data directory that is usually located in *C:\Program Files\MySQL\MySQL Server 4.1\data\[database_name]* on Windows and in */var/lib/mysql* on Unix variants such as Linux and Mac OS X.

To fully back up and restore a MySQL database using your current datafiles, all the files must be replaced in the same directory from which they were backed up. Then, the database must be restarted.

The mysqldump Command

It's better to use the MySQL command-line tool for making complete database backups. The same tools you'll use to back up and restore can also be used to change platforms or move your database from one server to another; mysqldump creates a text file containing the SQL statements required to rebuild the database objects and insert the data. The mysqldump command is accessible from the command line and takes parameters for backing up a single table, a single database, or everything. The command's syntax is:

```
mysqldump -u user -p objects_to_backup
```

The default mode for mysqldump is to export to backup and then to standard output, which is usually the screen.

Backing up

We're going to show you the commands to back up a database called test from the shell prompt.

```
mysqldump -u root -p test > my_backup.sql
```

This tells `mysqldump` to log into the database as the `root` user with a password of barney, and to back up the test database. The output of the command is saved to a file called *my_backup.sql* with the help of the redirect character also known as the greater-than symbol (>).

Example 8-1 shows the first portion of the output `mysqldump` creates.

Example 8-1. The contents of the my_backup.sql file

```
-- MySQL dump 10.9
--
-- Host: localhost    Database: test
-- -------------------------------------------------------
-- Server version         4.1.11-Debian_4-log
--
-- Table structure for table `authors`
--
DROP TABLE IF EXISTS `authors`;
CREATE TABLE `authors` (
  `author_id` int(11) NOT NULL auto_increment,
`title_id` int(11) NOT NULL default '0',
  `author` varchar(125) default NULL,
  PRIMARY KEY  (`author_id`)
) ENGINE=MyISAM DEFAULT CHARSET=latin1;
--
-- Dumping data for table `authors`
--
/*!40000 ALTER TABLE `authors` DISABLE KEYS */;
LOCK TABLES `authors` WRITE;
INSERT INTO `authors` VALUES (1,1,'Ellen Siever'),(2,1,'Aaron Weber'),(3,2,'Arno
ld Robbins'),(4,2,'Nelson  Beebe');
UNLOCK TABLES;
/*!40000 ALTER TABLE `authors` ENABLE KEYS */;
```

The two major sections in Example 8-1 are creating the authors table and populating the data for the table.

To back up only a single table from a database, simply add the table name after the database name. For example, the command below illustrates how to back up only the authors table:

```
$ mysqldump -u root -p test authors > authors.sql
```

Most of the time, you'll just want to back up everything in the database. To do this, use the `--all-databases` command-line switch. The resulting database backup file will contain the commands necessary to create the databases and users, making a complete database restore a snap. Here's how to use this parameter:

```
$ mysqldump -u root -p --all-databases > my_backup.sql
```

To create an empty copy of your database—just the structure—for testing, use the `--no-data` switch:

```
$ mysqldump -u root -p --no-data test > structure.sql
```

You can also do the opposite and just back up the data with the `--no-create-info` switch like this:

```
$ mysqldump -u root -p --no-create-info test > data.sql
```

Of course, having a backup of your database doesn't do you much good if you don't know how to restore the database from it.

Restoring a MySQL backup

The good news is it's not difficult to recreate your database from a `mysqldump` file. As you saw in Example 8-1, the contents of the backup file are simply SQL statements and can therefore be processed by the `mysql` command-line client to restore the backed-up data.

If you did a backup of your database using `mysqldump --all-databases` to a file called *my_backup.sql*, you could restore your database like this:

```
mysql -u root -p < my_backup.sql
```

If you did a selective backup of only one database, it's a bit more complex. To restore that type of backup file, use the `-D` command-line switch:

```
mysql -u root -p -D test < my_backup.sql
```

Now that you know how to restore default dump files, we can move on to some other applications regarding exporting and importing data.

Working with other formats

Although working with SQL-based files is convenient, there may be times when you want to save your data in other formats. For example, a common method of representing a list of data is in *CSV* (comma-separated values) format. The `mysqldump` command supports this format. All you need to do is specify the `--no-create-info`, `--tab`, and `--fields-terminated-by` arguments like this:

```
mysqldump -u root -p --no-create-info --tab=/home/jon --fields-terminated-by=',' test
```

This tells `mysqldump` to generate separate files for each table in the test database. They'll all be placed in the directory */home/jon*. Each file's name will be the name of the table that is being exported. Each file contains the records in the respective table separated by the comma character (**,**) that was specified on the command line.

The mysqlimport command

When you're setting up your database, you may need to bring in data from another database or a spreadsheet in CSV format. For example, if you're offering books for sale, you may bring in the existing catalog of books. To import the data displayed in Example 8-2, use the `mysqlimport` command.

Example 8-2. Book titles in CSV format

```
1,Linux in a Nutshell,476
2,Classic Shell Scripting,256
```

Like this:

```
mysqlimport -u root -p --fields-terminated-by=',' test /home/jon/books.txt
```

The main portion of the filename (not including the path or the file extension) determines the name of the table. In the example above, the table name is books. The table must already exist or an error displays. Another useful keyword is ENCLOSED BY *char;*, which allows you to specify characters, such as double quotes (") that enclose each field in the file. This is useful for avoiding the problem with a book title like *Classic Shell Scripting,* Second Edition, which would otherwise cause mysqlimport to process the "Second Edition" portion of the title as the start of the next field.

Backup best practices

Depending on how critical your data is and how often it changes, you can determine how often to back it up. As a rule, weekly, bi-weekly, and monthly are the most common schedules. If your business is completely dependent on your database, you should do a weekly backup schedule, if not backing up daily. Also, keeping a copy of the data in a separate location is a good idea in the event of large scale disasters, such as a fire. A client of ours keeps bi-monthly backups in a fire safe at the office, whereas another client sends the data to a backup service. A backup service can use physical hard drives, tapes, or CDs, or can log into your server and perform the backup electronically.

Advanced SQL

In this section, we'll introduce database concepts that, while not strictly necessary for developing your web sites, can increase performance and give your queries more flexibility.

Indexes

Indexes work the same way that an index of a book works. If you were to look for the keyword "create table" without an index, you'd need to spend a lot of time scanning through the pages of the book looking for a section that might be relevant. Then you'd have to scan the entire section. This certainly isn't an efficient use of your time or the database's. The solution is an index at the end.

The data in an index is sorted in order and organized to make finding a specific value as quickly as possible. Because the values are sorted, if you're looking for something specific, the database can stop looking when it finds a value larger than the item you're looking for.

You face the same problems as a book does, though. If an index is so great, why not index everything? There are numerous reasons:

- There's only a finite amount of space available.
- When writing books, it becomes inefficient to generate and maintain a gigantic, all-encompassing index.

So some intelligent decisions about which fields to index in your tables have to be made. Each index requires its own datafile for storage, which can add a bit of processing time when the contents of an indexed field changes in the database.

When indexes are used

If you do a simple SELECT statement with a WHERE clause, an index won't be used. There are three major areas where an index can be used:

In a WHERE clause
For example, the query SELECT * FROM `authors` WHERE `author` = 'Ellen Siever'; would use an index on the author column if it's available.

In an ORDER BY clause
For example, the query SELECT * FROM `contacts` ORDER BY `author`; would use an index on the author column if available.

In MIN and MAX clauses
For example, if the column that is specified in the MIN or MAX function has an index.

Just remember, indexes have to be defined before they can be used.

Where to specify the index

Database indexes can be specified as part of the CREATE TABLE command or they can be added to an existing table by using special SQL commands. If the index is created as part of the CREATE TABLE command, then it's specified at the end of the code block like this:

```
UNIQUE `authind` (`author`)
```

This UNIQUE command creates an index on the author name field. To create the same index using a SQL statement, use the code in Example 8-3.

Example 8-3. Creating a simple index

```
CREATE UNIQUE INDEX `authind` ON `authors` (`author`);
```

which returns the following:

```
Query OK, 4 rows affected (0.11 sec)
Records: 4  Duplicates: 0  Warnings: 0
```

Now to describe the table:

```
DESCRIBE `authors`;
```

This gives you this information:

```
+-----------+--------------+------+-----+---------+----------------+
| Field     | Type         | Null | Key | Default | Extra          |
+-----------+--------------+------+-----+---------+----------------+
| author_id | int(11)      |      | PRI | NULL    | auto_increment |
| title_id  | int(11)      |      |     | 0       |                |
| author    | varchar(125) | YES  | UNI | NULL    |                |
+-----------+--------------+------+-----+---------+----------------+
3 rows in set (0.00 sec)
```

Notice the new value of UNI in the key column for author.

Multicolumn indexes

It's also possible to create MySQL indexes that use more than one column. A multi-column unique index can be used to make sure that the combination of two or more keys is unique.

The best columns to index are those that are likely to be used in the WHERE clause, especially if you know that certain combinations of keys will be used. Those are good columns to add to a multicolumn index.

Unique indexes, similar to primary indexes, are also unique. Only one primary index is allowed per table. However, you can have as many unique indexes as your heart desires; there is no parameter on this.

We're going to do a query with a specific WHERE clause and then use EXPLAIN to get details about how it was processed by MySQL:

```
SELECT * FROM `authors` WHERE `author` = 'Arnold Robbins';
```

This returns:

```
+-----------+----------+----------------+
| author_id | title_id | author         |
+-----------+----------+----------------+
|         3 |        2 | Arnold Robbins |
+-----------+----------+----------------+
1 row in set (0.00 sec)
```

Use the EXPLAIN keyword on a database that doesn't have an index defined for the authors table:

```
EXPLAIN SELECT * `authors` WHERE `author` = 'Arnold Robbins';
```

EXPLAIN, in turn, gives you this output:

```
+----+-------------+---------+------+---------------+------+---------+------+---
---+-------------+
| id | select_type | table   | type | possible_keys | key  | key_len | ref  | ro
ws | Extra       |
+----+-------------+---------+------+---------------+------+---------+------+---
---+-------------+
|  1 | SIMPLE      | authors | ALL  | NULL          | NULL |    NULL | NULL |
 4 | Using where |
+----+-------------+---------+------+---------------+------+---------+------+---
---+-------------+
1 row in set (0.00 sec)
```

The EXPLAIN output provides a wealth of information about how MySQL processed the query.

It tells you that:

- You're using the authors table.
- The query type is ALL, so every record is scanned to check for the correct value.
- The possible_keys is NULL, because no index matches.
- The key used by this query; currently, none.
- The key_len is the key length; currently, NULL as no key was used.
- The ref column displays which columns or constants are used with the key; currently, none.
- The number of rows that must be searched through for this query.

After creating a unique index on authors called authind using the syntax from Example 8-3, rerun the EXPLAIN query:

```
+----+-------------+---------+-------+---------------+---------+---------+------
-+------+-------+
| id | select_type | table   | type  | possible_keys | key     | key_len | ref
 | rows | Extra |
+----+-------------+---------+-------+---------------+---------+---------+------
-+------+-------+
|  1 | SIMPLE      | authors | const | authind       | authind |     126 | const
 |    1 |       |
+----+-------------+---------+-------+---------------+---------+---------+------
-+------+-------+
1 row in set (0.12 sec)
```

Notice that many of the values have changed regarding the indexing.

Typing ref would mean that rows with matching index values are read from this table for matches.

- possible_keys displays a possible key of authind.
- key displays that the authind key was used.
- key_len displays the length of the key as 126.
- ref tells you that a constant key is being used.
- rows shows that one row was searched, which is much less than before.

The comparison shows that adding the index saves a lot of processing time, even for this small table.

Selecting Using the LEFT JOIN ON Clause

We've discussed performing joins in our SELECT statements using the WHERE clause, but there's another way to join tables. Instead of using the WHERE keyword, LEFT JOIN ON can be used to perform a *left* or *outer join*. A left join simply allows you to query two tables that are linked together by a relationship but allows one of the tables to return rows even if there isn't a matching row in the other table. Using the bookstore tables as an example, you might want to create a query that returns users and their purchases but also lists users who have yet to purchase anything.

Using the syntax:

```
SELECT fields FROM left_table LEFT JOIN right_table ON left_table.field_id = right_table.field_id;
```

your goal could be accomplished like this:

```
SELECT * FROM `users` LEFT JOIN `purchases` ON `users`.`user_id` =
`purchases`.`user_id`;
```

When doing a normal database query that links two tables, if both tables do not include the key values for the field being joined, nothing is returned for the entry.

Using Database Functions

Just like there are functions in PHP, you can also use functions within your MySQL queries. We'll discuss several categories of functions starting with string functions. The other major categories you'll learn about are date and time modification functions.

String functions

Since you'll frequently work with strings, MySQL provides many functions for doing a variety of tasks. You'll generally use the string functions with data that is being returned from a query. However, it's possible to use them without even referencing a table.

Concatenation. Just like the process of putting strings together with the PHP operator (.), which is a period, MySQL can paste together strings from data fields with the CONCAT function.

For example, if you want to return a single field that combines the title with the number of pages, you could use CONCAT. Example 8-4 shows how this is done.

Example 8-4. Using CONCAT to put fields together

```
SELECT CONCAT(`title`,' has ',`pages`,' pages.') FROM `books`;
```

Concatenating returns:

```
+----------------------------------------+
| concat(title,' has ',pages,' pages.')  |
+----------------------------------------+
| Linux in a Nutshell has 476 pages.     |
| Classic Shell Scripting has 256 pages. |
+----------------------------------------+
2 rows in set (0.02 sec)
```

The result is a string that's ready for displaying straight from the SQL query.

 When using field names in functions, don't enclose them in single or double quotes. MySQL will interpret them as literal text like the string ' has ' in Example 8-4.

The CONCAT function pastes together as many fields as you give it.

Concatenation with a predefined separator. Sometimes you might want to consistently put the same character or string between fields you're concatenating. This can be used for building a table export list. To do this, use the CONCAT_WS function.

For example, to return all of the fields in the authors table with commas as separators, you would use:

```
SELECT CONCAT_WS(',',`author_id`,`title_id`,`author`) FROM `authors`;
```

This returns the following:

```
+----------------------------------------+
| CONCAT_WS(',',author_id,title_id,author) |
+----------------------------------------+
| 1,1,Ellen Siever                       |
| 2,1,Aaron Weber                        |
| 3,2,Arnold Robbins                     |
| 4,2,Nelson Beebe                       |
+----------------------------------------+
4 rows in set (0.01 sec)
```

The separator could have been a space, which is useful for putting first and last name fields together for display.

Calculate a string length. To calculate the length of a string, use the LENGTH function, as shown in Example 8-5.

Example 8-5. Calculating the length of a string

```
SELECT CONCAT(`title`,' has ',LENGTH(`title`), ' characters.') FROM `books`;
```

This returns:

```
+------------------------------------------------------+
| CONCAT(title,' has ',LENGTH(title), ' characters.') |
+------------------------------------------------------+
| Linux in a Nutshell has 19 characters.               |
| Classic Shell Scripting has 23 characters.           |
+------------------------------------------------------+
2 rows in set (0.02 sec)
```

Example 8-5 shows the usage of LENGTH and CONCAT together.

Changing strings to upper- or lowercase. If you want to change the case of a string to all upper- or lowercase letters, you can use the UCASE and LCASE functions. For example, to covert the book title to all uppercase and then all lowercase, use the code in Example 8-6.

Example 8-6. Changing the case of the title

```
SELECT UCASE(`title`), LCASE(`title`) from `books`;
```

Example 8-6 returns:

```
+-----------------------+-----------------------+
| UCASE(title)          | LCASE(title)          |
+-----------------------+-----------------------+
| LINUX IN A NUTSHELL   | linux in a nutshell   |
| CLASSIC SHELL SCRIPTING | classic shell scripting |
+-----------------------+-----------------------+
2 rows in set (0.03 sec)
```

Trimming and padding strings. When working with forms, it's sometimes necessary to pad the length of a string to improve its display. The padding can be dots or some other character. VARCHAR type strings, in particular, are variable in length. The two functions that perform padding are LPAD and RPAD, they pad from the left and right, respectively. They both take three arguments: the string to pad, the size of the pad, and what character to use as padding. For example, we'll do a left pad on the title field of books to make it a uniform 30 characters with a period (.) as the padding character:

```
SELECT LPAD(`title`,30,'.') FROM `books`;
```

This returns your values all at the righthand margin:

```
+--------------------------------+
| LPAD(title,30,'.')             |
+--------------------------------+
| ..........Linux in a Nutshell  |
| .......Classic Shell Scripting |
+--------------------------------+
2 rows in set (0.00 sec)
```

This looks somewhat like the formatting you see in a table of contents.

To trim spaces or tabs (also known as whitespace) from a string, use `LTRIM` to remove them from the left and `RTRIM` to remove them from the right.

To trim nonwhitespace characters, use the `TRIM` function. It uses a syntax that's slightly different, because you're leading trimming:

```
TRIM(LEADING FROM string);
```

For trailing trimming, use:

```
TRIM(TRAILING FROM string);
```

In Example 8-7, `LEADING` is used to remove the leading zeros.

Example 8-7. Using the LEADING option to remove zeros

```
SELECT TRIM(LEADING '0' from '0000Example00000');
```

Example 8-7 returns:

```
+-------------------------------------------+
| TRIM(LEADING '0' from '0000Example00000') |
+-------------------------------------------+
| Example00000                              |
+-------------------------------------------+
1 row in set (0.00 sec)
```

To remove the trailing zeros, use the code in Example 8-8.

Example 8-8. Using TRIM with the TRAILING option

```
SELECT TRIM(TRAILING '0' from '0000Example00000');
```

Example 8-8 returns:

```
+--------------------------------------------+
| TRIM(TRAILING '0' from '0000Example00000') |
+--------------------------------------------+
| 0000Example                                |
+--------------------------------------------+
1 row in set (0.01 sec)
```

Notice that while Examples 8-7 and 8-8 don't reference any tables in the `SELECT` statements, they're still valid queries.

String location and position. Sometimes you'll want to know whether a string is within a string and what its position is in that string. To locate a string within a string, use the `LOCATE()` function. It takes the string to look for and the string to search in as its arguments. Example 8-9 shows how the location of a string is returned from a database field.

Example 8-9. Looking for the string in our author names

```
SELECT LOCATE`author`,LOCATE('on',`author`) FROM `authors`;
```

Example 8-9 returns:

```
+-------------------+---------------------+
| author            | LOCATE(on','author')|
+-------------------+---------------------+
| Aaron Weber       |                   4 |
| Arnold Robbins    |                   0 |
| Ellen Siever      |                   0 |
| Nelson  Beebe     |                   5 |
+-------------------+---------------------+
4 rows in set (0.01 sec)
```

The author names that don't contain the string on return a position of 0, indicating that the string was not found.

> The position counting for a match starts at 1, not 0, as with arrays in PHP. This is fortunate, since it would otherwise be impossible to tell the difference between a match at the beginning of the string and no match at all.

Keep in mind only the first occurrence of a string is matched, similar to a Find in an application. LOCATE() can also take a third argument to start looking at a position other than the start of the string.

Cutting up strings. The substring functions provide a way to extract a portion of a string. All that's needed is the string to work with, the position to start from, and how many characters to extract. Use the LEFT, RIGHT, and SUBSTRING functions to do the extraction.

LEFT
> Takes the string and the number of characters to extract from the start of the string.

RIGHT
> Takes the string and the number of characters to extract from the end of the string.

SUBSTR
> Takes the string and the number of characters to extract beginning with a certain position in the string.

For example, if a database has phone numbers stored in a 10-digit string without any formatting, the numbers could be displayed with the formatting by using the code in Example 8-10.

Example 8-10. Adding the formatting to a phone number using LEFT, RIGHT, and SUBSTR

```
SELECT CONCAT('(',
              LEFT('6128238193',3),
              ')',
```

Example 8-10. Adding the formatting to a phone number using LEFT, RIGHT, and SUBSTR (continued)

```
            SUBSTR('6128238193',4,3),
            '-',
            RIGHT('6128238193', 4));
```

These commands return:

```
+-----------------------------------------------------------------------------
-----------+
| CONCAT('(',LEFT('6128238193',3),')',SUBSTR('6128238193',4,3),'-',RIGHT('612823
8193', 4)) |
+-----------------------------------------------------------------------------
-----------+
| (612)823-8193
           |
+-----------------------------------------------------------------------------
-----------+
1 row in set (0.02 sec)
```

Example 8-10 shows how all three of these functions work together to reformat a phone number. The phone number could just as easily have been a database field instead of the number in the example.

Search and replace function. Another useful function is the `REPLACE` function. It does what the name implies, exactly like find/replace in a word-processing application. It takes a source string, a search string, and a replacement string and returns the string with the replacement.

For example, suppose you wanted to replace "Avenue" with "Ave" in an address, but only for the current query. Here's how it's done:

```
SELECT REPLACE('2323 Fulerton Avenue', 'Avenue', 'Ave.');
```

The `REPLACE` function displays:

```
+--------------------------------------------------+
| REPLACE('2323 Fulerton Avenue', 'Avenue', 'Ave.') |
+--------------------------------------------------+
| 2323 Fulerton Ave.                               |
+--------------------------------------------------+
1 row in set (0.00 sec)
```

Now that we've shown you just about all you could imagine you'll do with strings, it's time to work with dates and times.

Date and time functions

Again, you're dealing with territory that PHP had functions to work with, but what if you'd like to query for purchases from the last 30 days? It's nice to be able to do the date and time arithmetic in the query. The date and time functions can be used with or without a database table in the query. We'll show you both in the following examples.

Days, months, years, and weeks. Given a certain date, it's hard to remember if that day was a Tuesday or a Thursday. MySQL provides functions that tell you without having to do any of the thinking ourselves. How convenient! You could plot what day you were born just by establishing the date and year. PHP provides two very similar functions to do the calculation.

The WEEKDAY function takes a date as its argument and returns a number. The number represents the day of the week with Monday being 0. You could also use the DAYOFWEEK function, which, confusingly enough, does exactly the same thing but numbers the days differently, starting with Saturday as 1. Table 8-3 lists how each function numbers days of the week.

Table 8-3. WEEKDAY versus DAYOFWEEK

WEEKDAY value	DAYOFWEEK value	Day of the week
0	2	Monday
1	3	Tuesday
2	4	Wednesday
3	5	Thursday
4	6	Friday
5	7	Saturday
6	1	Sunday

For example, to find out what day of the week was October 12, 1964, use the WEEKDAY function in Example 8-11.

Example 8-11. Using WEEKDAY to get the day of the week

```
SELECT WEEKDAY('1964-10-12');
```

This then tells you:

```
+----------------------+
| WEEKDAY('1964-10-12') |
+----------------------+
|                    0 |
+----------------------+
1 row in set (0.00 sec)
```

Which means October 12, 1964 was a Monday. Pretty cool stuff!

It may seem a bit odd to return a number for the day of the week, so there's a function to return the day as its name. The DAYNAME function works like DAYOFWEEK or WEEKDAY but returns a string with the name instead, as shown in Example 8-12.

Example 8-12. Using DAYNAME to get the day of the week as a name

```
SELECT DAYNAME('1964-10-12');
```

As you can see, an alpha answer returns:

```
+----------------------+
| DAYNAME('1964-10-12') |
+----------------------+
| Monday               |
+----------------------+
1 row in set (0.00 sec)
```

Which proves that we were right in Example 8-11!

Similar to the DAYOFWEEK function are DAYOFMONTH and DAYOFYEAR. They take a date as their input and return a number. DAYOFMONTH returns the day of the month, and DAYOFYEAR returns days since the beginning of the calendar year, as demonstrated in Example 8-13.

Example 8-13. Finding days since the start of the year

```
SELECT DAYOFYEAR('2006-1-1'),
       DAYOFYEAR('2006-12-24');
```

From your DAYOFYEAR function, it returns the following:

```
+----------------------+------------------------+
| DAYOFYEAR('2006-1-1') | DAYOFYEAR('2006-12-24') |
+----------------------+------------------------+
|                    1 |                    358 |
+----------------------+------------------------+
1 row in set (0.00 sec)
```

Just like the relationship between DAYOFWEEK and DAYNAME, MONTH and MONTHNAME return the numeric month or its name, as shown in Example 8-14.

Example 8-14. Using MONTH and MONTHNAME on the purchases table

```
SELECT `day`,MONTH(`day`),MONTHNAME(`day`) FROM `purchases`;
```

Example 8-14 returns:

```
+------------+------------+----------------+
| day        | MONTH(`day`) | MONTHNAME(`day`) |
+------------+------------+----------------+
| 2005-02-15 |          2 | February       |
| 2005-02-10 |          2 | February       |
+------------+------------+----------------+
2 rows in set (0.00 sec)
```

If you want to find the week number for a certain date, you can use the WEEK function. It takes a date as its argument and returns the week number.

```
SELECT WEEK('2006-12-24');
```

This returns:

```
+--------------------+
| WEEK('2006-12-24') |
+--------------------+
|                 52 |
+--------------------+
1 row in set (0.00 sec)
```

This probably seems pretty easy compared to a lot of the information we've provided. Remember, though, based on how the calendar lays out, some years can have 53 weeks.

Hours, minutes, and seconds. When working with datetime, timestamp, or time data types, a specific time is stored in the field. MySQL provides several functions to manipulate these times. They take the logical names: HOUR, MINUTE, and SECOND. HOUR takes a time as an argument and returns the hour from 0 to 23. MINUTE returns the minute of a time from 0 to 59, and similarly, SECOND returns the second in the same range, as shown in Example 8-15.

Example 8-15. Using HOUR and MINUTE on a time

```
SELECT CONCAT_WS(':',hour('4:46:45'),MINUTE('4:46:45'));
```

Example 8-15 returns:

```
+--------------------------------------------------+
| CONCAT_WS(':',hour('4:46:45'),MINUTE('4:46:45')) |
+--------------------------------------------------+
| 4:46                                             |
+--------------------------------------------------+
```

Dates and times arithmetic. MySQL provides the functions DATE_ADD and DATE_SUB to allow you to add and subtract days from dates. Their syntax is:

```
DATE_ADD(date,INTERVAL expression type)
DATE_SUB(date,INTERVAL expression type)
```

The type can be one of those listed in Table 8-4.

Table 8-4. Types and their corresponding expected values

Type	Value that is expected
MICROSECOND	Number of MICROSECONDS
SECOND	Number of SECONDS
MINUTE	Number of MINUTES
DAY	Number of DAYS
WEEK	Number of WEEKS
MONTH	Number of MONTHS
QUARTER	Number of QUARTERS
YEAR	Number of YEARS

Table 8-4. Types and their corresponding expected values (continued)

Type	Value that is expected
SECOND_MICROSECOND	*SECONDS.MICROSECONDS*
MINUTE_MICROSECOND	*MINUTES.MICROSECONDS*
MINUTE_SECOND	*MINUTES:SECONDS*
HOUR_MICROSECOND	*HOURS.MICROSECONDS*
HOUR_SECOND	*HOURS:MINUTES:SECONDS*
HOUR_MINUTE	*HOURS:MINUTES*
DAY_MICROSECOND	*DAYS.MICROSECONDS*
DAY_SECOND	*DAYS HOURS:MINUTES:SECONDS*
DAY_MINUTE	*DAYS HOURS:MINUTES*
DAY_HOUR	*DAYS HOURS*
YEAR_MONTH	*YEARS-MONTHS*

For example, if you want to calculate the date of the current day minus 12, you would write code like that in Example 8-16.

Example 8-16. Using DATE_SUB to subtract days

```
SELECT DATE_SUB(NOW(), INTERVAL 12 DAY);
```

This returns (your time will be different based on when you run this query):

```
+----------------------------------+
| date_sub(NOW(), INTERVAL 12 day) |
+----------------------------------+
| 2005-11-03 04:27:09              |
+----------------------------------+
1 row in set (0.00 sec)
```

The NOW function returns the current time; we'll discuss this and some other special date/time functions shortly. In Example 8-16, the value after INTERVAL can be any expression that returns the format the type is expecting from Table 8-4.

Since Version 3.23, MySQL also supports the syntax of using + and – with dates, as in Example 8-17.

Example 8-17. Using the minus operator on a date

```
SELECT NOW()- INTERVAL 12 DAY;
```

Example 8-17 returns:

```
+------------------------+
| NOW()- INTERVAL 12 DAY |
+------------------------+
| 2005-11-03 04:32:30    |
+------------------------+
1 row in set (0.01 sec)
```

It's really all the same command but with an abbreviated syntax.

NOW function. The NOW function returns the current date and time according to the setting of your computer's system date and time. So, if your computer clock is off, the data from NOW will be as well. MySQL provides several functions for returning the current date or time, or the current date and time together. CURDATE and CURRENT_DATE both return the date in 'YYYY-MM-DD' format.

```
SELECT CURDATE();
```

This returns:

```
+------------+
| CURDATE()  |
+------------+
| 2005-11-15 |
+------------+
1 row in set (0.00 sec)
```

Use CURTIME or CURRENT_TIME to return the current time in the format 'HH:MM:SS':

```
SELECT CURTIME();
```

Computer setting for date and time returns:

```
+-----------+
| CURTIME() |
+-----------+
| 04:44:50  |
+-----------+
1 row in set (0.00 sec)
```

In addition to the NOW function, you can use SYSDATE and CURRENT_TIMESTAMP to return the current date and time in the 'YYYY-MM-DD HH:MM:SS' format:

```
SELECT SYSDATE();
```

Military formatted data is returned:

```
+---------------------+
| SYSDATE()           |
+---------------------+
| 2005-11-15 04:45:14 |
+---------------------+
1 row in set (0.00 sec)
```

Last but not least, MySQL provides the ability to display dates and times in a variety of formats.

Formatting for display. To display a date in a custom format, use the DATE_FORMAT function. It takes a date or timestamp as its input and a format string. In Table 8-5, the format strings are shown.

Table 8-5. Format strings for DATE_FORMAT

Format	Type	Example
%M	Month name	January–December
%W	Weekday name	Sunday–Saturday
%D	Day of the month with English suffix	0th, 1st, 2nd, 3rd
%Y	Year, numeric, four digits	2005
%y	Year, numeric, two digits	05
%X	Year for the week where Sunday is the first day of the week, numeric, four digits; used with %V	
%x	Year for the week, where Monday is the first day of the week, numeric, four digits; used with %v	
%a	Abbreviated weekday name	Sun, Sat
%e	Day of the month, numeric leading zero	00–31
%m	Day of the month, numeric	0–31
%c	Month, numeric leading zero	00–12
%b	Month, numeric	0–12
%m	Abbreviated month name	Jan, Dec
%b	Day of year	001, 366
%j	Hour	00–23
%H	Hour	0–23
%k	Hour	01–12
%h	Hour	01–12
%l	Hour	1–12
%I	Minutes, numeric	00–59
%r	12-hour (hh:mm:ss followed by AM or PM)	
%T	24-hour (hh:mm:ss)	
%S	Seconds	00–59
%s	Seconds	00–59
%f	Microseconds	000000–999999
%p	AM or PM	
%w	Day of the week (0=Sunday–6=Saturday)	
%U	Week (00–53), where Sunday is the first day of the week	
%V	Week (00–53), where Monday is the first day of the week	
%v	Week (01–53), where Monday is the first day of the week; used with %x	
%%	A literal %	%

If you use any other characters in the format string, they appear as they are, as shown in Example 8-18.

Example 8-18. Using DATE_FORMAT with a string to place colons between the segments

```
SELECT DATE_FORMAT('2006-12-24 09:09:23', '%h:%i:%s');
```

Adding colons displays:

```
+------------------------------------------------+
| DATE_FORMAT('2006-12-24 09:09:23', '%h:%i:%s') |
+------------------------------------------------+
| 09:09:23                                       |
+------------------------------------------------+
1 row in set (0.01 sec)
```

At this point, all the basics have been covered. In our next chapter, we'll walk through using PHP to connect and work with MySQL data.

Chapter 8 Questions

Question 8-1. What command is used to access MySQL from the command line?

Question 8-2. How do you back up a MySQL database called "blog" as the root database user?

Question 8-3. How would you restore the backup created in Question 8-2?

Question 8-4. What are the advantages and disadvantages to creating indexes on tables?

See the Appendix for the answers to these questions.

Getting PHP to Talk to MySQL

Now that you're comfortable using the MySQL client tools to manipulate data in the database, you can begin using PHP to display and modify data from the database. PHP has standard functions for working with the database.

First, we're going to discuss PHP's built-in database functions. We'll also show you how to use the PEAR database functions that provide the ability to use the same functions to access any supported database. This type of flexibility comes from a process called *abstraction*. Abstraction is the information you need to log into a database that is placed into a standard format. This standard format allows you to interact with MySQL as well as other databases using the same format. Similarly, MySQL-specific functions are replaced with generic ones that know how to talk to many databases.

In this chapter, you'll learn how to connect to a MySQL server from PHP, learn how to use PHP to access and retrieve stored data, and how to correctly display information to the user.

The Process

The basic steps of performing a query, whether using the `mysql` command-line tool or PHP, are the same:

- Connect to the database.
- Select the database to use.
- Build a `SELECT` statement.
- Perform the query.
- Display the results.

We'll walk through each of these steps for both plain PHP and PEAR functions.

Resources

When connecting to a MySQL database, you will use two new resources. The first is the link identifier that holds all of the information necessary to connect to the database for an active connection. The other resource is the results resource. It contains all information required to retrieve results from an active database query's result set. You'll be creating and assigning both resources in this chapter.

Querying the Database with PHP Functions

In this section, we introduce how to connect to a MySQL database with PHP. It's quite simple, and we'll begin shortly with examples, but we should talk briefly about what actually happens. When you try connecting to a MySQL database, the MySQL server authenticates you based on your username and password. PHP handles connecting to the database for you and allows you to immediately start performing queries and gathering data.

As in Chapter 8, we'll need the same pieces of information to connect to the database:

- The IP address of the database server
- The name of the database
- The username
- The password

If you're not sure what to use for these values, consult Chapter 7. And, before moving on, make sure you can log into your database using the mysql command-line client.

Figure 9-1 shows how the steps of the database interaction relate to the two types of resources. Building the SELECT statement happens before the third function call but is not shown. It's done with plain PHP code, not a MySQL-specific PHP function.

Including Database Login Details

You're going to create a file to hold the information for logging into MySQL. Storing this information in a file you include is recommended. If you change the database password, there is only one place that you need to change it regardless of how many PHP files you have that access the database.

> You don't have to worry about anyone directly viewing the file and getting your database login details,. The file, if requested by itself, is processed as a PHP file and returns a blank page.

Let's call this file *db_login.php* and place it in the same directory as your other PHP files. The file is represented in Example 9-1.

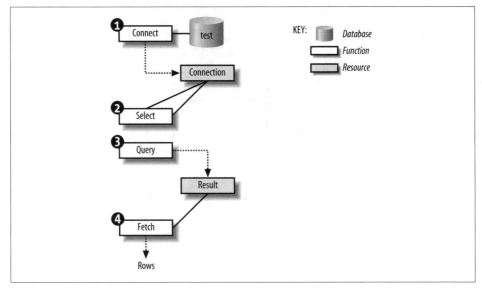

Figure 9-1. The interaction between functions and resources when using the database

Example 9-1. PHP file format

```
<?php
$db_host='hostname of database server';
$db_database='database name';
$db_username='username';
$db_password='password';
?>
```

In Example 9-2, we created this file to use a database on the same machine as the web server. We assign it a database name, username, and password.

Example 9-2. The db_login.php file with values filled in

```
<?php
$db_host='localhost';
$db_database='test';
$db_username='test';
$db_password='yourpass';
?>
```

Figure 9-2 illustrates how you're going to use this file with other PHP files. You're going to continue using the database that you started to set up in Chapter 7.

Example 9-3 is an abbreviated dump of the database created from the `mysqldump` command.

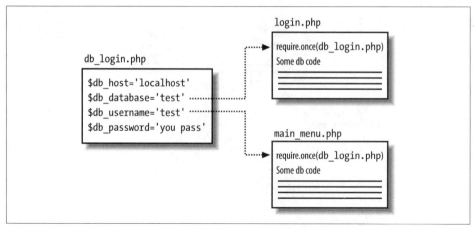

Figure 9-2. Reusing the login details in multiple files

Example 9-3. The SQL to recreate the test objects

```
--
-- Table structure for table `authors`
--
DROP TABLE IF EXISTS `authors`;
CREATE TABLE `authors` (
  `author_id` int(11) NOT NULL auto_increment,
  `title_id` int(11) NOT NULL default '0',
  `author` varchar(125) default NULL,
  PRIMARY KEY  (`author_id`)
) ENGINE=MyISAM DEFAULT CHARSET=latin1;
--
-- Dumping data for table `authors`
--
INSERT INTO `authors` VALUES (1,1,'Ellen Siever'),(2,1,'Aaron Weber'),(3,2,
'Arnold Robbins'),(4,2,'Nelson H.F. Beebe');
--
-- Table structure for table `books`
--
DROP TABLE IF EXISTS `books`;
CREATE TABLE `books` (
  `title_id` int(11) NOT NULL auto_increment,
  `title` varchar(150) default NULL,
  `pages` int(11) default NULL,
  PRIMARY KEY  (`title_id`)
) ENGINE=MyISAM DEFAULT CHARSET=latin1;
--
-- Dumping data for table `books`
--
INSERT INTO `books` VALUES (1,'Linux in a Nutshell',476),(2,'Classic Shell
Scripting',256);
--
-- Table structure for table `purchases`
--
```

Example 9-3. The SQL to recreate the test objects (continued)

```
DROP TABLE IF EXISTS `purchases`;
CREATE TABLE `purchases` (
  `id` int(11) NOT NULL auto_increment,
  `user` varchar(10) default NULL,
  `title` varchar(150) default NULL,
  `day` date default NULL,
  PRIMARY KEY (`id`)
) ENGINE=MyISAM DEFAULT CHARSET=latin1;
--
-- Dumping data for table `purchases`
--
LOCK TABLES `purchases` WRITE;
INSERT INTO `purchases` VALUES (1,'Mdavis','Regular Expression Pocket Reference',
'2005-02-15'),(2,'Mdavis','JavaScript & DHTML Cookbook','2005-02-10');
```

If you didn't create the tables in the last chapter, the code in Example 9-3 can be saved as *backup.sql* and run from the command prompt with the following:

```
mysql -u username -p password -D database_name < backupfile.sql
```

The database is called test, and it consists of three tables called books, authors, and purchases. Each table has a few sample rows. That's enough to get us started querying from PHP.

Connecting to the Database

The first thing you need to do is connect to the database and check to make sure there's a connection. Including the file that you set up to store your connection information allows you to use the variables instead of hardcoded values when you call the mysql_connect function, as shown in Example 9-4.

Example 9-4. Including the connection values and calling mysql_connect

```
<?php
include('db_login.php');
$connection = mysql_connect($db_host, $db_username, $db_password);
if (!$connection){
die ("Could not connect to the database: <br />". mysql_error());
}
?>
```

The mysql_connect function takes the database host, username, and password as parameters. If the connection is successful, a link to a database is returned. FALSE is returned if a connection can't be made. Check the return value from the function to make sure there's a connection. If there's a problem, such as an incorrect password, print out a polite warning and the reason for the error using mysql_error.

Instead of simply echoing an error message, use the die function to display the error, and then stop the program, Not being able to access the database makes most database-driven pages fairly useless and prevents the user from seeing numerous errors.

Notice that we didn't specify the database name yet.

Troubleshooting connection errors

One error you may get is:

```
Fatal error: Call to undefined function mysql_connect() in C:\Program Files\Apache
Group\Apache2\htdocs\test.php on line 4
```

This occurs because PHP 5.1.2 for Windows was downloaded, and MySQL support was not included by default. To fix this error, copy the *php_mysql.dll* file from the *ext/* directory of the PHP zip file to *C:\php*, and then edit lines 461 and 589 of *C:\WINDOWS\php.ini*. This will change the extension to include the directory to *C:/php* and uncommenting the MySQL extension line, respectively.

You'll need to restart Apache, and then MySQL support will be enabled.

Selecting the Database

Now that you're connected, the next step is to select which database to use with the mysql_select_db command. It takes two parameters: the database name and, optionally, the database connection. If you don't specify the database connection, the default is the connection from the last mysql_connect.

```
$db_select = mysql_select_db($db_database);
if (!$db_select){
die ("Could not select the database: <br />". mysql_error());
}
```

Again, it's good practice to check for an error and display it every time you access the database.

While it's possible to call mysql_select_db multiple times within the same script, it's not considered good practice. Generally, you should be able to do all of your work with one database. Maintaining connections and results to multiple databases are beyond this book's scope.

Now that you've got a good database connection, you're ready to execute your SQL query.

Building the SQL SELECT Query

Building a SQL query is as easy as setting a variable to the string that is your SQL query. Of course, you'll need to use a valid SQL query, or MySQL returns with an error when you execute the query. The variable name $query is used, but you can choose anything you'd like for a variable name. The SQL query in this example is SELECT * FROM books.

 Unlike when you used the mysql command-line client, the query does not have a semicolon at the end.

You can build up your query in parts using the string concatenate (.) operator:

```
$select = ' SELECT ';
$column = ' * ';
$from = ' FROM ';
$tables = ' `books` ';
$where = '';
$query = $select.$column.$from.$tables.$where;
```

Which is a more flexible version of this:

```
$query = "SELECT * FROM books";
```

The query string could also use a variable in the WHERE clause to limit which rows are returned based on user information or another query.

Now that you have your query assigned to a variable, you can execute it.

Executing the Query

To have the database execute the query, use the mysql_query function. It takes two parameters—the query and optionally the database link—and returns the result. Save a link to the results in a variable called, you guessed it, $result! This is also a good place to check the return code from mysql_query to make sure that there were no errors in the query string or the database connection by verifying that $result is not FALSE.

```
$result = mysql_query( $query );
if (!$result)
{
die ("Could not query the database: <br />". mysql_error());
}
```

When the database executes the query, all of the results form a result set. These correspond to the rows that you saw upon doing a query using the mysql command-line client. To display them, you process each row, one at a time.

Fetching and Displaying

Use `mysql_fetch_row` to get the rows from the result set. It takes the result you stored in $result from the query as a parameter. It returns one row at a time from the query until there are no more rows, and then it returns FALSE. Therefore, you do a loop on the result of `mysql_fetch_row` and define some code to display each row:

```
while ($result_row = mysql_fetch_row($result)){
        echo $result_row[2] . '<br />';
}
```

Fetch types

This is not the only way to fetch the results. Using `mysql_fetch_array`, PHP can place the results into an array in one step. It takes a result as its first parameter, and the way to bind the results as an optional second parameter. If MYSQL_ASSOC is specified, the results are indexed in an array based on their column names in the query. If MYSQL_NUM is specified, then the number starting at zero accesses the results. The default value, MYSQL_BOTH, returns a result array with both types. The `mysql_fetch_assoc` is an alternative to supplying the MYSQL_ASSOC argument.

If you rewrote the code above to use `mysql_fetch_array` with an associative indexed array, it would look like this:

```
while ($row = mysql_fetch_array($result, MYSQL_ASSOC)) {
                        echo $row[title]. '<br />';
}
```

Closing the Connection

As a rule of thumb, you always want to close a connection to a database when you're done using it. Closing a database with `mysql_close` will tell PHP and MySQL that you no longer will be using the connection, and will free any resources and memory allocated to it.

```
mysql_close($connection)
```

Putting It All Together

Now you're going to take all of the steps and put them into a single PHP file that you'll call *db_test.php*. You should place the PHP script shown in Example 9-5 in the same directory as the *db_login.php* file.

Example 9-5. Displaying the books and authors

```
<?php
// Include our login information
include('db_login.php');
// Connect
$connection = mysql_connect( $db_host, $db_username, $db_password );
```

Example 9-5. Displaying the books and authors (continued)

```php
if (!$connection)
{
    die ("Could not connect to the database: <br />". mysql_error());
}
// Select the database
$db_select=mysql_select_db($db_database);
if (!$db_select)
{
    die ("Could not select the database: <br />". mysql_error());
}
// Assign the query
$query = "SELECT * FROM `books` NATURAL JOIN `authors`";
// Execute the query
$result = mysql_query( $query );
if (!$result)
{
    die ("Could not query the database: <br />". mysql_error());
}

// Fetch and display the results
while ($result_row = mysql_fetch_row(($result)))
{
        echo 'Title: '.$result_row[1] . '<br />';
        echo 'Author: '.$result_row[4] . '<br /> ';
        echo 'Pages: '.$result_row[2] . '<br /><br />';
}
/ /Close the connection
mysql_close($connection);
?>
```

Here's the output from Example 9-5:

```
Title: Linux in a Nutshell<br />Author: Ellen Siever<br /> Pages: 476<br />
<br />Title: Linux in a Nutshell<br />Author: Aaron Weber<br /> Pages: 476<br />
<br />Title: Classic Shell Scripting<br>Author: Arnold Robbins<br /> Pages: 256<br />
<br />Title: Classic Shell Scripting<br />Author: Nelson H.F. Beebe<br /> Pages:
256<br /><br />
```

This displays in your browser as in Figure 9-3.

If you don't see the screen in Figure 9-3, then you'll see an error from whichever step in the process had a problem, giving you an idea of what went wrong and where it was wrong.

To make the display more appealing, you can put the information into a table, as shown in Example 9-6. You also add complete HTML headers.

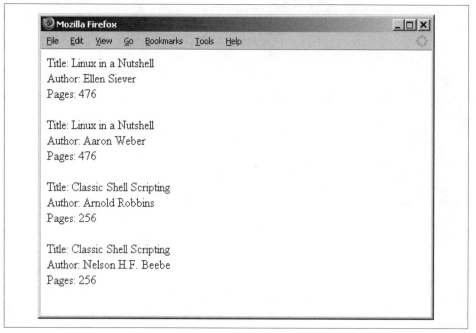

Figure 9-3. How Example 9-5 displays in the browser

Example 9-6. Displaying the results of a query in an HTML table

```
<!DOCTYPE HTML PUBLIC "-//W3C//DTD HTML 4.01 Transitional//EN"
"http://www.w3.org/TR/html401/loose.dtd">
<html>
<head>
<meta http-equiv="Content-Type" content="text/html; charset=iso-8859-1">
<title>Displaying in an HTML table</title>
</head>
<body>
<table border="1">
<tr>
<th>Title</th>
<th>Author</th>
<th>Pages</th>
</tr>
<?php
//Include our login information
include('db_login.php');
// Connect
$connection = mysql_connect($db_host, $db_username, $db_password);
if (!$connection){
die("Could not connect to the database: <br />". mysql_error());
}
// Select the database
$db_select = mysql_select_db($db_database);
if (!$db_select){
```

Example 9-6. Displaying the results of a query in an HTML table (continued)

```
die ("Could not select the database: <br />". mysql_error());
}
// Assign the query
$query = "SELECT * FROM `books` NATURAL JOIN `authors`";
// Execute the query
$result = mysql_query($query);
if (!$result){
die ("Could not query the database: <br />". mysql_error());
}
// Fetch and display the results
while ($row = mysql_fetch_array($result, MYSQL_ASSOC)){
$title = $row["title"];
$author = $row["author"];
$pages = $row["pages"];
echo "<tr>";
echo "<td>$title</td>";
echo "<td>$author</td>";
echo "<td>$pages</td>";
echo "</tr>";
}
// Close the connection
mysql_close($connection);
?>
</table>
</body>
</html>
```

Example 9-6 displays in your browser as shown in Figure 9-4.

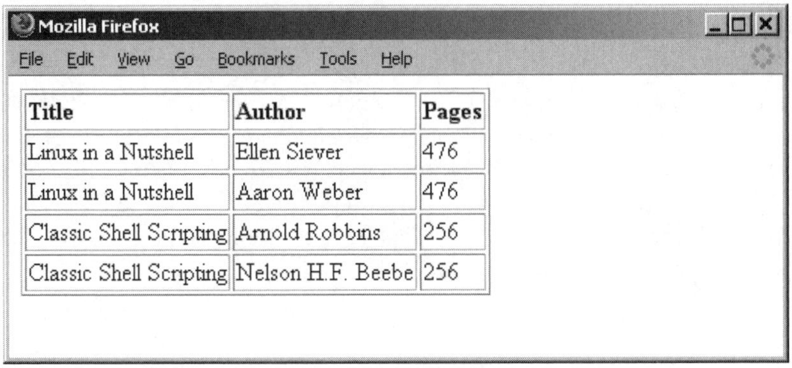

Figure 9-4. The same data but in an HTML table

Notice that you made use of the `MYSQL_ASSOC` fetch type in Example 9-6. You're probably saying to yourself, "That's great, but how do I display the book titles with the authors all on one line?" This is where we talk about PEAR.

Using PEAR

PEAR is a framework and distribution system for reusable PHP components. Actually, PEAR is a collection of add-on functionality for PHP development. There are many modules available to handle everything from session management to shopping cart functionality. Modules that are currently available are listed in Table 9-1.

Table 9-1. PEAR modules

Authentication	HTML	Processing
Benchmarking	HTTP	Science
Caching	Images	Semantic Web
Configuration	Internationalization	Streams
Console	Logging	Structures
Database	Mail	System
Date/Time	Math	Test
Encryption	Networking	Tools & Utilities
Event	Numbers	Validate
File Formats	Payment	Web Services
File System	PEAR	XML
GTK Components	PHP	

Our list is not complete. Visit *http://pear.php.net* to find out all of the modules that are available for download.

Installing

PEAR uses a Package Manager to manage which PEAR features you install. Whether you need to install the Package Manager depends on which version of PHP you installed. If you're running PHP 4.3.0 or newer, it's already installed. If you're running PHP 5.0, PEAR has been split out into a separate package. The DB package that you're interested in is also installed by default with the Package Manager. So if you have the Package Manger, you're all set.

Unix

You can install the Package Manager on a Unix system by executing the following from the shell (command-line) prompt:

```
lynx -source http://go-pear.org/ | php
```

This takes the output of the *go-pear.org* site (which is actually the source PHP code) to install PEAR and passes it along to the php command for execution.

Windows

The PHP 5 installation includes the PEAR installation script as *C:\php\go-pear.bat*. In case you didn't install all the files in Chapter 2, go ahead and extract all the PHP files to *C:/php* from the command prompt, and execute the *.bat* file. Figure 9-5 shows the initial screen after executing the PEAR installer.

```
C:\WINNT\system32\cmd.exe - go-pear.bat                           _ □ ×

C:\php>go-pear.bat
Welcome to go-pear!

Go-pear will install the 'pear' command and all the files needed by
it.  This command·is your tool for PEAR installation and maintenance.

Use 'php PEAR\go-pear.php local' to install a local copy of PEAR.

Go-pear also lets you download and install the PEAR packages bundled
with PHP: DB, Net_Socket, Net_SMTP, Mail, XML_Parser, PHPUnit.

If you wish to abort, press Control-C now, or press Enter to continue:
```

Figure 9-5. The go-pear.bat install script

You'll be asked a set of questions about paths. You can accept the defaults for all of them.

 The *php.exe* file must be in your path. Verify by typing php.exe from a command prompt. If it is not found, you'll need to add it to your PATH variable. To access your system path, navigate to Start → Control Panel → System → Environment and add an entry to the end of the path with C:\php.

The PEAR installer creates a file called *C:\php\PEAR_ENV.reg*. You need to double-click to set up the PEAR paths in the registry. This file is contingent on which PEAR version you installed. When the dialog box appears to verify your information, you will add this to the registry and click OK.

You may have to edit the *php.ini* file after running this *.bat* file to add the PEAR directory to the include path. Line 447 of *php.ini* now looks like this:

```
include_path = ".;c:\php\includes;c:\php\PEAR"
```

Apache must be restarted before the DB package can be used.

Hosted ISP

Most ISPs have PEAR DB installed. Ask your ISP to install it if they haven't already. You can tell if PEAR DB has been installed by trying the PHP code in Example 9-7 to see whether the require_once ('DB.php'); line causes an error when the script is executed.

Adding Additional Packages

Once that's complete, you can access the PEAR Package Manger by entering pear at the command prompt. Adding new modules is as easy as executing pear *packagename*. You won't need to do anything, since the DB package was installed along with the install by default.

However, if you're running Windows XP Home, you'll need to take these steps to install the PEAR DB:

```
C:\>cd c:\php
C:\>pear install DB
C:\>pear list
```

To find out what versions of PEAR packages are installed, execute pear list. That returns a listing such as the one shown in Figure 9-6.

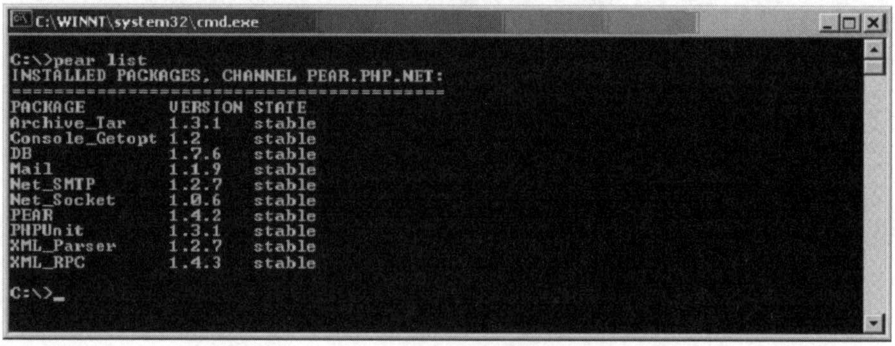

Figure 9-6. A listing of installed PEAR packages and versions

Once you've got PEAR installed, you're ready to try it out.

Rewriting the Books Example with PEAR

When using the PEAR DB package, you follow the same steps. However, the function syntax is slightly different. We'll go line by line and explain the differences as they appear in Example 9-7.

Example 9-7. Displaying the books table with PEAR DB

```
1 <?php
2
3 include('db_login.php');
4 require_once('DB.php');
5
6 $connection = DB::connect("mysql://$db_username:$db_password@$db_host/$db_database");
7
8 if (DB::isError($connection)){
```

Example 9-7. Displaying the books table with PEAR DB (continued)

```
9 die("Could not connect to the database: <br />".DB::errorMessage($connection));
10 }
11
12 $query = "SELECT * FROM `books` NATURAL JOIN `authors`";
13 $result = $connection->query($query);
14
15 if (DB::isError($result)){
16 die("Could not query the database:<br />".$query." ".DB::errorMessage($result));
17 }
18
19 echo('<table border="1">');
20 echo '<tr><th>Title</th><th>Author</th><th>Pages</th></tr>';
21
22 while ($result_row = $result->fetchRow()) {
23 echo "<tr><td>";
24 echo $result_row[1] . '</td><td>';
25 echo $result_row[4] . '</td><td>';
26 echo $result_row[2] . '</td></tr>';
27 }
28
29 echo("</table>");
30 $connection->disconnect();
31
32 ?>
```

Example 9-7 displays the screen shown in Figure 9-7.

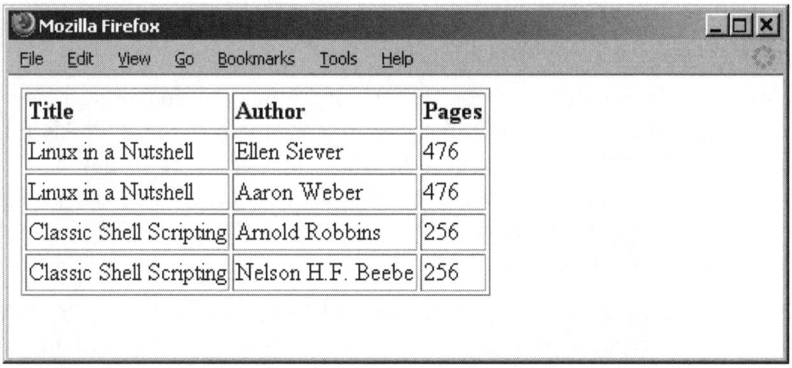

Figure 9-7. Switching to the PEAR DB functions didn't change the output

Notice that Figure 9-7 is identical to the output in Figure 9-4.

Line 3 includes your database login information and remains unchanged:

```
include('db_login.php');
```

Line 4 has a new require statement:

```
require_once( "DB.php" );
```

This requires the file *DB.php*, which provides the PEAR DB functions. The require_ once function errors out if the *DB.php* file is not found. It also will not include the file if it has been incorporated already. And, this would cause an error.

 The file *DB.php* is found in the */pear* subdirectory of the PHP distribution. The PEAR install should have added that directory to the include_path in the *php.ini* file. If this file is not found, verify that PEAR DB is installed and that the paths are set up correctly.

Creating a connect instance

The *DB.php* file defines a class of type DB. Refer to Chapter 5 for more information on working with classes and objects. We'll principally be calling the methods in the class. The DB class has a connect method, which we'll use instead of our old connect function mysql_connect. The double colons (::) indicate that we're calling that function from the class in line 4:

```
connection = DB::connect("mysql://$db_username:$db_password@$db_host/$db_database");
```

When you call the connect function, it creates a new database connection that is stored in the variable $connection. The connect function attempts to connect to the database based on the connect string you passed to it.

Connect string

The connect string uses this new format to represent the login information that you already supplied in separate fields:

```
dbtype://username:password@host/database
```

This format may look familiar to you, as it's very similar to the connect string for a Windows share. The first part of the string is what really sets the PEAR functions apart from the plain PHP. The phptype field specifies the type of database to connect. Supported databases include ibase, msql, mssql, mysql, oci8, odbc, pgsql, and sybase. All that's required for your PHP page to work with a different type of database is changing the phptype!

The *username*, *password*, *host*, and *database* should be familiar from the basic PHP connect. Only the type of connection is required. However, you'll usually want to specify all fields.

After the values from *dblogin.php* are included, the connect string looks like the following:

```
"mysql://test:test@localhost/test"
```

If the connect method on line 6 was successful, a $DB object is created. It contains the methods to access the database as well as all of the information about the state of that database connection.

Querying

One of the methods it contains is called query. The query method works just like PHP's query function in that it takes a SQL statement. The difference is the hyphen and greater-than syntax (->) is used to call it from the object. It also returns the results as another object instead of a result set.

```
$query = "SELECT * FROM `books`"
$result = $connection->query($query);
```

Based on the SQL query, this code calls the query function from the connection object and returns a result object named $result.

Fetching

Line 22 uses the result object to call the fetchRow method. It returns the rows one at a time, similar to mysql_fetch_row.

```
while ($result_row = $result->fetchRow()) {
    echo 'Title: '.$result_row[1] . '<br />';
    echo 'Author: '.$result_row[4] . '<br /> ';
    echo 'Pages: '.$result_row[2] . '<br /><br />';
}
```

You use another while loop to go through each row from fetchRow until it returns FALSE. The code in the loop hasn't changed from the non-PEAR example.

Closing

In line 30, you're finished with the database connection, so you close it using the object method disconnect:

```
$connection->disconnect();
```

PEAR error reporting

The function DB::isError will check to see whether the result that's been returned to you is an error or not. If it is an error, you can use DB::errorMessage to return a text description of the error that was generated. You need to pass DB::errorMessage the return value from your function as an argument.

Here you rewrite the PEAR code to use error checking:

```
<?php
if ( DB::isError( $demoResult = $db->query( $sql)))
{
    echo DB::errorMessage($demoResult);
} else {
    while ($demoRow = $demoResult->fetchRow()) {
            echo $demoRow[2] . '<br />';
    }
}
?>
```

Now that you have a good handle on connecting to the database and the various functions of PEAR, we're going to talk about forms. Forms provide a way to send substantial data from the user to the server where it can be processed.

Chapter 9 Questions

Question 9-1. Create a PEAR-style connect string to connect to this database:

> hostname: oreilly.com
> database name: survey
> username: joe
> password: my$ql

Question 9-2. Using the parameters in Question 9-1, write the non-PEAR PHP code to connect to a database and select the instance.

Question 9-3. Using the connection from Question 9-2, write the non-PEAR PHP code to fetch and display the results of the query select * from authors;.

Question 9-4. What are the advantages of using PEAR?

See the Appendix for the answers to these questions.

Working with Forms

HTML forms provide a way to send substantial data from the user to the server where it can be processed. You'll be using a lot of the PHP language concepts that you learned about in the first half of the book to process and validate the form data.

We'll begin by building a simple form and will then learn how to access the information in its fields after user submission. The basic types of input devices that can be placed on forms, as well as hidden values, will be discussed. Of course, the PHP code will be mixed in with all of these elements.

Forms work in a two-step process. The form must be presented to the user, who then enters some information and submits the form. Every form has a target for what page to load that will process the data when the user submits. Often, this is the same file that originally generated the form. The PHP code simply checks to see whether there's user input coming along with the request for the page to determine whether the file is being called to generate the form or process its data.

Searching a database is necessary in many different types of applications. Whether it's searching forum posts, users, or a blog, it can make a user's life much easier. On a database level, there are also many different ways to process a search and bring back results.

Building a Form

Since you'll need a place for the user to enter a search query, let's begin by building a form to handle the user's input. Every form must have these basic components:

- The submission type defined with the `method` keyword
- One or more input elements defined with the `input` tag
- The destination to go to when submitted defined with the `action` keyword

Let's build a simple form with a text input field called `search` and a `submit` button, as shown in Example 10-1.

Example 10-1. A simple form example

```
1  <html>
2  <head>
3    <title>Building a Form</title>
4  </head>
5  <body>
6    <form action="<?php echo($_SERVER['PHP_SELF']); ?>"
7          method="get">
8      <label>
9          Search: <input type="text" name="search" />
10     </label>
11       <input type="submit" value="Go!" />
12   </form>
13 </body>
14 </html>
```

Place the code in Example 10-1 into a file called *simple.php* in a web-accessible directory on your web server, such as the document root. Strictly speaking, forms are defined purely by HTML, but we're using some PHP code on line 6 to reference the super global PHP_SELF. This provides a shortcut to the name of the current PHP file that handles the submission of the form data.

The form in Example 10-1 allows you to capture the search sting from the user for a search. Notice how we wrapped a label tag around the input where the text was; this makes the form easier to use. Since clicking on the Search: text automatically sends the cursor to the search field. On line 7, we set the form submission method to GET. This is done to insure that users can bookmark their searches and not have to come back to the page and reenter their data. Line 9 does the bulk of the work by defining the text field.

Accessing the *simple.php* file from your browser should generate a form similar to Figure 10-1. It's not terribly useful, as any value you submit just brings the same form back again, but we'll take care of that soon.

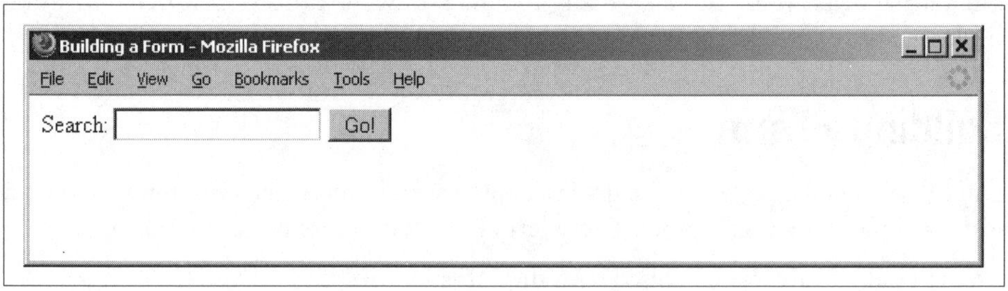

Figure 10-1. How the sample form appears in your browser

Accessing Submitted Form Values

Let's go ahead and modify the code in Example 10-1 to display back the search string when the form is submitted. To do this, check the value of a GET submitted field with the syntax $_GET[*field*]. Likewise, $_POST[*field*] is used to access a field when using the POST field submission.

Since search is the name of the field that we specified when building the form, we'll use $_GET["search"] in Example 10-2.

Example 10-2. Modifying our simple search to process the results

```
<html>
<head>
  <title>Building a Form</title>
</head>
<body>
<?php
$search = $_GET["search"];
$self=$_SERVER['PHP_SELF'];
if ($search != NULL )
{
('
<form action="'.$_SERVER["PHP_SELF"].'" method="GET">
<label>Search: <input type="text" name="search" />
</label>
<input type="submit" value="Go!" />

        </form>
        ');
}
?>
</body>
</html>
```

Example 10-2 generates this HTML:

```
<html>
<head>
  <title>Building a Form</title>
</head>
<body>
<form action="/oreilly/ch10/simple.php" method="GET" />
        <label> Search: <input type="text" name="search" id="search"> </label>
        <input type="submit" value="Go!" />
        </form>

        </body>
</html>
```

If you submitted a value of PHP in the search text box, you'd get output similar to Figure 10-2.

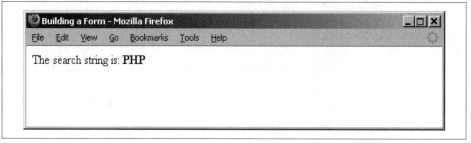

Figure 10-2. The same script is now able to echo back the search string

When the form is submitted, the if statement notices that the $search variable has a value assigned. Instead of the script returning the HTML form, the search string is returned. So, you have the same PHP file generating the form and processing its submitted values.

With forms, you can specify default values and use different form inputs. There are various ways you can submit the form. These will be explained in the following subsections.

Default Values

When doing searches on a database, you might need to actually have some default values in your forms. This is useful, for example, for searching within a price range. The user doesn't always want to insert values, and it makes it that much simpler when searching. Typically, the default value for a form element is set with the value attribute; there is an exception for checkboxes that use the checked keyword. Take Example 10-3.

Example 10-3. Form default values

```
<html>
<head>
  <title>Form Default Values</title>
</head>
<body>
  <form action="<?php echo($_SERVER['PHP_SELF']); ?>" method="GET" />
    <label>Min Price <input type="text" name="min_price" value="0" /></label><br />
    <label>Max Price <input type="text" name="max_price" value="1000" /></label>
<br />
    <input type="submit" value="Go! />
  </form>
</body>
</html>
```

In Figure 10-3, the default values reflect 0 and 1000 for the minimum and maximum prices that you want to search. Depending on the area, if the user searches for an apartment to rent, this is a good starting point. We already specified a default value for the submit button as Go! in Example 10-1.

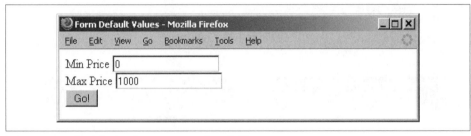

Figure 10-3. The default values appear in their fields

Types of Input

There are many different types of input, so which one should you use? Radio buttons, checkboxes, text input, text areas, buttons…oh my! We'll describe each of our input options.

Text boxes

Most of the time when dealing with input from a user, you might want a string of text. A text type element is used to capture these strings from the user. The `name` attribute is required to process the input after a form submission as it specifies how to reference the value. When it appears in the browser, the `size` parameter determines the length of the text box. The `maxlength` parameter determines the maximum number of characters the user can place in the field. The syntax is:

```
<input type="text" name="name" size="display size" maxlength="max characters allows" />
```

For example, the following:

```
<form>
<input type="text" name="search" size="10" maxlength="30" />
</form>
```

creates a text box like Figure 10-3.

Text areas

If you need a large chunk of text from a user or are going to be using a WYSIWYG editor, you need to use a text area. A text area is defined by using the `textarea` element. The `name`, `cols`, and `rows` attributes are required. The `name` attribute works like it did in a text box. The `cols` attribute specifies how many columns to create for your text area. The `rows` attribute specifies how many rows to create. The syntax is:

```
<textarea name="name" cols="# of cols" rows="# of rows"></textarea>
```

For example:

```
<form>
<label>Suggestion: <textarea name="suggestions" cols="40" rows="5"></textarea>
</label>
```

```
<input type="submit" value="Go! />
</form>
```

might display like Figure 10-4.

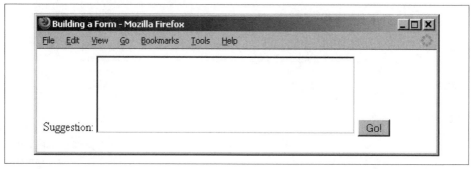

Figure 10-4. A simple form with a text area element

Checkboxes

A checkbox is useful when you want to give users several different options, especially when they're allowed to select each choice individually. Use checkboxes only when you have a few options to give to a user; otherwise, there is a different type of input that you would want to use. This is called a *select*, which we'll talk about in a bit. For a checkbox, set the input type to checkbox. The name and value attributes are also required. If the value is set to checked, the checkbox is checked by default.

The syntax is:

```
<input type="checkbox" name="name" value="checkbox value" />
```

For example:

```
<form>
<fieldset>
<label>Italian <input type="checkbox" name="food[]" value="Italian" /></label>
<label>Mexican <input type="checkbox" name="food[]" value="Mexican" /></label>
<label>Chinese <input type="checkbox" name="food[]" value="Chinese"
checked="checked" /></label>
</fieldset>
<input type="submit" value="Go! />
</form>
```

This displays the box shown in Figure 10-5.

Radio buttons

Radio buttons behave just like the presets on a radio. They are like checkboxes, except you can only select one radio button at a time. To create a radio button, set the type to radio. The name and value attributes are required. All of the radio buttons in a group must use the same name to allow for only one value. The syntax is:

```
<input type="radio" name="name" value="radio button value" />
```

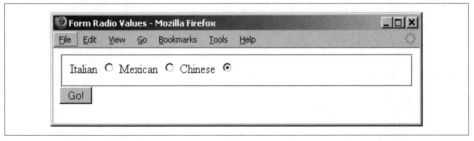

Figure 10-5. A sample form with checkboxes

For example:

```
<form>
<fieldset>
<label>Italian <input type="radio" name="food" value="Italian" /></label>
<label>Mexican <input type="radio" name="food" value="Mexican" /></label>
<label>Chinese <input type="radio" name="food" value="Chinese"
checked="checked" /></label>
</fieldset>
<input type="submit" value="Go! />
</form>
```

This looks like Figure 10-6.

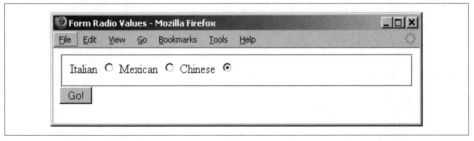

Figure 10-6. The same choices are available as before, but the radio buttons are round

Figure 10-6 allows only one type of food to be selected.

Hidden

Hidden form elements allow you to send information from the form to the script that processes the data without that information being visible to the user. This may be information such as whether the forms' submit button was pressed, or perhaps a username. The syntax is:

```
<input type="hidden" name="name" value="hidden value" />
```

For example:

```
<form>
<input type="hidden" name="submitted" value="true" />
</form>
```

HIDDEN is a TYPE attribute value to the INPUT element for forms. It indicates a form field that does not appear visibly in the document and that the user does not interact with. It can be used to transmit stale information about the client or server. Hidden fields can be viewed via the Page Source. Therefore, it's unadvisable to put passwords in a hidden field.

Selects

Selects present a list of options to the user. You can specify whether a user can select only one or many items from the list. The `<select>` element defines a select list. Each item on the list is specified with the option element. The syntax is:

```
<select name="name"> <option>Label of Option</option> </select>
```

Additionally, there are several attributes that can be set within `<select>`:

- The name attribute is required and specifies how to access the data after form submission.
- The size attribute specifies how many lines of the list appear in the browser window. The default is a drop-down list.
- The multiple attributes allow the user to select more than one item from the list.

There are two commonly used attributes for `<option>`:

- The selected attribute specifies a default selection.
- The value attribute specifies a value that is different from the label of the option. If no value is specified, the label of the option is used as the value.

 A selection list that doesn't have multiple attributes can have only one option selected by default.

A common use for a select list is providing options from which a user may choose, such as that created in Example 10-4.

Example 10-4. Multiple book types

```
<form>
<select name="media" multiple="multiple">
  <option></option>
  <option>Hard Cover</option>
  <option>Soft Cover</option>
  <option>Reference</option>
  <option>Audio Books</option>
</select>
</form>
```

Figure 10-7 shows the list built from the code in Example 10-4.

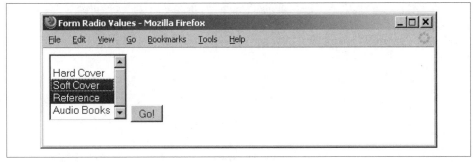

Figure 10-7. Multiple items selected from the list

The first option in the list is actually a blank entry. This is useful for detecting if a user hasn't made any changes to a list.

Working with Multiple Values

Having checkboxes and radio buttons creates a new problem. You can't use a single value when processing the results of a group of checkboxes with the same name or elements from a select list. Example 10-5 shows an example.

Example 10-5. A form with checkboxes using the same name to store multiple values

```
<html>
<head>
<title>Using Default Checkbox Values</title>
</head>
<body>
<?php
$food = $_GET["food"];
if (!empty($food)){
echo "The foods selected are: <strong>";
foreach($food as $foodstuff){
echo '<br />'.$foodstuff;
}
echo "</strong>.";
}
else {
echo ('
<form action="'.$_SERVER["PHP_SELF"].'" method="GET">
<fieldset>
<label>
Italian
<input type="checkbox" name="food[]" value="Italian" />
</label>
<label>
Mexican
<input type="checkbox" name="food[]" value="Mexican" />
</label>
<label>
```

Example 10-5. A form with checkboxes using the same name to store multiple values (continued)

```
Chinese
<input type="checkbox" name="food[]" value="Chinese" checked="checked" />
</label>
</fieldset>
<input type="submit" value="Go!" />');
}
?>
</body>
</html>
```

Example 10-5 produces something like Figure 10-8.

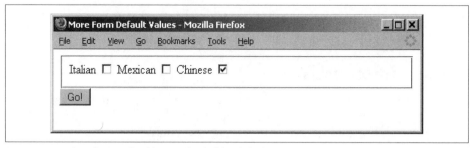

Figure 10-8. The Chinese checkbox is checked by default

You gave the user the choice of three different ethnic foods: Italian, Mexican, and Chinese. In this example, the user can check multiple checkboxes. Therefore, you need to access more than a single value from the name of the checkbox when you process the form submission in PHP. We'll place a pair of brackets ([]) after the field's name attribute to send the results in an array.

In the following code, the name attribute is set to food[] instead of food. Without the array, if a user checks multiple foods, his selections would be overwritten by the last food checked in the list. Placing closed brackets after the input name signifies an array. Since you want to have one choice checked already, give it an attribute of checked, and then set it to checked. This sets the checkbox to be set by default in a user's browser.

```
<html>
<head>
  <title>Using Default Checkbox Values</title>
</head>
<body>
<?php
$food=$_GET[food];
$self=$_SERVER['PHP_SELF'];
if (!empty($food))
{
  echo "The foods selected are:<br />";
  foreach($_GET[food] as $foodstuf)
  {
```

```
        echo "<strong>$foodstuf</strong><br />";
    }
}
else
{
    echo ("<form action=\"$self\" ");
    echo ('method="get">
     <fieldset>
      <label>Italian <input type="checkbox" name="food[]" value="Italian" /></label>
      <label>Mexican <input type="checkbox" name="food[]" value="Mexican" /></label>
      <label>Chinese <input type="checkbox" name="food[]" value="Chinese"
checked="checked" /></label>
     </fieldset>
     <input type="submit" value="Go!" >
         ');
}
?>
</body>
</html>
```

If you select two checkboxes, you'll see the screen in Figure 10-9.

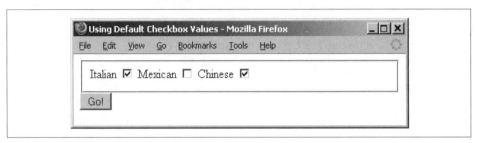

Figure 10-9. Selecting Italian and Chinese

The screen in Figure 10-9 produces the screen in Figure 10-10, when submitted.

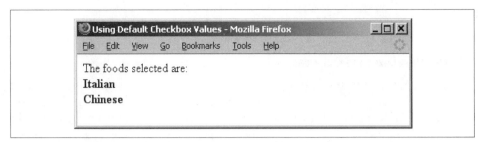

Figure 10-10. Each check field is displayed

You can set up radio buttons in the same way, but name should be set to food instead of food[], since radio buttons tell users they have only one choice.

Lastly, notice in the preceding code that the checkboxes are wrapped around a fieldset tag. This is used to logically define a set of data.

Validating Data

Whenever you are taking data from a user, you should always validate it. If you do not validate the user's input, it can cause many problems—most importantly, substantial security risks.

Validating input is not complicated. We'll go over the most common PHP functions that are used to sanitize data from users.

Validating checkboxes, radio buttons, and selects

Validating data that comes from checkboxes, radio buttons, or selects is easier than validating free format fields such as text boxes, because the value should only be one of the predefined values. To ensure this, store all of the options in an array and make sure the user input is part of the array when you process the data. We'll look at the code for checking input from a single selection (in other words, only one checkbox, radio button, or other selection), as shown in Example 10-6.

Example 10-6. Checking input from a radio button or a single select

```
<?php
$options = array('option 1', 'option 2', 'option 3');
// Coming from a checkbox or a multiple select statement
$valid = true;
if (is_array($_GET['input'])) {
$valid = true;
foreach($_GET['input'] as $input) {
if (!in_array($input, $options)) {
$valid = false;
}
}
if ($valid) {
// process input
}
}
?>
```

Validating text boxes and text areas

To validate text boxes and text areas, you first need to gather what information is valid and what isn't. Also, you don't want to allow the user to enter nothing. You can spend as little time as checking to see whether a string is empty, or you can build more complex expressions to check for the presence of certain characters, such as the @ in an email address. You can use the code in Example 10-7 to make sure the input is acceptable.

Example 10-7. Checking input from a checkbox or a multiple select

```
<?php
    $options = array('option 1', 'option 2', 'option 3');
```

Example 10-7. Checking input from a checkbox or a multiple select (continued)

```php
    //coming from a checkbox or a multiple select statement
    $valid = true;
    if (is_array($_GET['input'])) {
      $valid = true;
      foreach($_GET['input'] as $input) {
        if (!in_array($input, $options)) {
          $valid = false;
        }
      }
      if ($valid) {
        //process input
      }
    }
?>
```

Since we haven't given you much tangible, sink-your-teeth-into-it PHP code, we're going to give you a great example of how PHP can easily create a conversion tool. Using conversion tools, you could convert from Fahrenheit to Celsius, or U.S. Units of Measurement to Metric. Pretty cool, huh?

Building a Feet-to-Meters Converter in PHP

We're going to show you the power of PHP by creating a feet-to-meters converter application, shown in Example 10-8, which would be handy if your web site is used internationally.

Example 10-8. PHP feet-to-meters converter

```php
<head>
<title>Feet to meters conversion</title>
</head>
<body>
<?php
// Check to see if the form has been submitted
$feet = $_GET["feet"];
if ($_GET[feet] != NULL){
echo "<strong>$feet</strong> feet converts to <strong>";
echo $feet * 0.3048;
echo "</strong> meters.<br />";
}
?>
<form action="<?php echo($_SERVER['PHP_SELF']); ?>" method="GET">
<label>Feet:
<input type="text" name="feet" value="<?php echo $feet; ?>" />
</label>
<input type="submit" value="Convert!" />
</form>
</body>
</html>
```

This self-processing form collects a measurement in feet, multiplies that measurement by a standard conversion factor, and then prints out the results. Since you still have the original value for feet in the $feet variable from the form submission, you use it as an initial value when displaying the Feet user input field in the form. Figure 10-11 shows the results of entering 12 and clicking Convert.

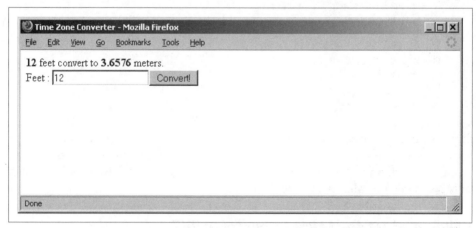

Figure 10-11. Simply convert feet to meters using a mathematical formula

Building a Time Zone Conversion Utility in PHP

Now that you've learned how to do a variety of tasks, let's put it all together to get an idea of what can be done in PHP. Example 10-9 uses forms, arrays, conditionals, looping, and date strings. These all work together to bring you a handy tool for converting between some common time zones.

Example 10-9. Converting between time zones based on user input

```
1 <html>
2 <head>
3 <title>Time Zone Converter</title>
4 </head>
5 <body>
6 <?php
7 // An array holds the standard time zone strings
8 $time_zones = array("Asia/Hong_Kong",
9 "Africa/Cairo",
10 "Europe/Paris",
11 "Europe/Madrid",
12 "Europe/London",
13 "Asia/Tokyo",
14 "America/New_York",
15 "America/Los_Angeles",
16 "America/Chicago");
17 // Check to see if the form has been submitted
18 if ($_GET["start_time"] != NULL){
```

```
19 $start_time_input = $_GET["start_time"];
20 $start_tz = $_GET["start_tz"];
21 $end_tz = $_GET["end_tz"];
22 putenv("TZ=$start_tz");
23 $start_time = strtotime($start_time_input);
24 echo "<p><strong>";
25 echo date("h:i:sA",$start_time)."\n";
26 echo "</strong>";
27 putenv("TZ=$end_tz");
28
29 echo "in $start_tz becomes ";
30 echo "<strong> ";
31 echo date("h:i:sA",$start_time)."\n";
32 echo "</strong>";
33 echo " in $end_tz.</p><hr />";
34 }
35 ?>
36 <form action="<?php echo($_SERVER['PHP_SELF']); ?>" method="GET">
37 <label>
38 Your Time:
39 <input type="text" name="start_time" value="<?php echo $start_time_input; ?>" />
40 </label> in
41 <select name="start_tz">
42 <?php
43 foreach ($time_zones as $tz) {
44 echo '<option';
45 if (strcmp($tz, $start_tz) == 0){
46 echo ' selected="selected"';
47 }
48 echo ">$tz</option>";
49 }
50 ?>
51 </select>
52 <p>Convert to:
53 <select name="end_tz">
54 <?php
55 foreach ($time_zones as $tz) {
56 echo '<option';
57 if (strcmp($tz, $end_tz) == 0){
58 echo ' selected="selected"';
59 }
60 echo ">$tz</option>";
61 }
62
63 ?>
64 </select>
65 <input type="submit" value="Convert!">
66 </form>
67 </body>
68
69 </html>
```

Here's what happened in Example 10-9 on a line-by-line basis:

- Lines 9 through 17 populate an array with a handful of time zones from around the world.
- Line 20 checks to see whether there is a value for the `$start_time`. It's assumed that if there's a value, then the code has been launched in response to the user submitting the form.
- Line 25 sets the environmental variable that defines the current time zone. PHP uses this for both the `strtotime` and `date` functions.
- Line 42 begins building the user input form. We'll give the user the chance to make another time comparison.
- Lines 43 through 49 and 55 through 61 loop through the time zones in the array. They also check whether the passed-in value from the form submission matches a time zone value. If it does, insert the `selected` attribute so that the time zone settings are remembered from the last form submission.

Figure 10-12 show an example of converting the time from Chicago to Paris.

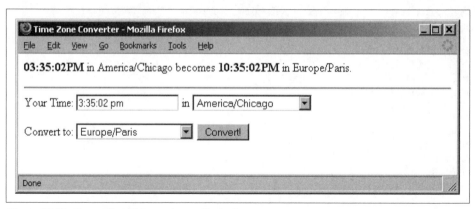

Figure 10-12. Converting Chicago time to Paris time

Querying the Database with Form Data

Once you've validated your data, you're ready to start using information from the forms in your database queries. Example 10-10 creates a function called `query_db` from the code in Chapter 7 for displaying authors with a change to line 11 that allows matching the title with a `LIKE` search clause. `LIKE` and `NOT LIKE` are usually used with strings and possibly with wildcards, such as the underscore (_) and the percentage sign (%).

- The underscore (_) matches a single character.
- The percent sign (%) matches zero or more characters.

In Example 10-10, the function takes a single parameter and searches for the specific book title you're looking to find.

Example 10-10. Combining form processing and database querying

```
1  ?php
2  function query_db($qstring) {
3  include('db_login.php');
4  require_once('DB.php');
5  $connection = DB::connect("mysql://$db_username:$db_password@$db_host/$db_database");
6
7  if (DB::isError($connection)){
8  die ("Could not connect to the database: <br />". DB::errorMessage($connection));
9  }
10 $query = "SELECT * FROM `books` NATURAL JOIN `authors`
11 WHERE `books`.`title` like '%$qstring%'";
12 $result = $connection->query($query);
13 if (DB::isError($result)){
14 die("Could not query the database:<br />".
15 $query." ".DB::errorMessage($result));
16 }
17 echo ('<table border="1">');
18 echo "<tr><th>Title</th><th>Author</th><th>Pages</th></tr>";
19 while ($result_row = $result->fetchRow()) {
20 echo "<tr><td>";
21 echo $result_row[1] . '</td><td>';
22 echo $result_row[4] . '</td><td>';
23 echo $result_row[2] . '</td></tr>';
24 }
25 echo ("</table>");
26 $connection->disconnect();
27 }
28 ?>
29 <html>
30 <head>
31 <title>Building a Form</title>
32 </head>
33 <body>
34 <?php
35 $search = $_GET["search"];
36 $self = $_SERVER['PHP_SELF'];
37 if ($search != NULL){
38 echo "The search string is: <strong>$search</strong>.";
39 query_db($search);
40 }
41 else {
42 echo ('
43 <form action="'.$self.'" method="get">
44 <label>Search:
45 <input type="text" name="search" id="search" />
46 </label>
47 <input type="submit" value="Go!" />
48 </form>
```

```
49 ');
50 }
51
52 ?>
53 </body>
54 </html>
```

Line 50 completes the processing of the form data. The search string is sent to the `query_db` function. This example shows a fairly simple search done by searching a words table, and then outputting the results on the pages that are being used, as shown in Figure 10-13.

Figure 10-13. We see our familiar text box for searching

Searching for "ing" matches one title, shown in Figure 10-14.

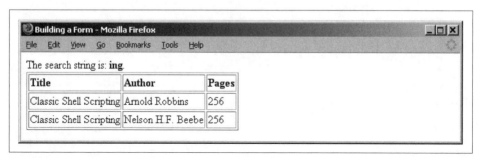

Figure 10-14. The book titles that contain "ing" are displayed

Shortening up the search string to `in` outputs an additional title, as shown in Figure 10-15.

While this code works pretty well, it's starting to get more complicated and intricate than some people are comfortable with. The solution is to break out the HTML from the PHP.

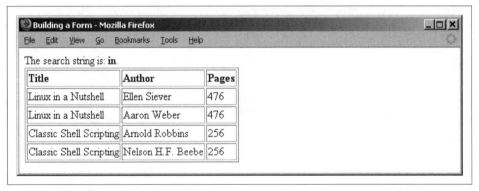

Figure 10-15. Shortening the search string gives more results

Templates

Templates separate the HTML code that defines the presentation or look of a page from the PHP code that's responsible for gathering the data. Once separated, it becomes easier for someone with HTML and perhaps CSS knowledge to modify the template without worrying about breaking the PHP code. Likewise, the PHP code can focus on the data instead of getting caught up in presentation details.

There are other advantages to using templates, too. If you make a mistake in the template, the error will be clearly returned from the template. The template itself can generally be loaded into a web browser or a graphical web development tool such as Dreamweaver, since it resembles the final state of the page when processed. Templates support very basic programming features for use with presentation, such as being able to tell whether a section of a page should be visible.

Of course, nothing's perfect; there are a couple of disadvantages to templates. Templates increase the number of files to maintain. They add a small amount of extra processing time. They also require installing the template engine and setting up directories. You need to be running at least PHP Version 4.0.6 to use Smarty, a popular template engine.

Template Engine

There are several template packages available on the Internet. Each uses its own *template engine* to process the templates and make them as efficient as possible. No matter which template engine you use, you'll always follow the same basic steps:

1. Retrieve your data.

2. Make calls to the template functions for each value that's used in a template.

3. Display the template using the template function.

We'll walk through this process with some examples shortly. One of the more popular template engines available is Smarty, shown in Figure 10-16. Smarty has many, many features, but what we're concerned most with is the basic template engine functionality.

Figure 10-16. Smarty template engine

Installation

While installing Smarty isn't as complex as installing and configuring Apache, PHP, and MySQL, it still deserves some attention.

1. Smarty can be downloaded from *http://smarty.php.net/download.php*. Download the latest stable release.
2. Extract the contents of the Smarty file to a convenient location.
3. Create a directory called *Smarty* in your document root. If you don't know what your document root is, you can use PHP to find out:

   ```
   <?php
   echo $_SERVER["DOCUMENT_ROOT"];
   ?>
   ```
4. Copy the contents of Smarty's *libs/* directory from the directory you extracted it to into the Smarty directory you just created.
5. You should now have the following file structure in your document root:

   Smarty/Config_File.class.php
   Smarty/debug.tpl
   Smarty/internals/
   Smarty/plugins/
   Smarty/Smarty.class.php
   Smarty/Smarty_Compiler.class.php

Application level directories

For each application with which you wish to use Smarty, you'll need to set up a set of four directories. The four directories are for templates, compiled templates, cached templates, and configuration files. Although you may not use all of those features, you should set up the directories just in case.

1. Create a directory called *myapp/* in your document root. (You can call it whatever you want, but for the remainder of the text, we will refer to it as *myapp/*.)
2. Create a directory named *smarty* inside the directory you just created (*myapp/smarty*).

3. In the *smarty* directory you just created, create four more directories: *templates*, *templates_c*, *cache*, and *config*. Ensure that the web server will have write access to the *templates_c* and *cache* directories that you created in the previous step.

All you need to do is create a template and a PHP file to try it out.

Creating sample scripts

Now set up your application in the document root. See Example 10-11.

Example 10-11. The index.php file to create

```
?php
// use the absolute path for Smarty.class.php
require($_SERVER["DOCUMENT_ROOT"].'/Smarty/Smarty.class.php');
$smarty = new Smarty();
$smarty->template_dir = $_SERVER["DOCUMENT_ROOT"].'/myapp/smarty/templates';
$smarty->compile_dir = $_SERVER["DOCUMENT_ROOT"].'/myapp/smarty/templates_c';
$smarty->cache_dir = $_SERVER["DOCUMENT_ROOT"].'/myapp/smarty/cache';
$smarty->config_dir = $_SERVER["DOCUMENT_ROOT"].'/myapp/smarty/configs';
?>
```

The bulk of what's happening in Example 10-11 is telling your PHP program where to find the Smarty class file to include and the location of the application directories.

Next, create *myapp/index.php*:

```
<?php
require_once("smarty.php");
$smarty->assign('test', '123');
$smarty->display('index.tpl');
?>
```

Create a sample template

Edit the *index.tpl* file in your *myapp/smarty/templates* directory, as shown in Example 10-12.

Example 10-12. The sample index.tpl template to create

```
<html>
<head>
<title>Smarty</title>
</head>
<body>
It's as easy as {$test}.
</body>
</html>
```

Now, go to your new application through the web browser (*http://www.domain.com/myapp/index.php*, in our example). You should see something like Figure 10-17.

Now you can convert the previous example to the version shown in Example 10-13.

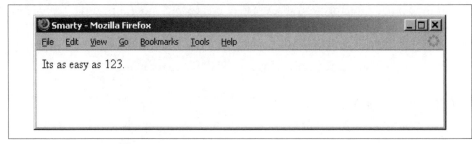

Figure 10-17. Web browser–displayed code

Example 10-13. Using the template to display the table

```php
<?php
function query_db($qstring){
require_once("smarty.php");
require_once("db_login.php");
require_once("DB.php");
$connection = DB::connect("mysql://$db_username:$db_password@$db_host/$db_database");
if (DB::isError($connection)){
die("Could not connect to the database: <br />". DB::errorMessage($connection));
}
$query = "SELECT * FROM `books`
NATURAL JOIN `authors`
WHERE `books`.`title` like '%$qstring%'";
$result = $connection->query($query);
if (DB::isError($result)){
die ("Could not query the database: <br>". $query. " ".DB::errorMessage($result));
}
while ($result_row = $result->fetchRow(DB_FETCHMODE_ASSOC)) {
$test[] = $result_row;
}
$connection->disconnect();
$smarty->assign('users', $test);
$smarty->display('index2.tpl');
}
?>
<html>
<head>
<title>Building a Form</title>
</head>
<body>
<?php
$search = $_GET["search"];
$self = $_SERVER['PHP_SELF'];
if ($search != NULL){
echo "The search string is: <strong>$search</strong>.";
query_db($search);
}
else {
echo '
<form action="'.$self.'" method="GET">
```

Example 10-13. Using the template to display the table (continued)

```
<label>
Search:
<input type="text" name="search" id="search" />
</label>
<input type="submit" value="Go!">
</form>';
}
?>
</body>
</html>
```

The template is a bit more complex, since you're dealing with rows coming back in arrays and there are multiple rows.

The *index2.tpl* file is shown in Example 10-14.

Example 10-14. The new table template

```
<table border=1>
<tr><th>Title</th><th>Author</th><th>Pages</th></tr>
{section name=mysec loop=$users}
  {strip}
  <tr>
    <td>{$users[mysec].title}</td>
    <td>{$users[mysec].author}</td>
    <td>{$users[mysec].pages}</td>
  </tr>
  {/strip}
{/section}
</table>
```

Example 10-14 outputs the screen shown in Figure 10-18.

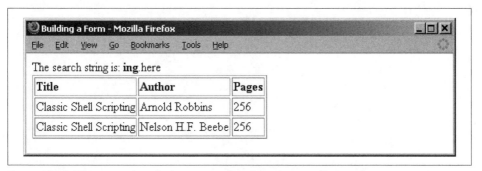

Figure 10-18. The output doesn't change even though you're using the template

The template incorporates the looping element of Smarty. We used an associative array for returning your results to make the template easier to read, as the field names are the column names and not numbers. Smarty could have easily added some nice decorations, such as alternating the color of the row backgrounds.

In the next chapter, we'll discuss more complicated database functions now that you have a good solid understanding of database functions.

Chapter 10 Questions

Question 10-1. Which super global variable is used to automatically call the same script to process the results of form input?

Question 10-2. Create a form that takes text field parameters for username and password and submits the values to the same script.

Question 10-3. Add code to echo the values of the form submission from Question 10-2.

Question 10-4. Write a SQL query to select only author names that begin with "A".

See the Appendix for the answers to these questions.

Practical PHP

In this chapter, we'll start working on some of the more common tasks that you'll perform when writing PHP programs, such as work with strings, display formats for strings, as well as dates and time. We'll also show you how to work with files that your PHP program creates or reads. Also, we'll provide an example of how to let a user upload a file and then validate its contents before making it accessible. Uploading files is useful but can be a security risk if files aren't properly validated.

When building HTML output for web pages, we spend quite a bit of time working with strings. PHP has a rich set of functions for doing all the tasks you may need to change the case of a string. You also need to be able to format dates and times. Performing any sort of addition or subtraction on dates—thanks to quirks such as leap years—can quickly become complicated without a little help from functions specifically designed to work with dates.

String Functions

Because you're working with essentially two languages that both support manipulating strings, you need to learn about string functions in PHP and MySQL. You may find it more appropriate to modify a string either in a query or in PHP, based on the particular situation. You're going to learn about the following string operations:

- Formatting strings for display
- Calculating the length of a string
- Changing a string's case to uppercase or lowercase
- Searching for strings within strings and returning the position of the match
- How to return just a portion of a string, which is a substring

We'll start with formatting strings, since that will help you throughout the rest of the topics.

Formatting Strings for Display

So far, you've been using echo and print to display strings without any modification. You'll learn about two functions called printf and sprintf. If you're familiar with other programming languages, such as C, you'll recognize that these functions work the same way as they do elsewhere. Don't worry if you haven't used them before—they're not too hard to work with. The only difference between the two is that printf displays a formatted string to the output like print does, while sprintf saves the string it builds as another string with a name specified by you.

Using printf

The printf function works by taking as its first parameter a special *formatting string*. The formatting string works like a template to describe how to plug in the rest of the parameters into one resulting string. You can specify details such as how to format numbers in the string or the padding of values. Each parameter that's placed into the resulting string has a placeholder in the formatting string. For example, to output a binary number, you use the code in Example 11-1.

Example 11-1. Displaying a number in binary format

```php
<?php
printf("The computer stores the number 42 internally as %b.",42);
?>
```

This code then produces the output shown in Figure 11-1.

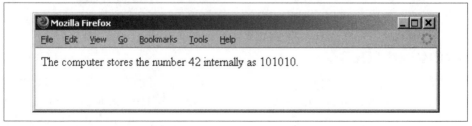

Figure 11-1. Displaying 42 in binary format

The formatting string in Example 11-1 contains a placeholder that specifies where to put the second parameter of 42. It begins with a percent sign (%), which is called the *conversion specification*. There can be any number of conversion specifications in the formatting string, but they must each have a corresponding parameter when printf is called.

The character after the percent sign is the type specifier. The *type specifier* defines how the parameter is formatted for display when it's placed in the output string, as demonstrated in Example 11-2.

Example 11-2. printf puts the numbers into the string

```php
<?php
printf("The computer stores the numbers 42, and 256 internally as %b and %b.",
42,256);
?>
```

When called from a web browser, the code in Example 11-2 displays Figure 11-2.

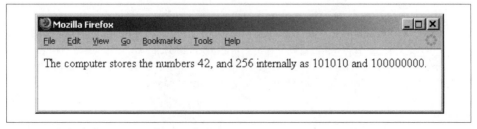

Figure 11-2. Including two numbers in the string

So far, the only type specifier we've used is b for binary, but there are more. Table 11-1 lists numeric type specifiers.

Table 11-1. Type specifiers for numbers

Specifier	Meaning	Example (using 42)
D	Display as a decimal number	42
B	Display as a binary number	101010
C	Display as ASCII equivalent	*
F	Display as a floating-point number, double precision	42.000000
O	Display as an octal number, base 8	52
S	Display as a string	42
X	Display as a lowercase hexadecimal	2a
X	Display as an uppercase hexadecimal	2A

The last column of Table 11-1 was generated with the code in Example 11-3.

Example 11-3. Displaying the same number in different formats

```php
<?php
$value=42;
printf("%d<br>",$value);
printf("%b<br>",$value);
printf("%c<br>",$value);
printf("%f<br>",$value);
printf("%o<br>",$value);
printf("%s<br>",$value);
printf("%x<br>",$value);
printf("%X<br>",$value);
?>
```

Example 11-3 gives you this column:

```
42
101010
*
42.000000
52
42
2a
2A
```

In practice, you might use this to convert from an integer to a hexadecimal number if you're building a string when specifying colors in HTML elements. Since you tend to relate better to the decimal value, you can use decimals and have them automatically formatted correctly for display in a tag such as `color="#2a11cc"`.

Padding

You can also specify padding for each field. To left pad a field with zeros, place a zero after the conversion specification percent sign (%) followed by the number of zeros to pad the type specifier, as shown in Example 11-4. If the output of the parameter uses fewer spaces than the number you specify, zeros are filled in on the left.

Example 11-4. Using left zero padding

```php
<?php
printf("Zero padding can help alignment %05d.", 42);
?>
```

Padding with zeros gives you the result shown in Figure 11-3.

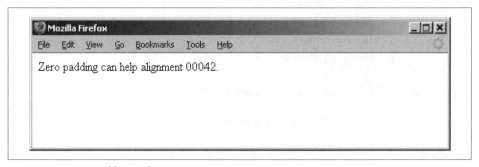

Figure 11-3. Zero padding to five spaces

Padding with leading spaces, shown in Example 11-5, works the same way, except you specify a space after the percent sign instead of a zero.

Example 11-5. Using left space padding

```php
<?php
printf("Space padding can be tricky in HTML % 5d.", 42);
?>
```

Using the left space padding displays the screen shown in Figure 11-4.

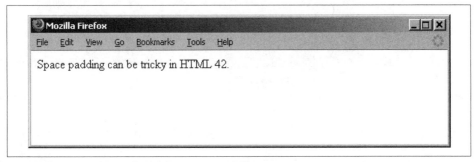

Figure 11-4. Left padding doesn't show up correctly

As you can see in Figure 11-4, the spacing before 42 was ignored by the web browser. You can fix that by using the HTML <pre> tag. The <pre> HTML markup is used to enclose preformatted text. In the tag, all spaces and line breaks are rendered literally. Additionally, the <pre> text renders in a fixed-pitch font. See Example 11-6.

Example 11-6. Adding the <pre> and </pre> tags so the spaces display

```php
<?php
printf("<pre>Space padding can be tricky in HTML % 5d.</pre>", 42);
?>
```

In Figure 11-5, we correctly see the spaces.

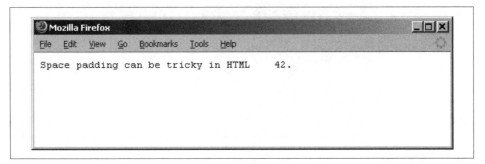

Figure 11-5. The spaces show up now

If you don't specify the character to pad, as happens in Example 11-7, printf assumes space padding and outputs a formatted string, like our example in Figure 11-5.

Example 11-7. Left padding using the default of spaces

```php
<?php
printf("<pre>Space padding can be tricky in HTML %5d.</pre>", 42);
?>
```

This code is equivalent to Example 11-5, and produces the same result, shown in Figure 11-6.

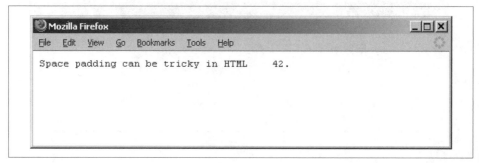

Figure 11-6. Still left padded

To right pad fields, simply put a negative number in the padding field, as in Example 11-8.

Example 11-8. Right padding with spaces

```php
<?php
printf("<pre>Space padding can be tricky in HTML %-5d.</pre>", 42);
?>
```

And the output from the negative number in the padding field displays Figure 11-7.

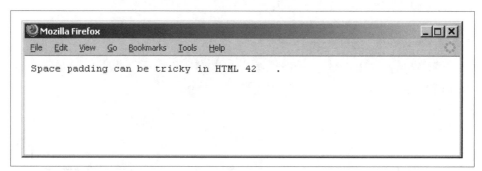

Figure 11-7. Padding on the right

Specifying precision

Sometimes you'll want to change how many digits appear after a decimal point for a real (floating-point) number. This is especially true if you need to print in currency format. To specify the number of digits to use after the decimal point, use a conversion specifier that has a decimal point after the percentage sign followed by the number of decimals. For example, the following code shows you how to do it:

```
%.number_of_decimals_to_displayf
```

Example 11-9 shows a value of 42.4242 set to display as currency.

Example 11-9. Displaying a real number in money format

```php
<?php
printf("Please pay $%.2f. ", 42.4242);
?>
```

Our code displays with the dollar sign and decimal correctly, as shown in Figure 11-8.

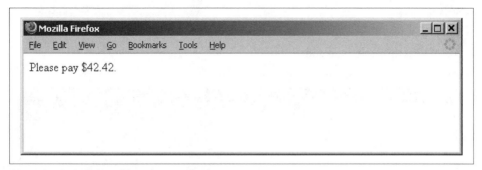

Figure 11-8. Only two decimal points display

Even if you replace the value of 42.4242 with 42, Example 11-9 would still print two zeros after the decimal point, since you told `printf` that you always want to print two digits after the decimal point.

```
Please pay $42.00.
```

Figure 11-9 breaks apart the conversion specifier %08.2f.

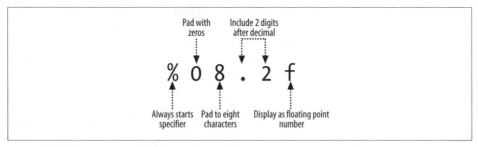

Figure 11-9. The segments of a conversion specifier

The conversion specification in Figure 11-9 means that you'll print the floating-point number left padded with zeros to eight total spaces. There'll be two digits after the decimal place.

Using sprintf

The `sprintf` function works exactly the same way as `print`, except its output is sent to a string.

In Example 11-10, the output string is assigned to the variable `$total`. From there, it could be used in further processing or, in this case, printed to the screen using echo.

Example 11-10. Using sprintf with a variable

```
<?php
$total=sprintf("Please pay $%.2f. ", 42.4242);
echo $total;
?>
```

Figure 11-10 displays the result.

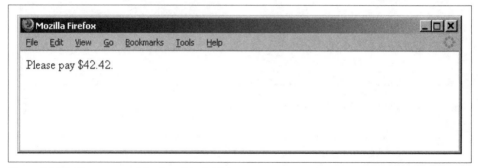

Figure 11-10. The output of the $total variable

Sometimes you'll be working with strings that come from external sources, so you'll need to find out information about them. This information might include whether they contain certain strings or may simply be their length. Remember that strings are more or less ordered lists of characters. Think of specific characters in a string as an exact numeric location of the string.

Length

The PHP function `strlen` can be used to find out how many characters are in a string. This is very useful for validating that there's data in a string, and that a string isn't larger than it should be. Example 11-11 shows how to use this.

Example 11-11. Calculating the length of a string

```php
<?php
  $password="secret1";

  if (strlen($password) <= 5)
  {
    echo("Passwords must be a least 5 characters long.");
  }
  else {
    echo ("Password accepted.");
  }
?>
```

Our password code above displays the screen in Figure 11-11.

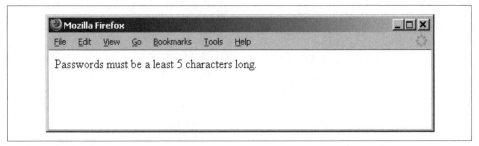

Figure 11-11. The password wasn't long enough to be secure

We're going to discuss changing the case of a string next. If you recall, this was an important bullet point when we started talking about string functions.

Changing Case

PHP provides functionality for changing the case of a string to all uppercase, all lowercase, or the first letter of a word to uppercase. The commands are strtoupper, strtolower, and ucwords, respectively. Example 11-12 uses each of them with the same string.

Example 11-12. Using the word case functions

```php
<?php
  $username="John Doe";
  echo("$username in upper case is ".strtoupper($username).".<br>");
  echo("$username in lower case is ".strtolower($username).".<br>");
  echo("$username in first letter upper case is ".ucwords($username).".<br>");
?>
```

The code in Example 11-12 displays lowercase, uppercase, and other details.

```
John Doe in upper case is JOHN DOE.
John Doe in lower case is john doe.
John Doe in first letter upper case is John Doe.
```

Number and other symbols are not affected.

Using `strtoupper` returns strings with all alphabetic characters converted to uppercase. Whereas `strtolower` returns a string with all alphabetic characters converted to lowercase. There's a caveat to this functionality, however: any characters with accents (circumflex, grave, tilde, umlaut, and all other accents on letters) won't be converted to lowercase. `ucwords` returns a string with the first character of each word capitalized, assuming that character is alphabetic. There's one more that we didn't show you in our code, but would be helpful to have in your back pocket: `ucfirst`, which performs the same as `ucwords` by making the first letter of every word an uppercase letter.

Checking for a String

To detect whether a string is part of another string, use `strstr`, shown in Example 11-13. This function takes two parameters: the string to search through and the string to search for. It is not case sensitive; if you want to use a function that is case sensitive, use `stristr`. Lastly, there is `strops`, which finds the position of every first occurrence of the string you specified.

Example 11-13. Detecting whether a string is contained in another string

```php
<?php
  $password="secretpassword1";

  if (strstr($password,"password")){
    echo('Passwords cannot contain the word "password".');
  }
  else {
    echo ("Password accepted.");
  }
?>
```

Example 11-13 outputs the following:

```
Passwords cannot contain the word "password".
```

Sometimes it's useful to also know the position of a string that matches another string.

Using String Position and Substring to Extract a Portion of a String

We're going to use several string functions together. Let's take the string `testing testing Username:Michele Davis` and retrieve only the name. Example 11-14 shows how several functions can be used together to search and extract a portion of string.

Example 11-14. Using several functions together to extract a portion of a string

```php
<?php
  $test_string="testing testing Username:Michele Davis";
  $position=strpos($test_string,"Username:");

  //add on the length of the Username:
  $start=$position+strlen("Username:");

  echo "$test_string<br>";
  echo "$position<br>";
  echo substr($test_string,$start);
?>
```

Use strpos to search for Username: and return its position in the string with zero being the first position. Use strlen to add on to that position to find where you need to start extracting from the $test_string. To extract the name, use substr, which takes the string as a parameter, returning everything after the $position character in the string. Figure 11-12 shows the end result of your labor.

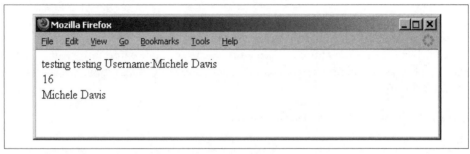

Figure 11-12. Pulling the username out of a larger string

The number 16 in our example is the position of our username. If you look at the code, it says:

```php
    echo "$position<br>";
```

This is where the 16 comes from.

Next up, we'll introduce how to display and work with dates and times.

Date and Time Functions

PHP uses the standard Unix-style timestamp to work with dates. This is simply the number of seconds since January 1, 1970. You get the current timestamp using the time function, shown in Example 11-15.

Example 11-15. A simple echo of the timestamp

```php
<?php
$timestamp= time();
```

Example 11-15. A simple echo of the timestamp (continued)

```
echo $timestamp;
?>
```

This results in Figure 11-13.

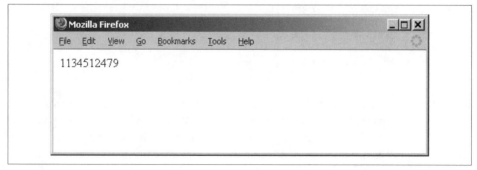

Figure 11-13. A Unix timestamp

```
1134511981
```

This is not exactly the most meaningful representation of the date and time. So instead, you can use the date function to translate the timestamp into a meaningful string. The date function takes a timestamp and a format string, as shown in Example 11-16.

Example 11-16. Making the date and time appear like we expect

```
<?php
$timestamp= time();
echo date("m/d/y G.i:s",$timestamp);
?>
```

This code returns the screen shown in Figure 11-14.

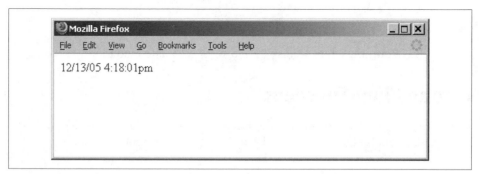

Figure 11-14. An easy-to-read date and time from the date function

Dates and times can be displayed in a variety of formats; these will be discussed next.

Display Formats

Date and times are displayed in a variety of formats. In Example 11-16, we used a date format string of m/d/y G.i:s. Table 11-2 shows other possible components for those formats.

Table 11-2. Time-formatting values

Format	Meaning	Example value
a	am or pm	Am
A	AM or PM	AM
d	Day of the month	01
D	Day or the week	Sun
F	Month name	January
h	Hours in 12-hour format with leading zeros	04
H	Hours in 24-hour format with leading zeros	16
g	Hours in 12-hour format without leading zeros	4
G	Hours in 24-hour format without leading zeros	16
i	Minutes	35
j	Day of the month	2
l	Day of the week as a name	Sunday
L	Leap year (1 for yes, 0 for no)	1
m	Month of the year abbreviated to three characters	Jul
M	Month of the year	July
N	Month of the year as number without leading zeros	7
s	Seconds of the hour	58
S	Suffix for the day	th, nd, st, rd
R	Standardized date format	Thu, 15 Dec 2005 16:49:39–0600
U	Timestamp	1134512479
y	Two-digit year	25
Y	Four-digit year	2025
z	Day of year	234
Z	GMT offset in seconds (Greenwich Mean Time)	−21600 (−6*60*60)

Arithmetic

Adding or subtracting days and hours can be done by adding or subtracting seconds. While this may sound odd, it's not hard. To add two days to a timestamp, add 2*24*60*60 (2 days*24 hours*60 minutes*60 seconds) to the timestamp, as shown in Example 11-17.

Example 11-17. Adding two days to the date

```php
<?php
$timestamp= time();
echo date("m/d/y G.i:s",$timestamp);
$seconds=2*24*60*60;
$timestamp+=$seconds;
echo "<br>new dates is:";
echo date("m/d/y G.i:s",$timestamp);
?>
```

This outputs:

```
12/13/05 16.28:32
new dates is:12/15/05 16.28:32
```

Let's see what else you need to create dates with validation.

Validating Dates

When you receive a user-supplied date, it's good practice, as with any other user-supplied data, to check that it's valid. You can use the checkdate function, shown in Example 11-18, to validate a date. It takes three parameters—the month, day, and year—for a date to validate. If the date is valid, it returns TRUE; otherwise, it returns FALSE.

Example 11-18. Validating two dates

```php
<?php
  echo("Validating: 4/31/2005<br>");
  if (checkdate(4,31,2005)) {
    echo('Date accepted.');
  }
  else {
    echo ('Invalid date.');
  }
  echo("<br>");
  echo("Validating: 5/31/2005<br>");
  if (checkdate(5,31,2005)) {
    echo('Date accepted.');
  }
  else {
    echo ('Invalid date.');
  }
?>
```

As you can tell by our example in Figure 11-15, the 31 April 2005 date was invalid, yet 31 May 2005 was valid. This can happen because of a typo or a user just entering wrong information.

Once you know that you have the valid segments of a date, you can create a timestamp.

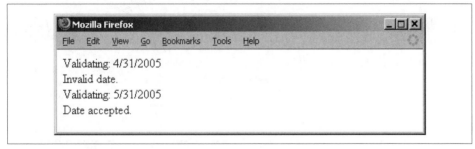

Figure 11-15. Only some months have 31 days

Using mktime to Create a Timestamp

It's fairly easy to get the current time and date using date, but if you're trying to create a date and all you have are the components of the date such as month, day, and year, you'll need to use the mktime function. The mktime function takes these parameters:

- Hour
- Minute
- Second
- Month
- Day of the month
- Year

You can omit some of the parameters when calling mktime, and they'll be filled in from the current time. mktime is a timestamp, which is an integer containing the number of seconds between the Unix Epoch of January 1 1970 00:00:00 GMT and the time specified. You can't omit them out of order though. Example 11-19 checks whether the date is valid, and then creates a timestamp.

Example 11-19. Creating a timestamp from the components of a date

```php
<?php
  echo("Validating: 5/31/2005<br>");
  if (checkdate(5,31,2005)) {
    echo('Date accepted: ');
    $new_date=mktime(18,05,35,5,31,2005);
    echo date("r",$new_date);
  }
  else {
    echo ('Invalid date.');
  }
  echo("<br>");
?>
```

When run, this code produces the screen shown in Figure 11-16.

```
Mozilla Firefox                                           _ □ ×
File   Edit   View   Go   Bookmarks   Tools   Help

Validating: 5/31/2005
Date accepted: Tue, 31 May 2005 18:05:35 -0500
```

Figure 11-16. A timestamp created from its components

Now that we've covered dates and times, it's time to head onto more exciting topics. Note that the number of the year might be a two- or four-digit value, between
0 to 69 mapping to 2000 to 2069 and 70 to 100 to 1970 to 2000. On systems where
time_t is a 32-bit signed integer, which is most common today, the valid range for
the year is somewhere between 1901 and 2038. This limitation is fixed since the
release of PHP 5.1.0.

File Manipulation

There may be times when you don't want to store information in a database and may
want to work directly with a file instead. An example is a logfile that tracks when
your application can't connect to the database. It'd be impossible to keep this information in the database, since it's not available at exactly the time you'd need to write
to it. PHP provides functions for file manipulation that can perform the following:

- Check the existence of a file
- Create a file
- Append to a file
- Rename a file
- Delete a file

We've already discussed the include and require functions for pulling information
directly into a PHP script. At this junction, we'll focus on working with file content.

> Since working directly with files from your PHP code can create secu-
> rity risks, it's a good idea to find solutions to problems that don't use
> files directly if possible; for example, storing information in a data-
> base instead of file. You must be very careful to not allow misuse of
> your PHP programs to either read or destroy the contents of impor-
> tant files either accidentally or as part of an attack.

Functions and Precautions

To check for the existence of a file, use the function file_exists, which takes the name of the file to check for its parameter, as shown in Example 11-20. If the file exists, it returns TRUE; otherwise, it returns FALSE.

Example 11-20. The file_exists.php script checks to see if the file is there

```php
<?php
  $file_name="file_exists.php";

  if(file_exists($file_name)) {
    echo ("$file_name does exist.");
  }
  else {
    echo ("$file_name does not exist.");
  }
?>
```

As you would expect, the file does exist:

```
The file exists.php does exist.
```

PHP provides several functions to tell you about various file attributes. PHP has the ability to read data from, and write data to, files on your system. However, it doesn't just stop there. It comes with a full-featured file-and-directory-manipulation API that allows you to:

- View and modify file attributes
- Read and list directory contents
- Alter file permissions
- Retrieve file contents into a variety of native data structures
- Search for files based on specific patterns

All of this file manipulation through the API is robust and flexible. These characteristics are why we're writing this book. PHP has a lot of great commands, including all the file manipulation ones.

Permissions

Now that you know a file exists, you may think you're done, but you're not. Just because it's there doesn't mean you can read, write, or execute the file. To check for these attributes, use is_readable to check for read access, is_writable to check for write access, and is_executable to check for the ability to execute the file. Each function takes a filename as its parameter. Unless you know the file is in the same directory as your script, you *must* specify a full path to the file in the filename. You can use concatenation to put the path and filename together, as in:

```php
$file_name = $path_to_file . $file_name_only;
```

Let's go ahead and expand the last example to also check for these details. Example 11-21 assumes the script is saved as *permissions.php*.

Example 11-21. Checking the permissions of a file

```php
<?php
  $file_name="permissions.php";

  if(is_readable($file_name)) {
    echo ("The file $file_name is readable.<br>");
  }
  else {
    echo ("The file $file_name is not readable.<br>");
  }
  if(is_writeable($file_name)) {
    echo ("The file $file_name is writeable.<br>");
  }
  else {
    echo ("The file $file_name is not writeable.<br>");
  }
  if(is_executable($file_name)) {
    echo ("The file $file_name is executable.<br>");
  }
  else {
    echo ("The file $file_name is not executable.<br>");
  }
?>
```

The code tells you the many details regarding permissions on the file in Figure 11-17.

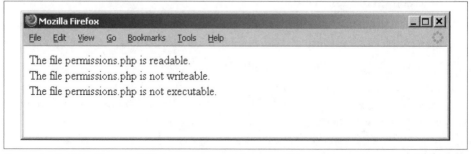

Figure 11-17. This file is readable but not executable or writable to PHP

Creating files

Files can be created with the touch command. This command takes a filename as its parameter. If a file doesn't already exist, it's created as an empty zero length file. If the file does exist, only its modification time is updated.

Deleting files

Files can be deleted with the unlink command. This command, shown in Example 11-22, takes a filename as its parameter. If a file exists and PHP has adequate permission, it'll delete the file. You must be very careful when deleting files not to accidentally delete a file that you still want. If you're using a filename that is derived from user input, you must also be very careful that the filename hasn't been crafted by the user to delete a different file than you intended. Example 11-22 shows how to use file_exists, touch, and unlink.

 Always be careful when deleting files, as you won't be able to retrieve your data!

Example 11-22. Using file_exists, touch, and unlink together

```php
<?php
  $file_name="test.txt";

  if(file_exists($file_name)) {
    echo ("$file_name does exist.<br>");
  }
  else {
    echo ("The file $file_name does not exist.<br>");
    touch($file_name);
  }
  if(file_exists($file_name)) {
    echo ("The file $file_name does exist.<br>");
    unlink($file_name);
  }
  else {
    echo ("The file $file_name does not exist.<br>");
  }
  if(file_exists($file_name)) {
    echo ("The file $file_name does exist.<br>");
  }
  else {
    echo ("The file $file_name does not exist.<br>");
  }
?>
```

The output looks like Figure 11-18.

Moving files

To move a file, you should use the rename function. It renames files or directories and takes the old name and the new name as its parameters. As of PHP 5.0, rename can also be used with some URL wrappers, and context support has been added. Example 11-23 assumes that you've recreated the *test.txt* file.

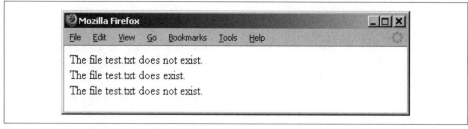

Figure 11-18. The test.txt file is created and removed

Example 11-23. Renaming a file

```php
<?php
  $file_name="test.txt";
  $new_file_name="production.txt";
  $status=rename($file_name,$new_file_name);
  if ($status) {
    echo ("Renamed file.");
  }
?>
```

The file has been renamed, as is demonstrated in the report from Example 11-23.

```
Renamed file.
```

URL Wrappers

Two URL protocols that PHP has built in for use with the filesystem functions include fopen and copy. In addition to these two wrappers, as of PHP 4.3.0, you can write your own wrappers using a PHP script and stream_wrapper_register. The default wrapper is *file://*, used with PHP, and it is the local filesystem. If you specify a relative path, which is one that doesn't begin with /, \, \\, or a Windows drive letter, such as *C://*, the path provided applies against the current working directory. Usually this is where the script resides, unless of course, it's been changed.

With some functions, such as fopen and file_get_contents, include_path can be used to search for relative paths as well. Table 11-3 provides a URL wrapper summary for reference.

Table 11-3. URL wrappers

Attribute	Supported
Restricted by allow_url_fopen	No
Allows reading	Yes
Allows simultaneous reading and writing	Yes
Allows writing	Yes
Allows appending	Yes
Supports stat	Yes

Table 11-3. URL wrappers (continued)

Attribute	Supported
Supports rename	Yes
Supports mkdir	Yes
Supports rmdir	Yes

Uploading Files

It's a fairly common requirement for a PHP-based site to allow file uploads. For example, on a blog site, a user may want to upload an image to go with her post. We'll walk through the steps to upload a file, because you'll be designing a blog in Chapter 16. PHP allows you to do this with the help of forms input.

When you use the file upload form field, the client's browser pulls up a file selection dialog, so you don't have to worry about doing that. The code to include in the file upload field is <input type="file" name="file">. You must also add enctype="multipart/form" to the form tag. This allows a file to be sent with the form submission. Finally, because of the increased size of the form submission, you must use the POST type submission instead of GET.

> The *php.ini* configuration file has a setting that globally limits the size of file upload, called upload_max_filesize. The default value is 2 MB. This helps prevent denial-of-service attacks in which an attacker uploads many huge files to slow your connection or fill up your server's storage.

Once the user selects a file from the HTML form produced by Example 11-24 and clicks Submit, Apache does some of the hard work by handling the upload and placing it into a temporary directory with a temporary filename. It's now up to you to validate the upload and move it if it passes validation.

Example 11-24. Prompting to upload a file

```
<html>
<head></head>
<body>
<form action="<?=$PHP_SELF?>" method="post" enctype="multipart/form-data">
<br><br>
Choose a file to upload:<br>
<input type="file" name="upload_file">
<br>
<input type="submit" name="submit" value="submit">
</form>

</body>
</html>
```

Accessing the file

Access the uploaded file like you access other attribute form submissions, by their name, which in this case is *upload_file*. The difference is that file upload variables are arrays that contain several attributes about the upload.

The attributes in Table 11-4 provide you with enough information to analyze the file.

Table 11-4. File upload attribute

Attribute	Meaning
`$HTTP_POST_FILES['`*upload_file*`']`	The array; replace *upload_file* with the name of your upload file submission variable
`$HTTP_POST_FILES['`*upload_file*`']['name']`	The original name of the file
`$HTTP_POST_FILES['`*upload_file*`']['tmp_name']`	The temporary name assigned during the upload process
`$HTTP_POST_FILES['`*upload_file*`']['type']`	The file's mime type
`$HTTP_POST_FILES['`*upload_file*`']['size']`	The file's size in bytes

Validation

You need to validate the file to ensure that it's not too big or—worse yet—in a file format that isn't allowed, such as a *.zip* file when you allow only *.jpg* files. You validate in this order:

1. Was a file actually sent?
2. Is it too big?
3. Is it the wrong type?

We'll start with the is_uploaded_file function to check that a file was indeed uploaded.

Example 11-25 verifies that the file exists in the temporary directory with the proper temporary name. If it doesn't, stop processing the file and warn the user that he needs to try again.

Example 11-25. Checking for the existence of an uploaded file

```php
<?php

if (!is_uploaded_file($HTTP_POST_FILES['upload_file']['tmp_name'])) {
  $error = "You must upload a file!";
  unlink($HTTP_POST_FILES['upload_file']['tmp_name']);
} else {
  //proceed to process the file
}

?>
```

Now in Example 11-26, we make sure the file isn't too big.

Example 11-26. Checking the file size

```php
<?php
$maxsize=28480;
if ($HTTP_POST_FILES['upload_file']['size'] > $maxfilesize) {
  $error = "Error, file must be less than $maxsize bytes.";
  unlink($HTTP_POST_FILES['upload_file']['tmp_name']);
} else {
  // proceed to process the file.
}
?>
```

To validate the size of a file, assign the maximum allowed file size in bytes to the variable $maxsize. In this case, you are checking for 28,480 bytes. You already have the file size stored in the $HTTP_POST_FILES array, so it's easy to check. If the file is too big, you need to tell the user about the problem and make him upload a different file. You also need to remove the file using the unlink function so that you don't end up with a million files sitting in the temporary directory.

 You might be tempted to validate the type of file by simply looking at its file extension, but this isn't a good idea, since it's trivial to modify the file extension of a file before uploading it.

Next, Example 11-27 checks the file type to make sure it's either a JPEG or a GIF file.

Example 11-27. Checking the file type

```php
<?php

if($HTTP_POST_FILES['upload_file']['type'] != "image/gif" AND
$HTTP_POST_FILES['upload_file']['type'] != "image/pjpeg" AND
$HTTP_POST_FILES['upload_file']['type'] !="image/jpeg") {
  $error = "You may only upload .gif or .jpeg files";
  unlink($HTTP_POST_FILES['upload_file']['tmp_name']);
} else {
   //the file is the correct format
}

?>
```

Use the $HTTP_POST_FILES['file']['type'] variable to compare the mime type against the types expected. This is much harder to alter than the file extension. If you find that the file type doesn't match, warn the user that he'll need to upload a different file and remove the temporary file.

The following line copies the file from the temporary directory into the *uploads* directory using the same filename:

```
copy($HTTP_POST_FILES['upload_file']['tmp_name'],"uploads/".
$HTTP_POST_FILES['upload_file']['name']);
```

Using unlink, let's remove the temporary file:

```
unlink($HTTP_POST_FILES['upload_file']['tmp_name']);
```

To help prevent misuse of the upload processing script, validate that the submit button was pressed. Take a look at the entire script in Example 11-28.

Example 11-28. Processing an uploaded file

```php
<?php
$maxsize=28480; //set the max upload size in bytes
if (!$HTTP_POST_VARS['submit']) {
  //print_r($HTTP_POST_FILES);
  $error=" ";
//this will cause the rest of the processing to be skipped
//and the upload form displays
}
if (!is_uploaded_file($HTTP_POST_FILES['upload_file']['tmp_name']) AND
!isset($error)) {
  $error = "<b>You must upload a file!</b><br><br>";
  unlink($HTTP_POST_FILES['upload_file']['tmp_name']);
}
if ($HTTP_POST_FILES['upload_file']['size'] > $maxsize AND !isset($error)) {
  $error = "<b>Error, file must be less than $maxsize bytes.</b><br><br>";
  unlink($HTTP_POST_FILES['upload_file']['tmp_name']);
}
if($HTTP_POST_FILES['upload_file']['type'] != "image/gif" AND
$HTTP_POST_FILES['upload_file']['type'] != "image/pjpeg" AND
$HTTP_POST_FILES['upload_file']['type'] !="image/jpeg" AND !isset($error)) {
  $error = "<b>You may only upload .gif or .jpeg files.</b><br><br>";
  unlink($HTTP_POST_FILES['upload_file']['tmp_name']);
}
if (!isset($error)) {
copy($HTTP_POST_FILES['upload_file']['tmp_name'],"uploads/".$HTTP_POST_FILES
['upload_file']['name']);
  unlink($HTTP_POST_FILES['upload_file']['tmp_name']);
  print "Thank you for your upload.";
  exit;
}
else
{
  echo ("$error");
}
?>

<html>
<head></head>
<body>
<form action="<?=$PHP_SELF?>" method="post" enctype="multipart/form-data">
```

Example 11-28. Processing an uploaded file (continued)

```
Choose a file to upload:<br>
<input type="file" name="upload_file" size="80">
<br>
<input type="submit" name="submit" value="submit">
</form>
</body>
</html>
```

Each validation checks to see whether a prior step failed; if so, it doesn't continue the validation. When you reach the end of the validation section, you print out the value in the $error variable. If there were no errors, no error message displays and you move the image to its final destination. If you encountered an error, or if this is the first time the script has been called, you display the file upload form.

Figure 11-19 shows what the form looks like.

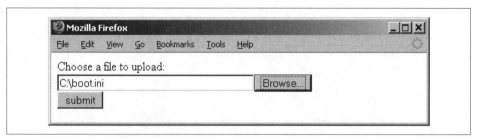

Figure 11-19. The upload form with an invalid file selected

When this file is submitted, you should see an error, shown in Figure 11-20, since it's not a *.jpg* or *.gif* file.

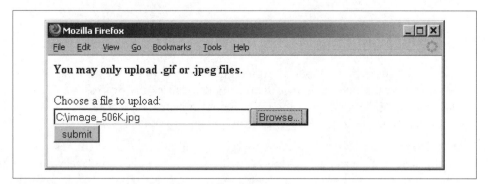

Figure 11-20. The .ini file was caught by the validation

Next, we'll try sending in a 506K image. Remember, the limit is 20K, so this is much larger than what you're allowing. Figure 11-21 shows what happens.

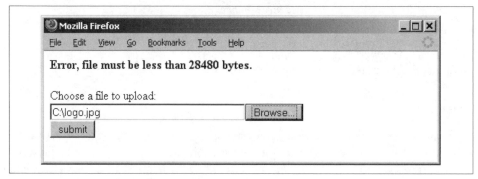

Figure 11-21. We caught the file size error, too

OK, now we'll try a file that meets the validation criteria, to get the happier result shown in Figure 11-22.

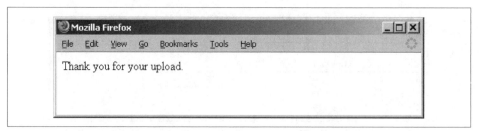

Figure 11-22. A successful upload!

There's now a file called *logo.jpg* in the *uploads* directory on your server. To increase security slightly, you could pick your own filenames instead of using a user-supplied name.

Calling System Calls

A system call is used by an application to request service from the operating system. System calls use machine code instructions, which causes the processor to change modes. Changing the mode gets the OS to perform restricted actions; for example, accessing hardware devices or server space available.

Every OS provides a library that sits between normal programs and the rest of the operating system, such as the Windows API. This library handles low-level details of passing information to the kernel and switching to supervisor mode.

You can use the exec function to call external functions.

> For maximum security, use exec only when PHP code doesn't provide the same functionality.

For example, if you'd like to get information about how much space is available on the server, execute the `df` command, shown in Example 11-29. However, this is assuming you're on a Unix host.

Example 11-29. Executing df and displaying the results

```
<?php
exec("df",$output_lines,$return_value);
echo ("Command returned a value of $return_value.");
echo "</pre>";
foreach ($output_lines as $output) {
  echo "$o";
}
echo "</pre>";
?>
```

For our system, we get the screen in Figure 11-23.

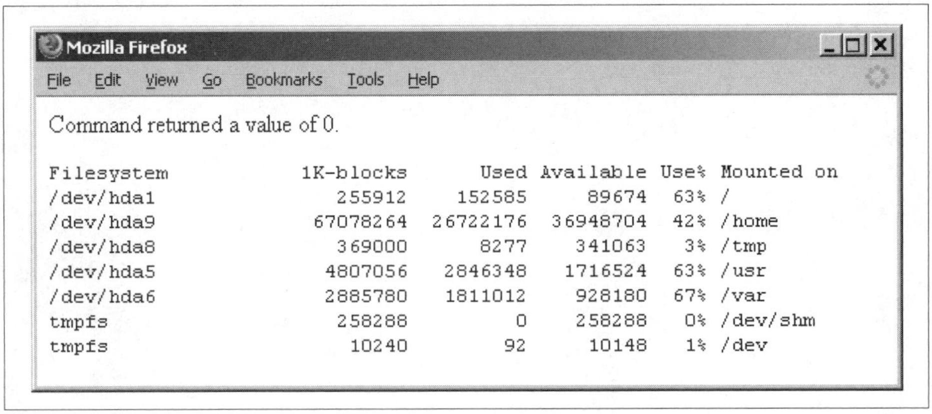
Mozilla Firefox
File Edit View Go Bookmarks Tools Help
Command returned a value of 0.
Filesystem 1K-blocks Used Available Use% Mounted on
/dev/hda1 255912 152585 89674 63% /
/dev/hda9 67078264 26722176 36948704 42% /home
/dev/hda8 369000 8277 341063 3% /tmp
/dev/hda5 4807056 2846348 1716524 63% /usr
/dev/hda6 2885780 1811012 928180 67% /var
tmpfs 258288 0 258288 0% /dev/shm
tmpfs 10240 92 10148 1% /dev

Figure 11-23. A synopsis of how full the hard disk is, from PHP

> Use extreme caution! Remember that while linking other commands in this chapter, you should avoid passing user input to exec because there's a substantial risk for misuse.

We're now going to discuss modifying objects in MySQL and working with data using PHP.

Chapter 11 Questions

Question 11-1. What's the difference between printf() and sprint()?

Question 11-2. Check that the date 1/31/2045 is valid.

Question 11-3. Display the day of the week for 1/31/2045.

Question 11-4. Rename the file *upload.tmp* to *sample.jpg*.

See the Appendix for the answers to these questions.

Modifying MySQL Objects and PHP Data

This chapter extends what you learned in Chapter 11 to show you how to perform more complicated database tasks from PHP. We'll learn how to create and modify both data and database objects from PHP. We'll go over a framework for dynamically creating links to expand on data from a database query. In fact, after you learn about sessions in the next chapter, you'll have everything you need to create full-fledged applications.

Changing Database Objects from PHP

The SQL query string remains the common tool for giving database commands. We can just as easily create and modify database objects with standard SQL that is called the same way we execute queries. We'll begin with creating a table.

Creating a Table

We've previously created the books and authors tables but we haven't created the purchases table. We'll create one using the PHP in Example 12-1.

Example 12-1. Creating a table from a PHP page in create_table.php

```php
<?php
include('db_login.php');
require_once( 'DB.php' );
$connection = DB::connect( "mysql://$db_username:$db_password@$db_host/
$db_database");
if (!$connection)
{
  die ("Could not connect to the database: <br>". DB::errorMessage());
};
$query = '
CREATE TABLE `purchases` (
  `purchase_id` int(11) NOT NULL auto_increment,
  `user_id` varchar(10) NOT NULL,
```

```
  `title_id` int(11) NOT NULL,
  `purchased` timestamp NOT NULL,
  PRIMARY KEY (`purchase_id`)
)
';
echo ("Table created successfully!");
$result = $connection->query($query);
if (DB::isError($result))
{
  die ("Could not query the database: <br>". $query. " ".DB::errorMessage($result));
}
$connection->disconnect();
?>
```

Example 12-1 has the same create statement bolded that you'd use directly from the command line. The statement is assigned to the $query variable as a string. When query is executed, you no longer get a result set. Instead, the table is created. We see this as the result:

```
Table created successfully!
```

Figure 12-1 shows the describe (desc) command for the table from the mysql command-line client.

![Screenshot of mysql command-line client showing the desc purchases command output with fields purchase_id, user_id, title_id, and purchased.]

Figure 12-1. Our purchases table defined from a PHP script appears everywhere

You could just as easily have substituted another database command.

In general, commands to modify databases and tables should be kept out of your PHP code to reduce the risk of a malicious user exploiting them or plain old programming mistakes that could wipe out a lot of data. We discuss them to illustrate what can be done from PHP. The only time you're likely to use these commands directly in PHP code is if you're writing a utility for web-based administration of MySQL databases such as phpMyAdmin.

If you really feel the need to use modification commands, place them in a portion of your site that is either password-protected at the Apache web server level or access-protected through your PHP code. We'll discuss restricting access to pages and logging in users in Chapter 13. With that caution in place, we'll discuss dropping tables next.

Dropping a Table

Example 12-2 drops the table you just created.

Example 12-2. Dropping the purchases table in drop.php

```php
<?php
require_once('db_login.php');
require_once('DB.php');
$connection = DB::connect("mysql://$db_username:$db_password@$db_host/$db_database");
if (DB::isError($connection)){
die ("Could not connect to the database: <br />". DB::errorMessage($connection));
}
$query = "DROP TABLE `purchases`";
$result = $connection->query($query);
if (DB::isError($result)){
die("Could not query the database: <br />". $query." ".DB::errorMessage($result));
}
echo "Table dropped successfully!";
$connection->disconnect();
?>
```

Example 12-2 returns:

```
Table dropped successfully!
```

That worked great, but you're going to need the purchases table, so let's recreate the table by calling the *create_table.php* code in Example 12-1.

Errors Happen

To make sure you handle an error properly—such as a typo in the create statement or, in this case, trying to create a table that already exists—execute the *create_table. php* script again. This produces the error in Figure 12-2.

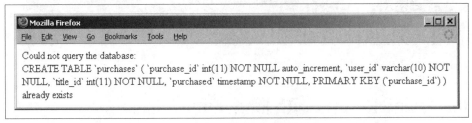

Figure 12-2. Attempting to create an existing table generates this error

Next, you'll add data to an existing table based on input from the user.

Manipulating Table Data

Since you've practiced executing a few SQL commands that manipulate database objects, you're ready to work with the data in your tables.

Adding Data

Naturally, you'll need to add rows to your tables. To add a purchase to your new purchases table, you'll use an INSERT statement in your query. Example 12-3 shows how this is done.

Example 12-3. Using a predefined INSERT statement in insert.php

```php
<?php
require_once('db_login.php');
require_once('DB.php');
$connection = DB::connect("mysql://$db_username:$db_password@$db_host/$db_database");
if (DB::isError($connection)){
die ("Could not connect to the database: <br />". DB::errorMessage($connection));
}
$query = "INSERT INTO `purchases` VALUES (NULL,'mdavis',2,NULL)";
$result = $connection->query($query);
if (DB::isError($result)){
die("Could not query the database: <br />". $query." ".DB::errorMessage($result));
}
echo "Inserted successfully!";
$connection->disconnect();
?>
```

When you call up *insert.php*, in your browser, you get:

```
Inserted successfully!
```

Figure 12-3 shows that the new row made it to the database by selecting all rows from purchases.

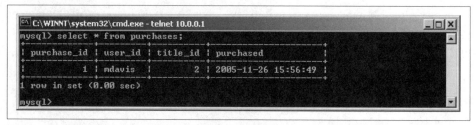

Figure 12-3. Validating that our new row is in the database

Displaying Results with Embedded Links

You may want to give your web user the ability to click on a hyperlink to launch an action that relates to the current row in the results from a query. You do this by adding URL links to the results of a query when they display on the screen. The links contain a unique identifier to the row and the script that handles the action.

The PHP script that is the target of the link typically queries the database based on the unique identifier that was passed to it. The types of action you can do range from

---

adding or deleting a row to expanding on details from a related table, such as authors for book titles.

In Example 12-4, let's display the list of titles with hyperlinks to purchase the titles.

Example 12-4. Using embedded links to provide a purchase button in pear_purchase_example.php

```php
<?php
require_once('db_login.php');
require_once('DB.php');
$connection = DB::connect("mysql://$db_username:$db_password@$db_host/$db_database");
if (DB::isError($connection)){
die ("Could not connect to the database: <br />". DB::errorMessage($connection));
}
$query = "SELECT * FROM `books`";
$result = $connection->query($query);
if (DB::isError($result)){
die("Could not query the database: <br />". $query." ".DB::errorMessage($result));
}
echo '<table border="1">';
echo "<tr><th>Title</th><th>Pages</th><th>Buy</th></tr>";
while ($result_row = $result->fetchRow(DB_FETCHMODE_ASSOC)) {
echo "<tr><td>";
echo $result_row["title"] . '</td><td>';
echo $result_row["pages"] . '</td><td>';
echo '<a href="purchase.php?title_id='.$result_row["title_id"].'">Click
to purchase</a></td></tr>';
}
echo "</table>";
$connection->disconnect();
?>
```

In Example 12-4, you modify the format of the last bolded table cell to build a hyperlink for purchasing the book. The target of that link is the file *purchase.php*, which is defined in Example 12-5. You send it a parameter called title_id, which is the primary key from the titles table. This unique ID specifies which book the user wants to purchase, and is used as a link in the table shown in Figure 12-4.

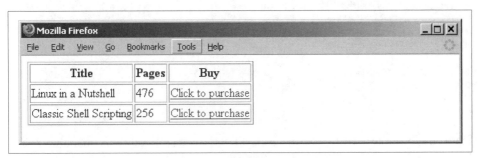

Figure 12-4. Users can click the purchase link to add the purchase to the purchases table

Next, you'll define the script that handles the purchase action in Example 12-5.

Example 12-5. The file purchase.php processes the user action based on the title_id parameter

```
1 <?php
2 require_once('db_login.php');
3 require_once('DB.php');
4 $connection = DB::connect("mysql://$db_username:$db_password@$db_host/$db_database");
5 if (DB::isError($connection)){
6 die ("Could not connect to the database: <br />". DB::errorMessage($connection));
7 }
8 $title_id = $_GET["title_id"];
9 $user_id = 'mdavis';
10 $query = "INSERT INTO `purchases` VALUES (NULL,'$user_id',$title_id,NULL)";
11 $result = $connection->query($query);
12 if (DB::isError($result)){
13 die("Could not query the database: <br />". $query." ".DB::errorMessage($result));
14 }
15 ?>
16 <html>
17 <head>
18 <title>Thanks for your purchase!</title>
19 <meta http-equiv="refresh" content="4; url=pear_purchase_example.php">
20 </head>
21 <body>
22 Thanks for your purchase!<br />
23 <?php
24
25 $query = "SELECT * FROM purchases NATURAL JOIN books NATURAL JOIN authors";
26 $result = $connection->query($query);
27 if (DB::isError($result)){
28 die("Could not query the database: <br />". $query." ".DB::errorMessage($result));
29 }
30 echo '<table border="1">';
31 echo "<tr><th>User</th><th>Title</th><th>Pages</th>";
32 echo "<th>Author</th><th>Purchased</th></tr>";
33 while ($result_row = $result->fetchRow(DB_FETCHMODE_ASSOC)) {
34 echo "<tr><td>";
35 echo $result_row["user_id"] . '</td><td>';
36 echo $result_row["title"] . '</td><td>';
37 echo $result_row["pages"] . '</td><td>';
38 echo $result_row["author"] . "</td><td>";
39 echo $result_row["purchased"] . "</td></tr>";
40 }
41 echo "</table>";
42
43 $connection->disconnect();
44 ?>
45 </body>
46 </html>
```

Since this example is fairly lengthy, we'll discuss the major additions on a line-by-line basis.

- Line 8 takes the parameter from the calling script and assigns it to a local variable called $title_id, which we'll reference in the insert statement.

- Line 9 sets a `$user_id` variable to `mdavis`. Ideally, the username wouldn't be hardcoded. In the next chapter, you'll learn about logging users into a session that holds their identity.
- Line 10 sets up the query with the `INSERT` statement using the user-supplied values.
- Line 19 uses a META tag to redirect users back to the page from which they came after briefly displaying a message that their purchases (that you processed as an `INSERT` to the database) were successful. The syntax for redirecting to another page after a delay is:

```
<meta http-equiv="refresh" content="seconds_before_refreshing; url=url_to_
redirect_to">
```

- The `META` statement should be placed in the `<head>` section of the HTML.
- Line 25 defines a new query to select all purchases. Subsequent lines display the results in an HTML table.

The end result is that a new purchase is added to the `purchases` table, and the user briefly sees the contents of the purchases table before returning to the previous page.

Figure 12-5 shows the purchase record we created in Example 12-3, plus the newly created entry from Example 12-4.

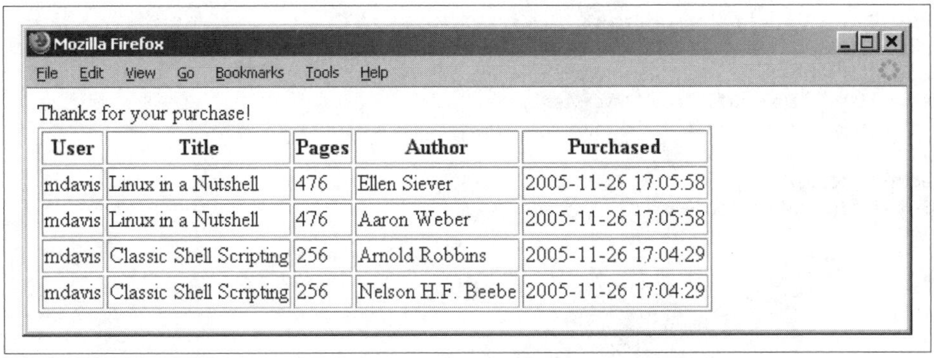

User	Title	Pages	Author	Purchased
mdavis	Linux in a Nutshell	476	Ellen Siever	2005-11-26 17:05:58
mdavis	Linux in a Nutshell	476	Aaron Weber	2005-11-26 17:05:58
mdavis	Classic Shell Scripting	256	Arnold Robbins	2005-11-26 17:04:29
mdavis	Classic Shell Scripting	256	Nelson H.F. Beebe	2005-11-26 17:04:29

Figure 12-5. After clicking "Click to purchase" for "Linux in a Nutshell"

With the click of a link, you can add customized data to your table. Let's integrate form submission and insert data.

Presenting a Form to Add and Process in One File

We're building a form that allows a web user to add a title to the `books` table. Example 12-6 is a slightly longer example, because we display and process the form in one file, but it should look familiar to you since we're simply combining several steps that we've done separately before.

Example 12-6. Using input from a form to add a title

```php
<?php
// Define a function to perform the database insert and display the titles
function insert_db($title, $pages){
require_once('db_login.php');
require_once('DB.php');
$connection = DB::connect("mysql://$db_username:$db_password@$db_host/$db_database");
if (DB::isError($connection)){
die ("Could not connect to the database: <br />". DB::errorMessage($connection));
}
// The query includes the form sumbission values that were passed to the function
$query = "INSERT INTO `books` VALUES (NULL,'$title','$pages')";
$result = $connection->query($query);
if (DB::isError($result)){
die("Could not query the database: <br />". $query." ".DB::errorMessage($result));
}
echo "Inserted OK.<br />";
// Display the table
$query = "SELECT * FROM `books`";
$result = $connection->query($query);
if (DB::isError($result)){
die("Could not query the database: <br />". $query." ".DB::errorMessage($result));
}
echo '<table border="1">';
echo "<tr><th>Title</th><th>Pages</th></tr>";
while ($result_row = $result->fetchRow(DB_FETCHMODE_ASSOC)) {
echo "<tr><td>";
echo $result_row["title"] . '</td><td>';
echo $result_row["pages"] . '</td></tr>';
}
echo "</table>";
$connection->disconnect();
}

?>
<html>
<head>
<title>Inserting From a Form</title>
</head>
<body>
<?php
// Retrieve the variable from the form submission
$title = $_GET["title"];
$pages = $_GET["pages"];
if (($title != NULL ) && ($pages != NULL)){
insert_db($title,$pages);
}
else {
// Display the form
echo '
<h1>Enter a new title:</h1>
<form action="'.$_SERVER["PHP_SELF"].'" method="GET">
<label>
```

Example 12-6. Using input from a form to add a title (continued)

```
Title:
<input type="text" name="title" id="title" />
</label>
<label>
Pages:
<input type="text" name="pages" id="pages" />
</label>
<input type="submit" value="Go!" />
</form>';
}
?>
</body>
</html>
```

Example 12-6 begins by displaying a form like Figure 12-6, using the code in the body of the file if the $title and $pages values do not have both values set.

Figure 12-6. This is how the form looks with some sample data in the field

Once the user enters values into both fields and clicks the Go! button, the same script handles the form submission processing. Since values exist for the two fields, the insert_db function is called with those values. The values are placed into the query string enclosed by single quotes (' '):

```
$query = "INSERT INTO 'books' VALUES (NULL,'$title','$pages')";
```

This query is then executed like any other query. Finally, the function queries the books table and displays the results in an HTML table.

Figure 12-7 shows what happens after clicking the Go! button with the sample data above.

You must take several precautions when working with strings submitted from a form that will be processed by the database.

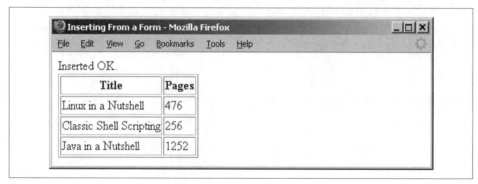

Figure 12-7. The results page shows the new entry

SQL Injection

Specifically, you need to be on guard for a tactic called SQL injection. *SQL injection* is when a malicious user enters another SQL query into a field such as 1,1);drop table users;. When this query is added to a query like this:

```
$query = "INSERT INTO 'books' VALUES (NULL,$title,$pages)";
```

here's what could happen:

```
$query = "INSERT INTO 'books' VALUES (NULL,1,1);drop table users; ,$pages)";
```

PHP and MySQL work together to thwart this kind of attack. What happens is the MySQL query command allows only one statement per query. So attempting to start a new query after the first one has already been started generates an error. Additionally, PHP uses a system by default called *magic quotes* with user input. Magic quotes automatically escape any special characters with a backslash (\), including single and double quotes.

Example 12-7 shows how to test whether magic quotes are enabled on your installation of PHP.

Example 12-7. Checking for magic quotes

```php
<?php
if (get_magic_quotes_gpc()) {
echo "Magic quotes are enabled.";
} else {
echo "Magic quotes are disabled.";
}
?>
```

The script should return:

```
Magic quotes are enabled.
```

Because the PEAR DB abstraction layer is being used, MySQL-specific escaping should not be used simultaneously. Use the PEAR escapeSimple($string) function to do your escaping with PEAR code.

If magic quotes are off, you can use the add_slashes function to accomplish the same thing with your input. Nonetheless, you should look out for these errors, since other databases may allow more than one statement per query. Be skeptical of user input, or you could end up with a compromised database.

Cross-Site Scripting Attacks

One last gotcha to look out for when using data from user input is the risk of *cross-site scripting* attacks. These attacks work slightly differently than SQL injection. They don't compromise the data on your server, but instead can lead to a user's browser giving out sensitive data to a third party because the browser thinks the command came from your trusted site. To guard against these attacks, you should pass any strings that came from a user through the htmlentities function. It takes the format:

```
htmlentities(string_to_clean)
```

For example:

```
print "The title of the book is: " .
htmlentities($_POST['title']);
```

Here's an example of what htmlentities does to the string:

```
<?php
$sample = "A sample is <i>italics</i>";
echo htmlentities($sample);
?>
```

When executed, this returns:

```
A sample is &lt;i&gt;italics&lt;/i&gt;
```

Essentially, you're guarding against the same problem as SQL injection, but the code that's vulnerable is the HTML. The special function HTML characters such as less than (<) and greater than (>) are escaped, preventing hostile HTML code from working when displayed from your site.

Here's a script to display the title table with the htmlentities functionality added:

```
<?php
require_once('db_login.php');
require_once('DB.php');
$connection = DB::connect("mysql://$db_username:$db_password@$db_host/$db_database");
if (DB::isError($connection)){
die ("Could not connect to the database: <br />". DB::errorMessage($connection));
}
// Dislplay the table
$query = "SELECT * FROM `books`";
$result = $connection->query($query);
if (DB::isError($result)){
die("Could not query the database: <br />".$query." ".DB::errorMessage($result));
}
echo '<table border="1">';
echo "<tr><th>Title</th><th>Pages</th></tr>";
```

```
while ($result_row = $result->fetchRow(DB_FETCHMODE_ASSOC)) {
echo "<tr><td>";
echo htmlentities($result_row["title"]) . '</td><td>';
echo htmlentities($result_row["pages"]) . '</td></tr>';
}
echo "</table>";
$connection->disconnect();
?>
```

Figure 12-8 shows that htmlentities didn't change the look of your table.

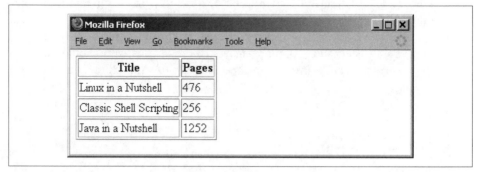

Figure 12-8. No change is made to the look of your table

You can be assured that you've prevented any malicious HTML that may have been entered by a user from confusing another user's browser.

Updating Data

Since you've been inputting table data, you can change existing records. You'll probably only do this if there are errors in your data, or in the instance that user data has changed and needs to be updated in the database. Updates are handled as shown in Example 12-8.

Example 12-8. Updating a field

```
<?php
require_once('db_login.php');
require_once('DB.php');
$connection = DB::connect("mysql://$db_username:$db_password@$db_host/$db_database");
if (DB::isError($connection)){
die ("Could not connect to the database: <br />". DB::errorMessage($connection));
}
$query = "UPDATE `books` SET `pages`=558 WHERE `title_id`=2";
$result = $connection->query($query);
if (DB::isError($result)){
die("Could not query the database: <br />".$query." ".DB::errorMessage($result));
}
echo "Updated successfully!";
$connection->disconnect();
?>
```

If you have multiple columns to edit in one record at a single time, you'd separate the code with a comma (,). Again, you could have used a dynamic value such as a form input in the WHERE clause. If you use a WHERE clause, you'd have to specify what rows the update affects; otherwise, the change applies to every row.

Updates and deletions are two of most important reasons to use a primary key. The primary key number, which never should change, can be a point of reference in the WHERE clause. In Figure 12-9, you see the new value in the books table from the mysql client.

```
C:\WINNT\system32\cmd.exe - telnet 10.0.0.1
4 rows in set (0.00 sec)

mysql> select * from books where title_id =2;
+----------+------------------------+-------+
| title_id | title                  | pages |
+----------+------------------------+-------+
|        2 | Classic Shell Scripting |   558 |
+----------+------------------------+-------+
1 row in set (0.00 sec)

mysql>
```

Figure 12-9. The new page count of 558 appears in the table

Since updates and deletions are so important, you'll perform a delete operation. As a precaution against accidentally updating too many rows, apply a limit clause with your update.

 Never update a primary key column. This value should never change. If you change a primary key in one table, it could affect the data in another table.

Deleting Data

Use the DELETE command to completely remove existing data from the database. Remember though, once you've deleted data, it can no longer be retrieved; it is permanently gone. Make sure you have appropriate checks and balances in place for the deletion of existing data. Use the WHERE command so that you don't delete data from all the rows in your table.

The command TRUNCATE TABLE `tablename` deletes an entire table, which means the table structure and the records, and then recreates the structure. Technically, your final result is the same, but our example is a safer way to perform a delete. The advantage of TRUNCATE is that it's much faster for deleting large tables.

 While it's great to be able to DROP and TRUNCATE tables from PHP, you probably don't want to leave this capability anywhere on your web site for an average user.

There is a way to safeguard against erroneous selections by running the query using SELECT instead of DELETE. Deleting data from a MySQL database through PHP works similarly to any of the other queries. If you do this, query results display which row or rows are going to be affected by your deletion. Let's modify the example to provide a link that deletes the current row. In Example 12-9, you'll delete a purchase.

Example 12-9. Providing a link to delete a purchase in deletion_link.php

```php
<?php
require_once('db_login.php');
require_once('DB.php');
$connection = DB::connect("mysql://$db_username:$db_password@$db_host/$db_database");
if (DB::isError($connection)){
die ("Could not connect to the database: <br />". DB::errorMessage($connection));
}
$query = "SELECT * FROM `purchases` NATURAL JOIN `books`";
$result = $connection->query($query);
if (DB::isError($result)){
die("Could not query the database: <br />".$query." ".DB::errorMessage($result));
}
echo '<table border="1">';
echo "<tr><th>User</th><th>Title</th><th>Purchased</th><th>Remove</th></tr>";
while ($result_row = $result->fetchRow(DB_FETCHMODE_ASSOC)) {
echo "<tr><td>";
echo $result_row["user_id"] . '</td><td>';
echo $result_row["title"] . '</td><td>';
echo $result_row["purchased"] . '</td><td>';
echo '<a href="delete.php?purchase_id='.$result_row["purchase_id"].'">Click to
remove from purchases</a></td></tr>';
}
echo '</table>';
$connection->disconnect();
?>
```

In Example 12-9, you're using the SELECT command so that data won't be erroneously deleted when the query is run. The results of this query display which row(s) are affected by the deletion. The script that handles the actual deletion is shown in Example 12-10.

Example 12-10. The delete.php code for performing a delete

```php
<?php
require_once('db_login.php');
require_once('DB.php');
$connection = DB::connect("mysql://$db_username:$db_password@$db_host/$db_database");
if (DB::isError($connection)){
die ("Could not connect to the database: <br />". DB::errorMessage($connection));
}
$purchase_id = $_GET["purchase_id"];
$query = "DELETE FROM `purchases` WHERE `purchase_id`=$purchase_id";
$result = $connection->query($query);
if (DB::isError($result)){
```

Example 12-10. The delete.php code for performing a delete (continued)

```
die("Could not query the database: <br />".$query." ".DB::errorMessage($result));
}
?>
<html>
<head>
<title>Item deleted!</title>
<meta http-equiv="refresh" content="4; url=deletion_link.php">
</head>
<body>
Item deleted!<br />
<?php
$query = "SELECT * FROM `purchases` NATURAL JOIN `books` NATURAL JOIN `authors`";
$result = $connection->query($query);
if (DB::isError($result)){
die("Could not query the database: <br />".$query." ".DB::errorMessage($result));
}
echo '<table border="1">';
echo "<tr><th>User</th><th>Title</th><th>Pages</th>";
echo "<th>Author</th><th>Purchased</th></tr>";
while ($result_row = $result->fetchRow(DB_FETCHMODE_ASSOC)) {
echo "<tr><td>";
echo $result_row["user_id"] . '</td><td>';
echo $result_row["title"] . '</td><td>';
echo $result_row["pages"] . '</td><td>';
echo $result_row["author"] . "</td><td>";
echo $result_row["purchased"] . "</td></tr>";
}
echo "</table>";
$connection->disconnect();
?>
</body>
</html>
```

Figure 12-10 shows how the browser window looks after going to *deletion_link.php*.

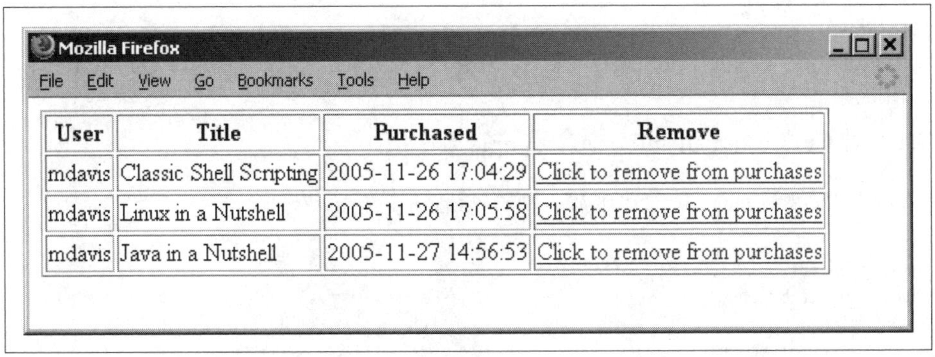

Figure 12-10. Each purchase has a link for its removal

Click on the last removal link to see Figure 12-11.

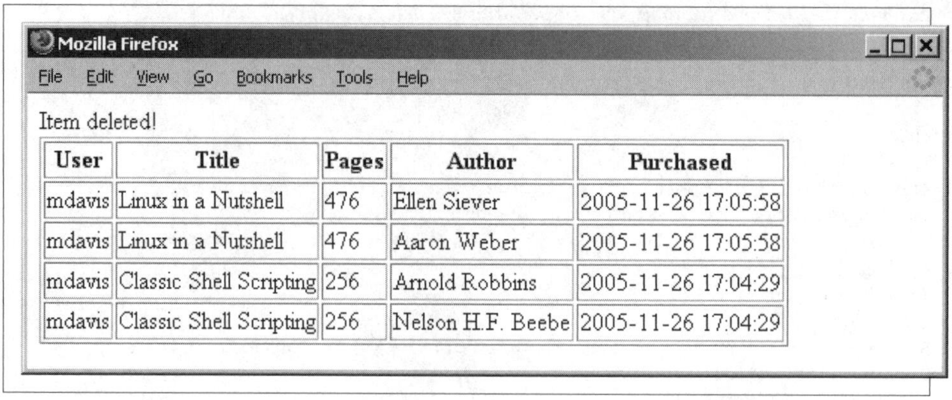

Figure 12-11. A successful delete, and the book is removed from the purchases

The purchase is no longer in the table. It's a good idea to confirm with the user before completing a deletion. This is usually handled by an intermediate screen that summarizes what's going to be deleted and requires the user to click a button that confirms the deletion.

Generating Unique Identifiers

In our examples so far, we always let MySQL pick the primary key when doing inserts by sending NULL in the key field. The downside of this is that you don't know what key value MySQL assigned your row. If you add a book and then an author, how do you know what the foreign key value is for the book to add in the authors table? Well, you can use the mysql_insert_id command to get the last auto-assigned primary key from an AUTO_INCREMENT column.

Its syntax is:

```
int mysql_insert_id ( [resource link_identifier] )
```

If the last query generated an auto-increment, that value is returned. Zero is returned if the last query didn't generate a key. FALSE is returned if there isn't a valid database connection.

We'll add a title and an author in Example 12-11.

Example 12-11. Using mysql_insert_id to link up an author to a title

```php
<?php
require_once('db_login.php');
require_once('DB.php');
$connection = DB::connect("mysql://$db_username:$db_password@$db_host/$db_database");
if (DB::isError($connection)){
die ("Could not connect to the database: <br />". DB::errorMessage($connection));
}
$query = "INSERT INTO `books` VALUES (NULL,'Python in a Nutshell',600)";
$result = $connection->query($query);
```

Example 12-11. Using mysql_insert_id to link up an author to a title (continued)

```
if (DB::isError($result)){
die("Could not query the database: <br />".$query." ".DB::errorMessage($result));
}
$last_value = mysql_insert_id();
echo "The id that was created is: $last_value<br />";
$query = "INSERT INTO `authors` VALUES (NULL,$last_value,'Alex Martelli')";
$result = $connection->query($query);
if (DB::isError($result)){
die("Could not query the database: <br />".$query." ".DB::errorMessage($result));
}
echo "Inserted successfully!";
$connection->disconnect();
?>
```

Execute mysql_insert_id directly after the INSERT statement to minimize the possibility of another INSERT statement being executed before you read the value. In a multitasking environment, you have to be aware that other processes or users may also be using the data to execute queries. Figure 12-12 shows the output of the PHP code.

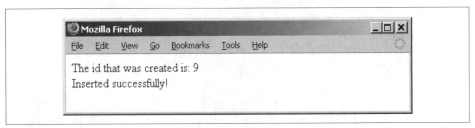

Figure 12-12. We can see that the book was assigned a key value of 9

Let's check Figure 12-13 to make sure that the values were saved correctly in the database by selecting from both tables in the mysql command-line client.

Title	Pages	Authors
Linux in a Nutshell	476	Ellen Siever, Aaron Weber
Classic Shell Scripting	558	Arnold Robbins, Nelson H.F. Beebe
Java in a Nutshell	1252	none
Python in a Nutshell	600	Alex Martelli

Figure 12-13. Our new entries for the book and author are present

The title_id value of 9 was correctly added to the authors table.

Performing a Subquery

Sometimes you'll want to display the data in a linked table as a list instead of repeating all of the values from the joined table. For example, when listing books, it would look nicer to list authors in one cell of your table. Example 12-12 uses a second query and a loop to accomplish this.

Example 12-12. Displaying the authors in a list

```php
<?php
require_once('db_login.php');
require_once('DB.php');
$connection = DB::connect("mysql://$db_username:$db_password@$db_host/$db_database");
if (DB::isError($connection)){
die ("Could not connect to the database: <br />". DB::errorMessage($connection));
}
// Display the table
$query = "SELECT * FROM `books`";
$result = $connection->query($query);
if (DB::isError($result)){
die("Could not query the database: <br />".$query." ".DB::errorMessage($result));
}
echo '<table border="1">';
echo "<tr><th>Title</th><th>Pages</th><th>Authors</th></tr>";
while ($result_row = $result->fetchRow(DB_FETCHMODE_ASSOC)) {
echo "<tr><td>";
echo htmlentities($result_row["title"]) . '</td><td>';
echo htmlentities($result_row["pages"]) . '</td><td>';
$author_query = "SELECT * FROM `authors` WHERE `title_id`=".$result_row["title_id"];
$author_result = $connection->query($author_query);
if (DB::isError($author_result)){
die("Could not query the database: <br />".$author_query."
".DB::errorMessage($author_result));
}
$author_count = $author_result->numRows();
if (0 == $author_count) {
echo 'none';
}
$counter = 0;
while ($author_result_row = $author_result->fetchRow(DB_FETCHMODE_ASSOC)) {
$counter++;
echo htmlentities($author_result_row["author"]);
if ($counter != $author_count) {
echo ', ';
}
}
echo '</td></tr>';
}
echo '</table>';
$connection->disconnect();
?>
```

Define a second query and result set for the authors. For each title, a query of the authors table can retrieve a variable number of authors. Count the result set using the numRows function. To avoid an empty cell, if there were no authors, you display None. Use the $author_count variable again while looping so as not to put a comma after the last author name in the list. The result is this nicer format, shown in Figure 12-14.

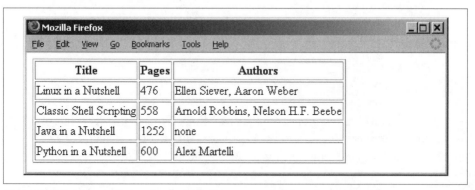

Figure 12-14. Authors displayed on a single line

In Chapter 13, we'll talk about storing information in sessions and how to limit access to pages.

Chapter 12 Questions

Question 12-1. Add another column to the books table called published_date that stores a date in a PHP page.

Question 12-2. What are the two major categories of security risks when working with user input?

Question 12-3. Which function tells you whether the PHP interpreter has magic quotes turned on?

Question 12-4. Which function prevents cross-site scripting attacks when used before displaying user-supplied input?

See the Appendix for the answers to these questions.

Cookies, Sessions, and Access Control

As your applications grow more complex, you'll need to keep better track of which user your program is working with. Cookies, sessions, and access control all provide an opportunity to interact more appropriately with specific users.

Cookies

You can track certain user details like the number of visits, names, or the date of the last visit using *cookies*, which are small bits of text stored on the client that have been available since Netscape 1.0. The client machine stores this information and sends it to the web server whenever there is a request. Cookies data is sent along with the HTTP headers.

After the first visit to a web site, the browser returns a copy of the cookie to the server each time it connects. For security reasons, cookies can be read only from the domain that created them. Additionally, cookies have an expiration date after which they're deleted. The maximum size of data that a cookie can hold is 4 KB.

Cookies are different from sessions, because cookies are stored on the client's disk, whereas a session stores the bulk of its data on the server. Sessions are basically like tokens, which are generated at authentication. This means that a session is available as long as the browser is opened. Sessions actually use a single cookie by default to track their token or session identifier.

Figure 13-1 illustrates where cookies are stored when a web browser requests pages; in this example, *http://example.com/set.php* followed by *http://example.com/read.php*. The actual key storage resides on the client's browser after the first page is requested. When the client requests the second page, it also sends the cookie data to the server.

Sessions are popularly used, as there's a chance of your cookies getting blocked if the user's browser security setting is high. Sessions provide a fall back of passing the session identifier from page to page if cookies are disabled.

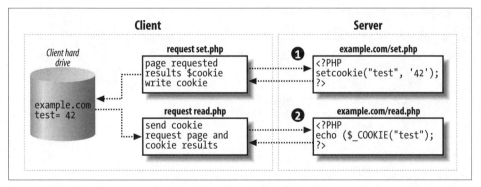

Figure 13-1. Client browser and server interaction with cookies

When you issue _session_start, it generates a session ID and places that on the client side in a cookie. There are ways to avoid this, such as using the tag rewrite.

Mostly the server uses the cookie to remember the user and maintain the illusion of a session that spans multiple pages. Everything you could possibly want to know about cookies can be found at *http://www.w3.org/Security/Faq/wwwsf2.html#CLT-Q10*.

Setting a Cookie

PHP provides an easy way to set a cookie: the function setcookie.

Because cookies are generated as part of HTML page headers, it's important that you call setcookie before sending any other output.

The function takes a name for the cookie as a parameter. You can optionally specify other details; for example:

    setcookie (name , value , expire , path, domain , secure)

Table 13-1 lists the parameter values and their meanings for setcookie.

Table 13-1. setcookie parameters

Parameter	Meaning	Example value
name	The name that the cookie will use for storage and retrieval.	username
value	The value stored in the cookie.	michele
expire	A Unix timestamp when the cookie expires. If not set, the cookie expires when the user closes her browser.	Time()+60*60*24*7 tells the cookie to expire in a week
path	The URL paths on the site that can access the cookie. Defaults to /, which means all directories can access the cookie.	/testing

Table 13-1. setcookie parameters (continued)

Parameter	Meaning	Example value
domain	Similar to a path, except access can be limited to a subdomain of a site.	To limit access to only *www* on site *example.com* use www.example.com. To grant access to all domains, use .example.com.
secure	If set to 1, cookies are sent only over a secure HTTPS connection. HTTPS connections use encryption between the client and the browser to secure data.	0 for secure and 1 for insecure, which is the default.

Example 13-1 shows how to create a cookie with the name username and the value michele.

Example 13-1. Creating a cookie

```php
<?php
//remember that setcookie must come before any other line that generates output
setcookie("username","michele");
echo 'Cookie created.';
?>
```

The cookie was set, but you won't be able to read it until the client reloads the page or browses to another page.

Accessing a Cookie

Cookies can be accessed one of two ways. They're accessible from the $_COOKIE environmental variable with the syntax $_COOKIE['*cookiename*'], as demonstrated in Example 13-2.

Example 13-2. Viewing the username cookie

```php
<?php
if (!isset($_COOKIE['username']))
{
  echo ("Opps, the cookie isn't set!");
}
else
{
  echo ("The stored username is ". $_COOKIE['username'] . ".");
}
?>
```

This code displays with the stored username:

```
The stored username is michele.
```

You can also see all cookies by accessing the super global variable $_SERVER[HTTP_COOKIE].

Destroying a Cookie

Cookies can be destroyed or deleted by the client or the server. Clients can easily delete their cookies by locating the *Cookies* folder on their system and deleting them. The server can delete the cookies by:

- Resetting a cookie by specifying expiration time
- Resetting a cookie by specifying its name only

In both instances, you'd use the setcookie command. To destroy a cookie by specifying the expiration time, simply call setcookie with a past expiration date, as is done in Example 13-3.

Example 13-3. Destroying a cookie by expiring it in the recent past

```php
<?php
//remember that setcookie must come before any other line that generates output
setcookie("username","", time()-10 );
echo 'Rosebud.';
?>
```

Example 13-3 returns:

```
Rosebud.
```

Now if you called the code in Example 13-2 again, you'd get:

```
Oops, the cookie isn't set!
```

Sometimes you may want to restrict pages from being viewed by everyone. Do this by using PHP to get authentication from the HTTP server.

PHP and HTTP Authentication

PHP can use authentication from the Apache web server. PHP sends a header request to the browser requesting an authentication dialog on the client's browser. You'll recognize this prompt as a standard browser login prompt. Because the authentication head must come before any other HTML output, this works only with the module-based PHP installation, not the CGI version.

Example 13-4 shows how to use HTTP authentication.

Example 13-4. Using HTTP authentication with a PHP script

```php
<?php
if (!isset($_SERVER['PHP_AUTH_USER']) || !isset($_SERVER['PHP_AUTH_PW'])) {
header('WWW-Authenticate: Basic realm="Member Area"');
header("HTTP/1.0 401 Unauthorized");
echo "Please login with a valid username and password.";
exit;
} else {
echo "You entered a username of: ".$_SERVER['PHP_AUTH_USER']." ";
```

Example 13-4. Using HTTP authentication with a PHP script (continued)

```
echo "and a password of: ".$_SERVER['PHP_AUTH_PW'].".";
}
?>
```

The code from Example 13-4 displays a prompt like the one in Figure 13-2.

Figure 13-2. The prompt for authentication to the Member Area realm

If the user clicks Cancel, he'll see Figure 13-3.

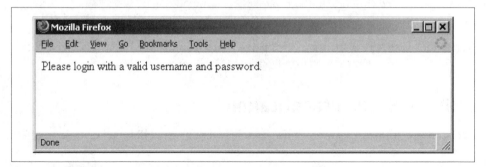

Figure 13-3. Clicking Cancel causes a message that the user must log in

That's a fairly simple example. We checked to see if the username and password were set, then displayed them to the user. The realm field provides a way for grouping related pages together for access restrictions. Any PHP page that presents the authentication headers within the same realm as the login page is accessible after a successful login. This spares the user from having to re-authenticate for each PHP page.

Example 13-5 validates the username and password retrieved from an authentication prompt. If they don't match, access to all pages in that realm is denied.

Example 13-5. Checking the values returned from the authentication prompt

```php
<?php
$username = 'jon_doe';
$password = 'MyNameIsJonDoe';
if (!isset($_SERVER['PHP_AUTH_USER']) || !isset($_SERVER['PHP_AUTH_PW'])) {
header('WWW-Authenticate: Basic realm="Member Area"');
header("HTTP/1.0 401 Unauthorized");
echo "You must enter in a username and password combination!";
exit;
}
elseif (strcmp($_SERVER['PHP_AUTH_USER'], $username) !== 0 ||
strcmp($_SERVER['PHP_AUTH_PW'], $password) !== 0) {
header('WWW-Authenticate: Basic realm="Member Area"');
header("HTTP/1.0 401 Unauthorized");
echo "Your username and password combination was incorrect!";
exit;
}
echo("You have successfully logged in!");
?>
```

Example 13-5 checks that the authentication was set. If it wasn't, request a username and password. The elseif clause checks to see whether the strings are equal to each other.

This is different than simply comparing two strings with the equality (==) operator. When comparing input, the == operator can cause unexpected results. Therefore, use the strcmp function. The strcmp function returns 0 only when the two strings are identical. If either the username or password comparison returns a value other than 0, you deny access; otherwise, access is granted. If they don't match, request another authentication prompt from the user by sending authentication headers again. They then must come before any other output.

Storing a Username and Password in a Database

Let's revisit some of the knowledge you picked up back in Chapter 5. We're going to create a new table for users. Instead of comparing a username and password to values that are set in your PHP script, you'll check them against a database table called USERS. As explained in Chapter 5, you'll want to log into the command prompt and create a table using the syntax in Example 13-6.

Example 13-6. Creating the users table to store login information

```sql
CREATE TABLE `users` (
`user_id` INT NOT NULL AUTO_INCREMENT,
`first_name` VARCHAR(100),
`last_name` VARCHAR(100),
`username` VARCHAR(45),
`password` CHAR(32),
PRIMARY KEY (`user_id`));
```

This code returns:

```
Query OK, 0 rows affected (0.23 sec)
```

To add a user, you create an entry in the database for a user with an encrypted password, as shown in Example 13-7.

Example 13-7. Creating the entry in the database for a user with an encrypted password

```
INSERT INTO users (`first_name`, `last_name`, `username`, `password`)
VALUES
('Michele','Davis', 'mdavis', MD5('secret'));
```

This yields:

```
Query OK, 1 row affected (0.01 sec)
```

To check that your row was created and see what the MD5 encoding function returned, you query the users table:

```
SELECT * FROM users;
```

Presto:

```
+---------+------------+-----------+----------+----------------------------------+
| user_id | first_name | last_name | username | password |
+---------+------------+-----------+----------+----------------------------------+
|       1 | Michele    | Davis     | mdavis   | 5ebe2294ecd0e0f08eab7690d2a6ee69 |
+---------+------------+-----------+----------+----------------------------------+
1 row in set (0.00 sec)
```

Now that you've created the table, let's set up the login script to test a username and password. You encoded the password using MD5 to provide an extra layer of security. The password that created the encoded string cannot be determined from the stored string. This means that even if a malicious user finds out another user's encoded password, she can't use it to log in. However, this method is for testing only, and more secure options will be discussed later in the book.

Example 13-10 reuses much of the same code from the example in the previous section, so don't worry about having to rewrite too much! The major difference is that instead of using the strcmp command to check the username and password, you place them into a query and use the database to check for a match.

Don't forget that you still need your database login information in a file called *db_login.php*, shown in Example 13-8.

Example 13-8. The database login details

```php
<?php
$db_host='localhost';
$db_database='test';
$db_username='test';
$db_password='yourpass';
?>
```

The values from Example 13-8 are used in Example 13-9.

Example 13-9. Verifying a username and password against the database

```php
<?php
require_once('db_login.php');
require_once('DB.php');
if (!isset($_SERVER['PHP_AUTH_USER']) ||
!isset($_SERVER['PHP_AUTH_PW'])) {
header('WWW-Authenticate: Basic realm="Member Area"');
header("HTTP/1.0 401 Unauthorized");
echo "You must enter in a username and password combination!";
exit;
}
$web_username = $_SERVER['PHP_AUTH_USER'];
$web_password = $_SERVER['PHP_AUTH_PW'];
$connection = DB::connect("mysql://$db_username:$db_password@$db_host/$db_database");
if (DB::isError($connection)){
die ("Could not connect to the database: <br />". DB::errorMessage($connection));
}
$query = "SELECT `user_id`, `username` FROM `users` WHERE
`username`='".$web_username."' AND `password`=MD5('".$web_password."') LIMIT 1";
$result = $connection->query($query);
if (DB::isError($result)){
die("Could not query the database: <br />".$query." ".DB::errorMessage($result));
}
if (!$row = $result->fetchRow(DB_FETCHMODE_ASSOC)) {
header('WWW-Authenticate: Basic realm="Member Area"');
header("HTTP/1.0 401 Unauthorized");
echo "Your username and password combination was incorrect!";
exit;
}
echo("You have successfully logged in as ".$row['username']."!");
?>
```

You may have to change display_errors = Off in the *php.ini* file if you get the following error.

    Warning: headers already sent message causing the message box not to display.

This may be a little too much to consume at the moment, but save the script and run it, which displays the screen in Figure 13-4. Then try logging in with the username of mdavis and a password of secret.

You should see that the script handles the login, shown in Figure 13-5, with the database because there is a successful match of data.

If you entered something invalid, you'll see an unauthorized page such as Figure 13-6 telling you that the username and password are incorrect.

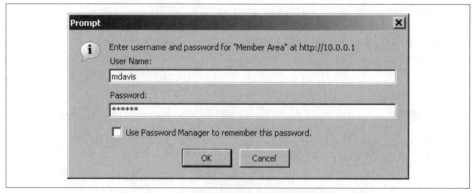

Figure 13-4. Prompting for username and password before checking the database

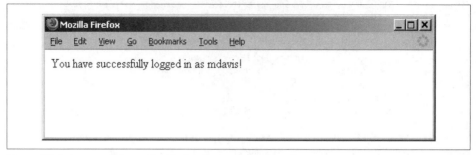

Figure 13-5. A successful match with the database's credentials

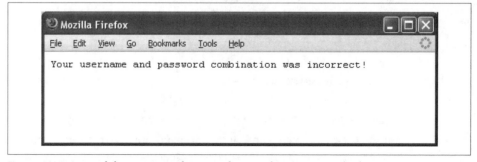

Figure 13-6. An invalid username and password causes this message to display

Sessions

HTML and web servers by default don't keep track of information that was entered on a page when the client's browser loads another page. This makes doing anything that involves using the same information from a user on several pages difficult.

Sessions help solve this problem by maintaining data during a user's visit to your web site from page to page on your site. Each session can store many variables that are maintained throughout that session. The server keeps track of users' sessions by assigning them a unique session ID, generated by the server, when the session starts. This identifier is called the *session identifier* and must be sent to the server each time a page is requested once a session begins. Figure 13-7 illustrates the interaction between the client browser and web server for a session.

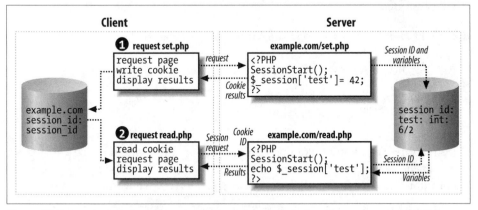

Figure 13-7. A typical session stores some information on both the client and server hard disks

Sessions are stored on the server. The session variables are stored in a file and are *serialized*. When a variable is serialized, it's written out to a file as its name, type, and value all in a sequential string. On a Unix-based server, this file is usually written out to a directory under the */tmp* (temporary) filesystem.

PHP doesn't actually create a record for a session until a session variable has been assigned a value. That makes sense since without any values to manage, the session doesn't really do anything.

The browser sends the session ID to the server each time it requests a page. The browser can send the session ID to the server either through a cookie or as a URL parameter. The default is to use the cookie, but because it's possible for a user to turn off cookies in his browser preferences, we also discuss passing the session ID in the URL string.

Using Sessions

To start a session, place the session_start function at the beginning of your PHP script before you can store or access any data during in the session. The session_ start function, used in Example 13-10, needs to execute before any other header calls or other output is sent to the browser; otherwise, your session may not work properly.

Example 13-10. Simply starting a session

```php
<?php
    session_start();
?>
```

First, we'll discuss the way variables used to be assigned to a session, since you may see this in code you get off the Web. The old school way is to use the session_register function, shown in Example 13-11. Don't use this method in your code, as it will cause an error.

Example 13-11. Registering a variable with session_register

```php
<?php
//DON'T USE THIS APPROACH
session_start();
session_register("hello");
$hello = "Hello World";
?>
```

Once the variable is bound like this in a PHP script, any changes to the variable are stored in the session. If the session isn't already started, the session_register command automatically starts it. Modern PHP interpreters return a warning with this code:

```
Warning: Unknown(): Your script possibly relies on a session side-effect which
existed until PHP 4.2.3. Please be advised that the session extension does not
consider global variables as a source of data, unless register_globals is enabled.
You can disable this functionality and this warning by setting
session.bug_compat_42 or session.bug_compat_warn to off, respectively. in Unknown
on line 0
```

The correct way is to store and access session variables by the $_SESSION global variable with the name of the variable supplied within brackets. Assigning a new variable to the $_SESSION global automatically adds it to the session. The session must be started before you can access the session variables.

> The use of session_register is considered to be less secure than using $_SESSION because of the possibility of a malicious user sending a value as a GET parameter with the same name as a registered session variable. For example, an attacker could send a bogus value for $username and make your PHP script believe a user is logged in who really didn't pass authentication.

For instance, Example 13-12 registers the same variable.

Example 13-12. Registering a variable by including it in $_SESSION

```php
<?php
    session_start();
    $_SESSION['hello'] = 'Hello World';
    echo $_SESSION['hello'];
?>
```

Now if the user was to follow a link to another page on your site that starts a session, the $_SESSION global variable contains a key called hello with the string value of Hello World, as shown in Example 13-13.

Example 13-13. Referencing a variable set on a prior page in the session

```php
<?php
    session_start();
    echo $_SESSION['hello'];
?>
```

Therefore, the code in Example 13-13 displays this information, as shown in Figure 13-8.

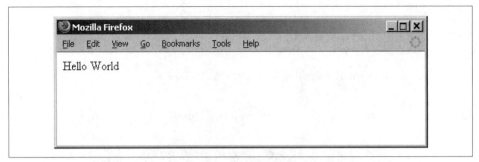

Figure 13-8. The value set previously in the session is accessible

Either Examples 13-11 or 13-12 can be used to register the session variable before it's requested in Example 13-13.

Expanding Our Login Example

Most login systems use session variables to pass useful information around without having to re-retrieve them from the database. In Example 13-14, we're checking to see whether a user is valid, and then setting a few session variables.

Example 13-14. Checking to see whether a user is valid

```php
<?php
session_start();
require_once('db_login.php');
require_once('DB.php');
if (empty($_SESSION['user_id'])) {
DELETE THIS PAR AFTER MOVING THE FIGURE ANCHOR --->
if (!isset($_SERVER['PHP_AUTH_USER']) || !isset($_SERVER['PHP_AUTH_PW'])) {
header('WWW-Authenticate: Basic realm="Member Area"');
header("HTTP/1.0 401 Unauthorized");
echo "You must enter in a username and password combination!";
exit;
}
```

Example 13-14. Checking to see whether a user is valid (continued)

```
$connection = DB::connect("mysql://$db_username:$db_password@$db_host/$db_database");
if (DB::isError($connection)){
die ("Could not connect to the database: <br />". DB::errorMessage($connection));
}
$username = mysql_real_escape_string($_SERVER['PHP_AUTH_USER']);
$password = mysql_real_escape_string($_SERVER['PHP_AUTH_PW']);
$query = "SELECT `user_id`, `username` FROM `users` WHERE
`username`='".$username."' AND `password`=MD5('".$password."') LIMIT 1";
$result = $connection->query($query);
if(!($row = $result->fetchRow(DB_FETCHMODE_ASSOC))) {
header('WWW-Authenticate: Basic realm="Member Area"');
header("HTTP/1.0 401 Unauthorized");
echo "Your username and password combination was incorrect!";
exit;
}
$_SESSION['user_id'] = $row['user_id'];
$_SESSION['username'] = $row['username'];
}
echo "You have successfully logged in as ".$_SESSION["username"].".";
?>
```

Example 13-14 displays Figure 13-9, followed by Figure 13-10, if you were successful.

Figure 13-9. The login prompt before entering our credentials

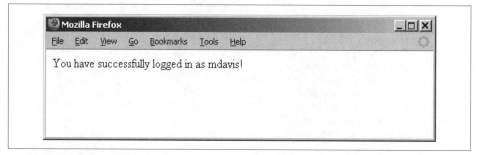

Figure 13-10. A successful login

The code first checks the session to see if the user_id session variable already has a value assigned to it. Subsequent pages can check for the session variables that were set at the end of Example 13-14 instead of doing another HTTP realm-based authentication and verifying that against the database.

If the session has the key user_id, you know the variable was set and you can continue without any further checking. However, email addresses and URLs are difficult to validate with 100% accuracy. Obviously, you'd mandate that an email address have an @ that is followed by some combination of letters, numbers, and the period. Lastly, there is a period followed by a two- to four-letter string—for example, .nl, ca, com, edu, uk, or info. If you mandate certain parameters, you'll be more successful during validation.

When you're trying to validate a URL, you should check for the optional *http://*. After this, you want to see letters, numbers, or a dash, followed by a period, and then a two- to four-letter string as just described for email addresses.

Ending a Session

There are times when you want to end a session before the session times out. An example of this is when you provide a logout button or link on your page. The logout is actually done by ending the user's session. To end a session, use the session_destroy function. Of course, you must first start a session for it to make sense to destroy it.

Keep in mind that ending a session doesn't make the values from that session unavailable to the rest of the currently executing PHP page. Example 13-15 provides a simple script that both ends the session and makes the session values unavailable to the rest of the PHP script.

Example 13-15. Destroying a session

```php
<?php
session_start();
// Do some miscellaneous work
$_SESSION['username'] = 'Michele';
// Logout of the site
session_destroy();
echo "At this point we can still see the value of username as
".$_SESSION['username']."<br />";
$_SESSION = array();
echo "Now the value of username is blank: ".$_SESSION['username'];
?>
```

The code in Example 13-15 produces something like Figure 13-11.

When you destroy the session, the session data is deleted from the server's session files. To wipe out the values in the $_SESSION global variable, set it to an empty array.

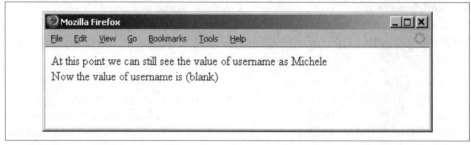

Figure 13-11. Destroying a session and clearing out the values

Although you're using $_SESSION to destroy the values from the session, if you used session_register to add variables to a session, you need to use one of two functions to remove the values from the running script. The function session_unset removes all session variables while session_unregister removes only the variable name that's sent as a parameter.

We're going to address garbage collection—and no, this isn't about when your garbage is collected at the curb, this is when a session is destroyed or times out.

Garbage collection

Garbage collection determines what happens to the contents of a session on the server after a session is destroyed or simply times out from inactivity. If the server didn't do periodic clean up of old sessions, they'd accumulate, endlessly wasting space, and creating clutter on the server. Garbage collection happens automatically and deletes all old session data.

PHP has a load-balancing feature for garbage collection, so that old session files aren't deleted for every session request. The default timeout for session files is 1440 seconds or 24 minutes. That probably doesn't seem like a lot of time if you have a very robust site, but PHP has commands that can delete garbage following parameters you set. A session file can be deleted after that timeout, but it could reside on the server longer, depending on the amount of sessions created.

The following PHP *.ini* variables deal with the garbage collector:

- session.gc_maxlifetime
- session.gc_probability
- session.gc_divisor

In the above variables, gc equals garbage collector. If you have enough disk space on your server, you can set the session file timeout pretty long in order to preserve most or even all sessions until the browsers are closed. However, in many cases, the session needs to expire after a certain time, so you have to change the lifetime of the session cookie itself.

We'll discuss setting the session's timeout values so you get a better understanding of what you're going to need to do.

Setting a session's timeout

After a certain time period, it's reasonable to expect that a user's session should automatically log out, which is essentially an expiration period. PHP allows you to specifically set this duration. The best way to do this is to modify the *.htaccess* file.

The *.htaccess* file affects the HTML and PHP files in the same directory as the file. It allows you to make configuration changes without modifying Apache's configuration files. Any changes made in the *.htaccess* file also apply to files in subdirectories unless another *.htaccess* file is in a subdirectory. In Example 13-16, we're using the session.gc_maxlifetime variable.

Example 13-16. Session timeout

```
<IfModule mod_php4.c>
  php_value session.gc_maxlifetime "14400"
</IfModule>
```

The value that comes after sessions.gc_maxlifetime is in 100ths of a second, so, if you want a session timeout of 30 minutes, you would use a value of 18000.

> The cookie path can be / or */directoryx* if the cookie needs to be valid for a certain directory only. *directoryx* could be any directory or folder you have named specifically for the cookies.

As seen in Example 13-16, we have a session cookie with a custom-defined lifetime and a defined garbage collector timeout. This ensures that the current session data is available as long as the session cookie in the browser is valid. Authentication with Auth_HTTP is going to be discussed.

Using Auth_HTTP to Authenticate

Similar to the way you use PEAR to improve and simplify database access, there's also a PEAR module called Auth_HTTP that streamlines the process of authenticating users against a database table. Because the code is prewritten, it reduces the risk that you'll make a mistake when authenticating users. You may notice that there's also a module called Auth. This module is similar to Auth_HTTP, except it displays the login screen using an HTML page instead of the pop-up authentication that Auth_HTTP uses.

As far as how it looks, the user can't tell that there is a difference between using the manually applied HTTP authentication dialogs that were previously used in this chapter and the Auth_HTTP module.

If you haven't already installed the `Auth_HTTP` module, you can do so by entering `pear install Auth` from the command line. But you must be logged in as root on a Unix host to do it. The `pear install Auth` command displays Example 13-17.

Example 13-17. pear install Auth output

```
downloading Auth-1.2.3.tgz ...
Starting to download Auth-1.2.3.tgz (24,040 bytes)
........done: 24,040 bytes
Optional dependencies:
package `File_Passwd' version >= 0.9.5 is recommended to utilize some features.
package `Net_POP3' version >= 1.3 is recommended to utilize some features.
package `MDB' is recommended to utilize some features.
package `Auth_RADIUS' is recommended to utilize some features.
package `File_SMBPasswd' is recommended to utilize some features.
install ok: Auth 1.2.3
```

If you follow the code in Example 13-17 with `pear install Auth_HTTP`, you'll get the output found in Example 13-18.

Example 13-18. pear install Auth_HTTP output

```
downloading Auth_HTTP-2.1.6.tgz ...
Starting to download Auth_HTTP-2.1.6.tgz (9,327 bytes)
.....done: 9,327 bytes
install ok: Auth_HTTP 2.1.6
```

Now, Example 13-19 automates checking usernames and passwords against the database.

Example 13-19. Using Auth_HTTP to authenticate a user

```php
<?php
// Using Auth_HTTP to limit access
require_once('db_login.php');
require_once("Auth/HTTP.php");
// We use the same connection string as the pear DB functions
$AuthOpts = array(
'dsn' => "mysql://$db_username:$db_password@$db_host/$db_database",
'table' => "users", // your table name
'usernamecol' => "username", // the table username column
'passwordcol' => "password", // the table password column
'cryptType' => "md5", // password encryption type
);
$authenticate = new Auth_HTTP("DB", $AuthOpts);
// Set the realm name
$authenticate->setRealm('Member Area');
// Authentication failed error message
$authenticate->setCancelText('<h2>Access Denied</h2>');
// Request authentication
$authenticate->start();
// compare username and password to stored values
if ($authenticate->getAuth()){
```

Example 13-19. Using Auth_HTTP to authenticate a user (continued)

```
echo "Welcome back to our site ".$authenticate->username.".";
}
?>
```

What's happening here is that we include the `Auth_HTTP` code with a `require_once` line. The `AuthOpts` array contains the parameters that define how you connect to the database, which table contains user information, and the exact fields to be checked. These parameters are listed in Table 13-2.

Table 13-2. Auth options

Key	Description	Example
dsn	The same database connect string that we used with PEAR DB	mysql://$db_username:$db_password@$db_host/$db_database
table	The database table that holds login information	users
usernamecol	The database field that holds the username	username
passwordcol	The database field that stores the possibly encrypted password	password
cryptType	How the password is encrypted in the database	none, md5
dbFields	Which additional fields to retrieve from the login information table	*, first_name, user_id

Once you have the options set, use `new` to start a new authentication object. Reference the `setRealm` method to set the realm, start the authentication with `start`, and compare the results with `getAuth`. The method `setRealm` is used to set the name of the realm for HTTP authentication, and then it appears in the login box, which the browser displays.

Figure 13-12 shows the authentication dialog before entering the username and password.

Figure 13-12. We see our familiar authentication prompt before clicking OK

Once validated against the values in the database, we see the page in Figure 13-13.

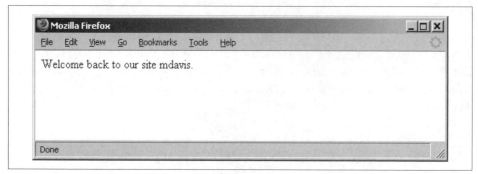

Figure 13-13. Telling the user that she is logged in now

If you were to refresh this page, you wouldn't be prompted again for a username and password as long as your session stays active.

A second example retrieves more information from the users table if the username and password match, as shown in Example 13-20.

Example 13-20. Retrieving additional information for the user

```php
<?php
// Example of Auth_HTTP the also returns additional information
require_once('db_login.php');
require_once("Auth/HTTP.php");
// We use the same connection string as the pear DB functions
$AuthOptions = array(
'dsn'=>"mysql://$db_username:$db_password@$db_host/$db_database",
'table'=>"users", // your table name
'usernamecol'=>"username", // the table username column
'passwordcol'=>"password", // the table password column
'cryptType'=>"md5", // password encryption type in your db
'db_fields'=>"*", // enabling fetch for other db columns
);
$authenticate = new Auth_HTTP("DB", $AuthOptions);
// Set the realm name
$authenticate->setRealm('Member Area');
// Authentication failed error message
$authenticate->setCancelText('<h2>Access Denied</h2>');
// Request authentication
$authenticate->start();
// compare username and password to stored values
if($authenticate->getAuth()){
echo "Welcome back to our site ".$authenticate->username.".<br />";
echo "Your full name is ";
```

Example 13-20. Retrieving additional information for the user (continued)

```
echo $authenticate->getAuthData('first_name');
echo " ";
echo $authenticate->getAuthData('last_name').".";
}
?>
```

Figure 13-14 shows that the first and last names were also stored in the database and can now be used without doing a separate query. Any columns that were part of the users table can be accessed with getAuthData as long as db_fields is set to retrieve them all with "*".

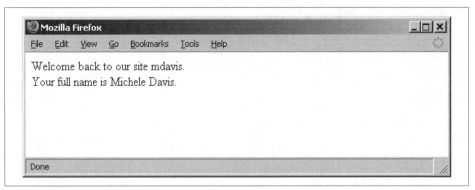

Figure 13-14. We can now display more information from the users table without a new query

As you can see, using this module reduces the amount of manual interaction that's necessary to log in users against a database. This saves you time, because you don't need to construct a database query anymore. To make life even simpler, you could place the code from the last example into a separate *include* file placed at the beginning of each script that has restricted access. If the user is already logged in, it doesn't display anything but instead prompts the user for a password if she isn't logged in. That way, all your pages are protected with the same chunk of code.

We're going to move on to something very important: security. As you know, hackers, benign and malicious, are everywhere. Keeping your site free of problems created by the malicious ones requires knowing a lot about security. There'll also be additional resources in the last chapter of the book for more security resources that are beyond the scope of this book. We've touched on security in many places so far, now we'll summarize what you've learned all in one place and introduce some advanced techniques to make your site as secure as possible. Regardless of whether your site contains sensitive customer data or just your favorite recipes, you still don't want to log in to find your data missing or altered.

Chapter 13 Questions

Question 13-1. Where is the data for a cookie stored?

Question 13-2. What function can be used to encode passwords for storage in the database so that users' plain-text passwords aren't exploited?

Question 13-3. Create a session and store the value 1 in the session variable user_id.

Question 13-4. Display the user_id session variable created in Question 13-3.

See the Appendix for the answers to these questions.

Security

Once your code is working, you may be tempted to think that you're done with it. In reality, you may have some security issues that don't affect normal usage but still provide an opening for an attack. The unfortunate reality of web-accessible applications is that they're only as secure as their weakest link. Therefore, you must be conscious of security on every level, from the database to the web server and the PHP processing itself.

Although you can't make every system truly unbreakable, you can perform the equivalent of dead-bolting doors and locking windows. If you make your system difficult enough to compromise, then it's generally not worth a hacker's effort, though keep in mind that some may still try. We've had our own server locked up from hackers trying to get in, or boatloads of spam that cause the server to belch and stop working temporarily.

We're going to reiterate some of the security concepts that we discussed while learning the basics of PHP and MySQL. That reduces the risk that you'll build a site without reading about security and so will end up with an easily compromised site. We'll also expand on those topics to give you some more options for making hackers' lives difficult and your life easier.

Limit Access to Administrative Pages

When installing software packages that include a control panel or setup script, you should always either change the script's directory or, in the case of setup scripts, remove them after you're done installing. These scripts can provide a way for a random web surfer to mess up your configuration for the package you installed. While that isn't so bad, in a worst case scenario, it could lead to hackers uploading PHP code of their choice and doing quite unpleasant things with your system. Most web-based packages recommend doing this in their installation instructions. Follow their advice; they wrote the installation manual for a reason: for you to read it! As most technical writers say, "Always published, never read." How many people do you know personally who actually read their alarm clock setup, DVD player setup, or manuals for any number of electronic devices?

An alternate means of securing directories containing administrative scripts is to create an *.htaccess* file in the same web directory as the scripts. This file tells Apache to require a user to authenticate it before it returns any of the information in that directory.

To require authentication for a specific directory, place the code in Example 14-1 into a file called *.htaccess* in the directory you created for the code.

Example 14-1. Using Apache authentication to restrict access to scripts

```
AuthType Basic
AuthName "Administrators Only"
AuthUserFile /usr/local/apache/passwd/passwords
Require valid-user
```

Requesting a directory or subdirectory where this file was saved causes the prompt in Figure 14-1 to display in Firefox; Internet Explorer also displays a similar prompt.

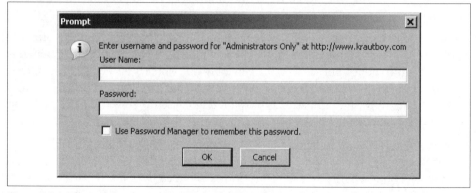

Figure 14-1. The authentication prompt your browser displays because of the Apache authentication request

Failure to supply a correct username and password causes the warning in Figure 14-2 to display.

For best results, this file shouldn't be readable by users—only by the web server process. On a Unix system, this can be set with the command:

```
chmod 644 /usr/local/apache/passwd/passwords
```

Apache has a special command, the *htpasswd* file, which contains valid usernames and encrypted passwords for your web site. The path to the *htpasswd* file needs to be specified in the *htaccess* file as the AuthUserFile.

As you probably know, usernames and passwords are completely arbitrary; unfortunately, there's no correspondence between the usernames and passwords used in

Authorization Required

This server could not verify that you are authorized to access the document requested. Either you supplied the wrong credentials (e.g., bad password), or your browser doesn't understand how to supply the credentials required.

Figure 14-2. The browser won't return any information for a protected directory without a valid login

your *htaccess* file. For example, if your login name is mdavis, your username for the *htaccess* file could also be mdavis, or it could be Michele.

> Keep in mind that you need to set up usernames that are understandable for your site, and then you need to create passwords for those usernames.

It's important to know that the htpasswd command is used to create the username and password pairs. The full path for the command on a Unix/Linux server is */usr/local/bin/htpasswd*. Remember, the htpasswd command reflexively encrypts every single password before writing it to the *htpasswd* file. In other words, the htpasswd command takes the name of the password file and the username to set its parameters. Look at Example 14-2 for the correct format.

Example 14-2. Creating an Apache password for .htaccess

```
htpasswd -c /usr/local/apache/passwd/passwords mdavis
```

The -c option is required only for adding the first entry to a password file. You'll be prompted to enter the password twice to ensure that you don't have a typo. If the passwords match, you'll see the following:

```
Adding password for user mdavis
```

As stated above, keep in mind that if the password is valid, it's automatically encrypted. When you do this, only users who respond correctly to the authentication prompt are able to access pages in the directory in which *.htaccess* resides in any subdirectories.

> On Windows, the procedure is quite similar, but instead of using *htpasswd*, use *htpasswd.exe*. It's usually located in *C:\Program File\ Apache Group\Apache2\bin*. You can also place the *.htpasswd* file in the *C:\Program Files\Apache Group\Apache2* directory.

Including Files

Because no one ever wants to recreate the wheel, there are ways to reuse code. It probably sounds like plagiarism, but in the world of open source, it's a bonus to reuse code using include files.

Obviously, the ability to reuse code by including makes your life easier by not having the same blocks of code repeated over and over in your programs. It also improves the maintainability of your pages, because code used on multiple pages need only be modified once in the PHP source file.

The downside to look out for is using filenames for your included code that allows the web server to return the contents of the file without being processed by PHP. This has two major security risks. First, it allows a user to see your PHP source code, which could allow someone to look for weaknesses in the code and then know how to easily exploit them. Second, you could expose passwords that may be stored in an *include* file. In order to thwart these problems, make sure that you always name your included file with the *.php* extension and not something such as *.inc* that won't be processed if viewed directly. But, there is a caveat when using include.

For PHP versions before 4.0.2, require always attempts to read the target file, even if the line it's on never executes. The good news is that the conditional statement won't affect the require statement. Then again, if the line on which require occurs doesn't execute, neither will any of the code in the target file. Additionally, looping structures don't affect the operation of the require statement. Remember that the code in the target file is still subject to the loop, even though the require statement occurs only once.

Figure 14-3 shows what can happen by simply requesting your *db_login.php* script if it ends in an *.inc* extension—for example, *http://10.0.0.1/db_login.inc*.

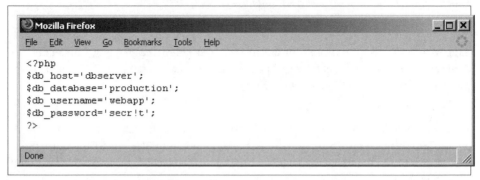

Figure 14-3. Nothing that we want the world to see!

You should avoid ending the login script with a *.inc* extension; there's a better way. The files should be renamed with a *.php* extension. You can put your include files that have sensitive information in a directory that's not under the published web root. Another good way is to place it in a directory that's protected by an *.htaccess* file, at the very least.

Storing Passwords in the Database

In general, it's never a good idea to store passwords for users in the database without encoding them. The principal reason for this is that if someone is able to gain access to your database, even just read-only access, he can get all of your users' passwords. This allows that person to log in as other users, and he could attempt to use the same password on other web sites, since many users use common passwords across numerous sites.

We see password violation on a weekly basis. Our teenager uses instant messaging, and his friends know what he likes and he knows what they like, so all the teens can extrapolate someone's password just based on their knowledge of their friends. Then they can log in as someone else and raise havoc by pretending to be soccergrrl, as opposed to their own login, randomkid.

There are only a few downsides to encrypting passwords, including slightly increased complexity and the need to change a password for a user instead of being able to relay the forgotten password. One way to work around this problem is to store a password hint in the database. This is something that a user can enter when registering that'll help her remember what password she used. For example, if your password is your dog's name, you might use "dog" as a reminder.

So far, we've only discussed a single way to encrypt a password using the md5 one-way encrypt function. There's actually another function that can be used that is more secure. It's called sha1, which stands for *secure hash algorithm*. Instead of returning a 128-bit string such as md5, sha1 returns a 160-bit string. The added length helps make it harder to guess the original password value. Additionally, the algorithm that's used in sha1 is more advanced that md5, making it more difficult to break the code.

For example, try Example 14-3 and see what you get when you run the code.

Example 14-3. Comparing the output of md5 to that of sha1

```php
<?php
echo "Encrypting <b>testing</b> using md5: ".md5("testing");
echo "<br />";
echo "Encrypting <b>testing</b> using sha1: ".sha1("testing");
?>
```

This displays the result shown in Figure 14-4.

The Problem with Automatic Global Variables

Sometimes making life easy for developers can cause problems. Early versions of PHP (before version 4.2.0) by default allowed you to access variables for a GET or

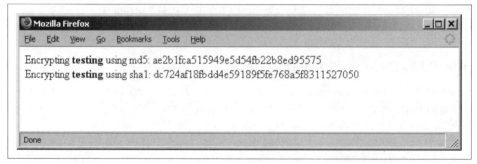

┌───┐
│ Mozilla Firefox   _ □ ✕   │
│ File   Edit   View   Go   Bookmarks   Tools   Help   │
│   │
│ Encrypting **testing** using md5: ae2b1fca515949e5d54fb22b8ed95575   │
│ Encrypting **testing** using sha1: dc724af18fbdd4e59189f5fe768a5f8311527050│
│   │
│ Done   │
└───┘

Figure 14-4. The output from sha1 is slightly longer than md5's

POST operation automatically as global variables with the name of variable coming from whatever came from the GET or POST operation. While this was very convenient, it also created a big security hole.

> The actual setting that changed its default value is called register_ globals. It could be set to OFF in the *php.ini* configuration file before. Most people didn't change the default value though.

It wasn't really that register_globals was a terrible idea, it's just that most people didn't properly check the source of a variable before use. The danger was that because PHP doesn't require variables to be predefined, it's possible for a malicious user to call your PHP script with a GET or POST parameter that you aren't anticipating. If that variable matches the name of a variable that you're using for something important, such as indicating whether a password matches, then the malicious user might be able to change the functionality of your program just by adding a false parameter.

Unfortunately, admitting that this was a mistake and having to change the default value wasn't without some pain. Because many people assumed that they could automatically reference form-submitted values as globals, scripts that used to work now find no value where they expect it. Code had to be rewritten, and worse yet, you may still find some code that hasn't been fixed and therefore doesn't work and won't even tell you the problem.

> If you've just downloaded a set of PHP scripts from the Internet and find that they run but essentially ignore form-inputted data, there's a good chance that they were written with the assumption that register_ globals was on. You'll need to either expand out the variables or change the references within the scripts to the appropriate $_GET or $_POST superglobals.

Example 14-4 shows how the globals could be misused (assuming the function check_username_and_password is defined already).

Example 14-4. Not initializing a variable was a hole in sample.php

```php
<?php
if (check_username_and_password()) {
   //they logged in successfully
   $access = TRUE;
}
if ($access) {
   echo "Welcome to the administrative control panel.";
   //more privileged code here…
}
else {
  echo "Access denied";
}
?>
```

What should have happened in the code for Example 14-4 is to set $access to FALSE before it was used. Had a malicious user called a script such as *http://sample.php?access=1*, she'd see Figure 14-5.

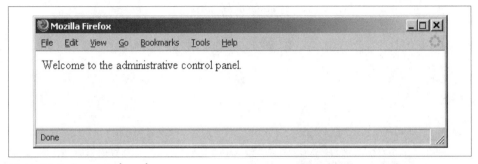

Figure 14-5. A security breach

The value for $access of TRUE from the GET parameter would cause the check for access to return TRUE when register_globals is on. Modifying the code to look like this:

```php
<?php
//predefining the value is good coding practice anyway
$access = FALSE;
if (check_username_and_password()) {
   //they logged in successfully
   $access = TRUE;
}
if ($access) {
   echo "Welcome to the administrative control panel.";
   //more privileged code here…
}
else {
  echo "Access denied";
}
?>
```

causes the correct message to come up, as shown in Figure 14-6.

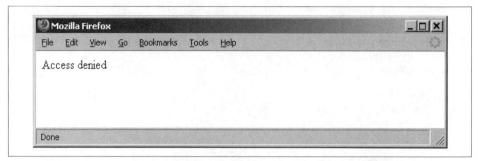

Figure 14-6. Access is correctly denied regardless of the register_globals setting

The legacy of register_globals doesn't stop with data supplied from forms. It's possible to read session variables when register_globals is on. In Example 14-5, $username could also come from other sources, such as GET, which is part of the URL request.

Example 14-5. Sessions with register_globals on or off in session_test.php

```php
<?php
session_start();
if (isset($username)) {
  echo "Hello $username";
} else {
  echo "Please login.";
}
?>
```

Requesting *http://10.0.0.1/session_test.php?username="test"* with register_globals on returns what is shown in Figure 14-7.

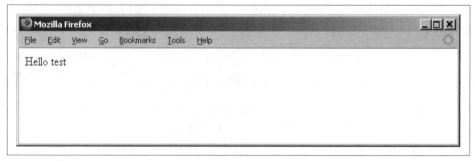

Figure 14-7. Any security has been effectively circumvented

The correct way is to access the variable from the $_SESSION super global, as in Example 14-6.

Example 14-6. Session using the proper $_SESSION super global

```php
<?php
session_start();
$username=$_SESSION['username'];
if (isset($username)) {
  echo "Hello $username";
} else {
  echo "Please login.";
}
?>
```

The code in Example 14-6 returns Figure 14-8.

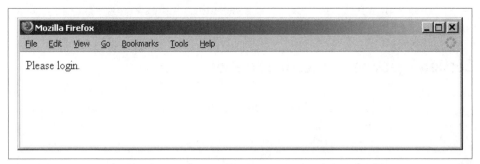

Figure 14-8. Users must log in and cannot bypass the login with a global variable

To continue to access a user-supplied variable without caring about where it came from, you can use the $_REQUEST superglobal, as shown in Example 14-7.

Example 14-7. Detecting simple variable poisoning

```php
<?php
if (isset($_COOKIE['MAGIC_COOKIE'])) {
    // MAGIC_COOKIE comes from a cookie.
    // Be sure to validate the cookie data!
} elseif (isset($_GET['MAGIC_COOKIE']) || isset($_POST['MAGIC_COOKIE'])) {
    mail("admin@example.com", "Possible breakin attempt", $_SERVER['REMOTE_ADDR']);
    echo "Security violation, admin has been alerted.";
    exit;
} else {
    // MAGIC_COOKIE isn't set through this REQUEST

}
?>
```

While register_globals is turned off by default to improve security, it doesn't mean that the problem of validating has gone away.

Remember to always initialize variables. This simple step can thwart a malicious attempt to send data through an alternate source. It also helps the readability of your code at almost no cost.

Superglobal arrays such as $_GET, $_POST, and $_SERVER have been available since PHP 4.1.0.

Session Security

Because a session may contain sensitive information, you need to treat the session as a possible security hole. Session security is necessary to create and implement a session. If someone is listening in or snooping on a network, it's possible that he can intercept a session ID and use it to look like he is someone else. It's also possible to access session data from the local filesystem on multiuser systems such as ISP hosting machines.

Session Hijacking and Session Fixation

Session hijacking is when someone accesses either a client's cookie or session ID, and then attempts to use this data. *Session fixation* is attempting to set your own session ID. Session fixation and hijacking are easy to combat. We'll make use of the super global variables for the client's IP address and browser type to keep things secure.

Example 14-8 demonstrates encoding the information with an md5 function call to thwart these potential security holes.

Example 14-8. Checking for session hijacking

```
<?php
session_start();
$user_check = md5($_SERVER['HTTP_USER_AGENT'] . $_SERVER['REMOTE_ADDR']);
if (empty($_SESSION['user_data'])) {
session_regenerate_id();
echo ("New session, saving user_check.");
$_SESSION['user_data'] = $user_check;
}
if (strcmp($_SESSION['user_data'], $user_check) !== 0) {
session_regenerate_id();
echo ("Warning, you must reenter your session.");
$_SESSION = array();
$_SESSION['user_data'] = $user_check;
}
else {
echo ("Connection verified!");
}
?>
```

When a browser first requests the page in Example 14-8, a session is started. In that session, we stored the encoded combination of the IP address and browser type. That way, when the user returns to this page, we can compare the value stored in the session versus a fresh computation of the IP address and browser type. If the two don't match, we potentially have a hijacker, so we pick a new ID and clear out any saved data for that session. That way, the hijacker cannot retrieve any of the private information stored in the session. This doesn't cause a problem for legitimate users, because they aren't going to change browser or IP addresses in the middle of a session with your web site.

Figure 14-9 shows the newly created session the first time the script runs.

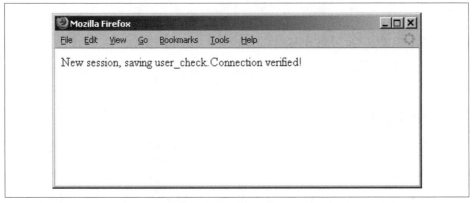

Figure 14-9. The session is created and validates since it is a new session

Figure 14-10 shows what happens if the same script is executed again right away from the same browser.

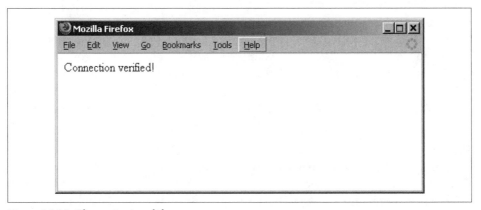

Figure 14-10. The session is valid

Figure 14-11 mixes things up by copying the session ID cookie from the browser in Figure 14-9 and setting Internet Explorer on the same client machine to send a request with the same session ID.

Because our script checks the type of browser, and it's changed from Firefox to Internet Explorer, the session is regenerated to prevent a security lapse.

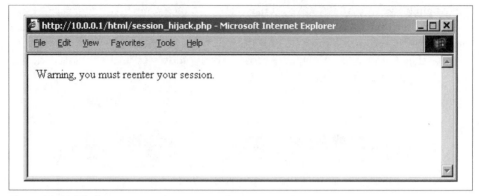

Figure 14-11. The browser type change is caught

Trusting User Data

You know that trusting data from a user isn't a great idea. But what exactly do you consider to be user data versus system data that you trust?

GET

Data from GET operations is inherently user data since it usually comes from form submissions.

POST

Data from POST operations is inherently user data since it usually comes from form submissions.

Cookies

Cookies may seem like they could be trusted since they are automatically sent, but in reality, since they are stored on the client's computer, they could be intentionally altered. Therefore, they're considered user data.

Session data

Session data can be trusted as long as the session value is set based on validated data. If it's set to a user-supplied value without validation, it's not trustworthy.

User input should be checked and escaped properly. Data that's bound for the database must have all special characters such as single and double quotes escaped. If PHP is not running with magic quotes on (discussed later in this chapter), then you'll need to pass user input through addslashes before sending it to the database.

Any user input that displays should be checked for embedded HTML that could be used for cross-site scripting attacks. The htmlspecialcharacters function is useful for escaping characters that have special meaning in HTML like less than (<) and greater than (>).

Shared Hosting Concerns

If you don't have your own dedicated server or are on a server that has multiple users, it can be very dangerous to use the default PHP settings to store your user's session data in a temporary directory. Normally, all users have access to that temporary directory, so they can easily pilfer private data from the session, including the session ID.

To make your session data more secure, you can set the session.save_path configuration parameter with the ini_set function to change the path where sessions are stored, as shown in Example 14-9. Make sure that these are stored below the web root directory.

Example 14-9. session.save_path functionality

```php
<?php
    ini_set('session.save_path', '/home/user/sessions/');
    session_start();
?>
```

Example 14-9 stores the sessions in the */home/user/sessions* directory. Be sure that whichever folder you choose is created and has the correct permissions for the PHP interpreter to write the session data. Typically, this means the file must be writable by the permission group www-data. This folder shouldn't be readable or writable by general users at large.

Preventing Access to the Database

There are a couple of ways to reduce the chance that a malicious user can access your database. First, if there is a problem connecting to the database, the default MySQL error code reveals the location of the database—in other words, the IP address of the host. You'd like to suppress that information.

To prevent the standard error message from PHP, add the Error Control Operator, which is the at sign (@), to the front of the database function call. You'll experience a more closed-lipped or dubious error message in Example 14-10 before calling die to stop all processing.

Example 14-10. Suppressing the standard database error message

```php
<?php
require_once('db_login.php');
$error = "Site down for maintenance, please check back.";
$db_link = @mysql_connect($db_host, $db_username, $db_password) or die($error);
@mysql_select_db($db_database, $db_link) or die($error);
?>
```

Without the at sign (@) before the function calls, you'll see Figure 14-12.

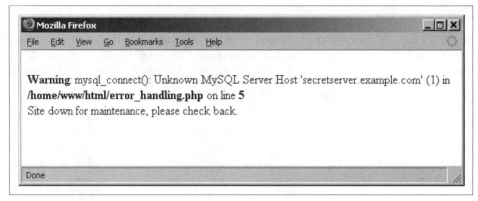

Figure 14-12. The database server's location is revealed in the error message

From a security standpoint, notice how little the error message in Figure 14-13 reveals to a potential attacker about the environment.

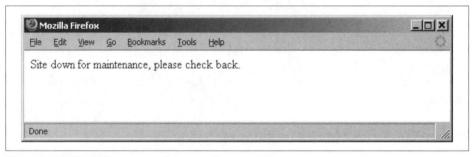

Figure 14-13. We no longer give out more information than is necessary

While this may seem like a minor point, minimizing information available to hackers makes getting in much harder, providing you with more security.

Blocking Access to the Database for External Hosts

If your MySQL database server is on the same host as the web server, then it makes good sense to block access to the database port for external users. This can be done through the firewall setup utilities that are part of your operating system. The standard TCP/IP port number for MySQL is 3306. The *port number* is used to differentiate between services on the same host.

Create Separate Database Users

If you're running more than one application on your server, you should set up separate database users within MySQL for each application. That way, if there is a security breach in one of the applications, the data for the other application wouldn't be compromised. For example, if you have a bookstore web site, you can create all of your database objects to be accessible from a bookstore database account. Another site for employees to check their timesheets could then be set up using a separate database login. Each application continues to work well, and in the event of a security breach, the extent of damage is limited.

Magic Quotes

PHP attempts to shield developers from the danger of special characters being used in user input by a process called *magic quotes*. The escape characters such as single quotes (') and double quotes (") are escaped with slashes (\). By default, any data that comes from GET, POST, and cookies operations is automatically escaped. The escaping process is the same using the addslashes function on a string. When you send data that has special characters escaped to MySQL for insertion, MySQL automatically knows to convert the string back to the original values for storage in the database.

While magic quotes are good for beginners, they tend to create as many problems as they solve. Specifically, they waste some processing time, since all input is escaped regardless of whether it is bound for a database or may have been displayed.

Example 14-11 shows how magic quotes add an escape character to a value collected from a form.

Example 14-11. Seeing the results of magic quotes

```php
<?php
$search=$_GET[search];
$self=$_SERVER['PHP_SELF'];
if ($search != NULL )
{
  echo "The search string is: <strong>$search</strong>.";
}
else
{
  echo ("<form action=\"$self\" ");
  echo ('method="get">
        <label> Search: <input type="text" name="search" id="search"> </label>
        <input type="submit" value="Go!">
        </form>
        ');
}
?>
```

The entry in Figure 14-14 returns the screen in Figure 14-15.

Another annoyance with magic quotes is that you can't always assume magic_quotes are enabled if you're writing PHP code that might end up being installed on a variety of servers. The solution is to check whether it is enabled from within your code and call addslashes manually if it isn't. To check to see whether magic_quotes escaping is

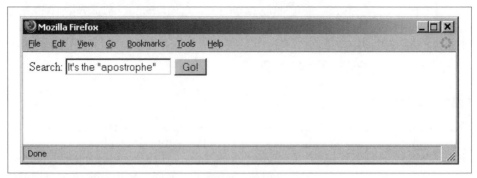

Figure 14-14. Sending some test data with special characters

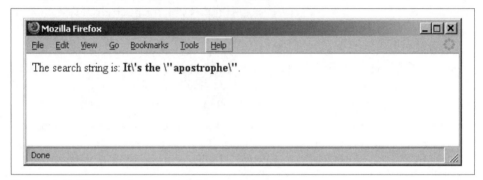

Figure 14-15. The string has its special characters escaped

active, use the get_magic_quotes_gpc function. Example 14-12 shows how to check for magic quotes and call add_slashes if they are off.

Example 14-12. Checking for magic quotes

```php
<?php
$search = $_GET["search"];
if (!get_magic_quotes_gpc()) {
$search = addslashes($search);
}
if ($search != NULL ){
echo "The search string is: <strong>$search</strong>.";
}
else {
echo '<form method="'.$_SERVER["PHP_SELF"].'" method="GET">
<label>
Search:
<input type="text" name="search" id="search" />
</label>
<input type="submit" value="Go!" />
</form>';
}
?>
```

Again, whether magic quotes are enabled or not, it's up to you to be knowledgeable about how PHP and MySQL treat special characters. Be sure that your site not only works but is secure.

We've covered security and numerous issues to help you secure your web site. Next, we'll be discussing validation and error handling. We're very close to creating your blog. How exciting!

Chapter 14 Questions

Question 14-1. Why should you use the *.php* extension for include files when other extensions such as *.inc* could be used instead?

Question 14-2. What's a more secure function than md5() for encoding passwords before they're stored in the database?

Question 14-3. Why shouldn't you use automatic global variables in your code?

Question 14-4. What is considered to be untrustworthy user data?

See the Appendix for the answers to these questions.

Validation and Error Handling

We've already discussed performing validation within our PHP code. In this chapter, we'll explore our options for validating form data before a form submission. We'll also discuss what to do when validation fails, and how to process other errors. We can check information on the client side in the user's browser using JavaScript. We can also check the data when it's submitted directly in PHP.

There's some information that can go out as part of a production error message that is not harmful for end users. For example, it's OK to say that you're having a problem connecting to your database. However, you don't want to reveal more information than is necessary in an error messages that may go out to end users. For example, you don't want to disclose the IP address of your database and certainly not the username that was attempted when you tried to connect. Both of those could aid a potential attacker in breaking in when the database comes back online.

Validating User Input with JavaScript

On the client side, your best tool for validating data is JavaScript. JavaScript is different than PHP, because it's designed to execute in the user's browser instead of on the server. Because it executes in the client's computer, JavaScript is not allowed to access anything that could be a security risk, such as the local filesystem or network resources. JavaScript is primarily used in web pages. Although its name sounds like Java, it has no relationship to it.

Since this processing is built into most modern browsers, it's not difficult for end users to disable it. Therefore, even when you use JavaScript, always take precautions to handle the possibility of it not being present on the browser.

Some of the practical things you can do with JavaScript are checking fields and alerting the user to a problem before the data is submitted to the server. The validation can be as simple as checking for an empty field or more complex checks such as validating an email address.

Although JavaScript provides immediate feedback to a user if a field doesn't pass validation, it shouldn't be relied upon as the only validation method. Your PHP code should always perform the final validation.

JavaScript has many functions built in for validating fields. They range from the familiar length function to more complex and powerful *regular expressions*. We'll discuss regular expressions in more detail later. For now, all you need to know is that they provide a way of concisely describing what a string should look like. For example, an email address should have an at (@) sign with alphanumeric characters before and after it, such as *michele@krautgrrl.com*.

There is one non-JavaScript tactic you can use to reduce client-side errors. You can set the MAXLENGTH attribute in your form's text fields. This prevents users from entering strings that are too large.

Let's go ahead and work with Example 15-1, which validates before submission.

Example 15-1. Building a form that validates its fields before submission

```
<SCRIPT LANGUAGE="JavaScript1.2" SRC="source.js">
</SCRIPT>

<HTML>
<HEAD>
    <TITLE>Sample Form</TITLE>
</HEAD>

<SCRIPT LANGUAGE="JavaScript1.2">
    function check_valid(form) {
    var error = "";
    error += verify_username(form.username.value);
    error += verify_password(form.password.value);
    error += verify_phone(form.phone.value);
    error += verify_email(form.email.value);
    if (error != "") {
       alert(error);
       return false;
    }
return true;
}
</SCRIPT>

<BODY BGCOLOR="#FFFFFF">
    <FORM action="process.php" METHOD="post"
onSubmit="return check_valid(this)" id="test1" name="test1">
    <TABLE BORDER="0" WIDTH="100%" CELLSPACING="0" CELLPADDING="0">
        <TR>
            <TD WIDTH="30%" ALIGN="right">Username</TD>
            <TD WIDTH="70%">: <INPUT TYPE="text" NAME="username"></TD>
        </TR>
        <TR>
            <TD ALIGN="right">Password</TD>
```

```
            <TD>: <INPUT TYPE="password" NAME="password"></TD>
        </TR>
        <TR>
            <TD ALIGN="right">Phone</TD>
            <TD>: <INPUT TYPE="phone" NAME="phone"></TD>
        </TR>
        <TR>
            <TD ALIGN="right">Email</TD>
            <TD>: <INPUT TYPE="email" NAME="email"></TD>
        </TR>
        <TR>
            <TD> </TD>
            <TD><INPUT TYPE="SUBMIT" VALUE="Submit"></TD>
        </TR>
    </TABLE>
    </FORM>
</BODY>
</HTML>
```

Example 15-1 includes the JavaScript in Example 15-2. The SRC= tag within the
SCRIPT element includes the script that makes the functions available within the
HTML source file.

Example 15-2. The file source.js contains functions to check the various fields

```
// verify username - 6-10 chars, uc, lc, and underscore only.
function verify_username (strng) {
var error = "";
if (strng == "") {
   error = "You didn't enter a username.\n";
}
    var illegalChars = /\W/; // allow letters, numbers, and underscores
    if ((strng.length < 6) || (strng.length > 10)) {
       error = "The username is the wrong length. It must be 6-10 characters.\n";
    }
    else if (illegalChars.test(strng)) {
    error = "The username contains illegal characters.\n";
    }
return error;
}

// verify password - between 6-8 chars, uppercase, lowercase, and numeral
function verify_password (strng) {
var error = "";
if (strng == "") {
   error = "You didn't enter a password.\n";
}
    var illegalChars = /[\W_]/; // allow only letters and numbers
    if ((strng.length < 6) || (strng.length > 8)) {
       error = "The password is the wrong length. It must be 6-8 characters.\n";
    }
    else if (illegalChars.test(strng)) {
```

```
      error = "The password contains illegal characters.\n";
   }
   else if (!((strng.search(/(a-z)+/)) && (strng.search(/(A-Z)+/)) &&
(strng.search(/(0-9)+/)))) {
      error = "The password must contain at least one uppercase letter, one
lowercase letter, and one numeral.\n";
   }
return error;
}

// verify email
function verify_email (strng) {
var error="";
if (strng == "") {
   error = "You didn't enter an email address.\n";
}

   var emailFilter=/^.+@.+\..{2,3}$/;
   if (!(emailFilter.test(strng))) {
      error = "Please enter a valid email address.\n";
   }
   else {
//test email for illegal characters
      var illegalChars= /[\(\)\<\>\,\;\:\\\"\[\]]/
         if (strng.match(illegalChars)) {
            error = "The email address contains illegal characters.\n";
         }
   }
return error;
}

// verify phone number - strip out delimiters and verify for 10 digits
function verify_phone (strng) {
var error = "";
if (strng == "") {
   error = "You didn't enter a phone number.\n";
}
//strip out acceptable non-numeric characters
var stripped = strng.replace(/[\(\)\.\-\ ]/g, '');
   if (isNaN(parseInt(stripped))) {
      error = "The phone number contains illegal characters.";

   }
   if (!(stripped.length == 10)) {
   error = "The phone number is the wrong length. Make sure you included an area
code.\n";
   }
return error;
}
```

Figure 15-1 shows a form with some invalid data, and Figure 15-2 shows the result.

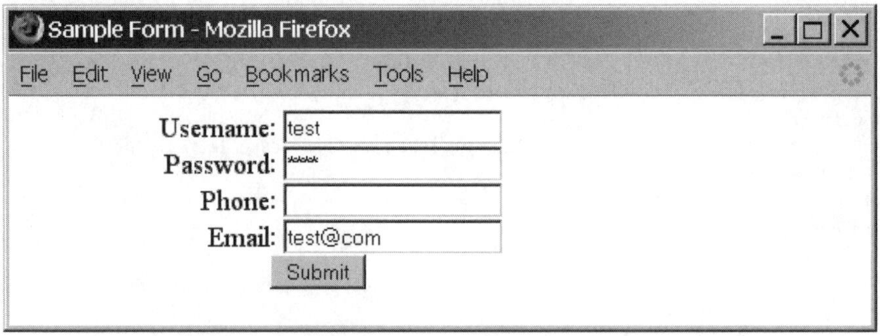

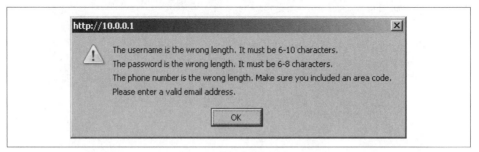

Figure 15-1. Entering some invalid data into the form

Figure 15-2. The JavaScript alert window lists the validation problems

Pattern Matching

Pattern matching allows you to build expressions that match strings using a specific matching syntax called a *regular expression*. Regular expressions allow you to perform searching tasks such as separating out a certain tag for an incoming text file, or validating user input such as email addresses.

The easiest way to use regular expressions in PHP is to use the PCRE (Perl-compatible regular expressions) extension. This extension is installed by default, so it should be part of your PHP environment. PHP also supports a style of regular expression matching functions called ereg that are older and less compatible than PCRE functions.

A regular expression is really just a string. The string uses a combination of special characters and literals to allow matching of other strings. For example, the following string describes an email address:

    \b[A-Z0-9._%-]+@[A-Z0-9._%-]+\.[A-Z]{2,4}\b

It does this by searching for:

1. Sequential alphanumeric and punctuation characters, which form the username
2. The at symbol (@)

3. A group of alphanumeric and punctuation characters, which forms the first part of the domain name

4. A period, which separates the domain name from the extension

5. A two- to four-character alpha string, which signifies the top level domain—for example, com and net

The descriptors used in the regular expression are:

\b

A boundary point of a word

[aAbB]

One of anything inside the brackets: a, A, b, B

{2,4}

A total of between 2 and 4 of anything preceding the brackets

A-Z

Any letter between A and Z, such as A, B, and C

\.

A literal period

+

Match the preceding block one or more times

There are two types of characters in the regular expression string. Those that match themselves, such as the at (@) symbol, are called *literals*, meaning they literally match. The other type is called *metacharacters*, which describe matching by specifying repetition, ranges, and combinations within the expression.

Quantifiers

Quantifiers are metacharacters that specify how many times you wish to match the preceding pattern in a string.

Quantifiers include:

*

Zero or more

+

One or more

?

Zero or one

{*num*}

Exactly *num* times

{num,}
> At least *num* times

{min,max}
> At least *min* but not more than *max* times

For example, the regular expression [a-f]?ex matches both alex and ex, but not ax.

Anchors

Anchors define a specific location for a match to take place. To match the start of a line, the caret character (^) is used. To match the end of a line, the dollar character ($) is used. To match a string that begins with I, use the regular expression ^I.

Other anchors deal with *word boundaries*. Words are made up of consecutive letters, digits, and underscores. All other characters, such as spaces, punctuation, and newline characters, are word boundaries. To match a word boundary, the backslash b (\b) character is used. To match everywhere that isn't a word boundary, the backslash capital B (\B) character is used. Table 15-1 lists other word boundaries.

Table 15-1. Escaped word boundaries

Character	Anchor type
\b	A word boundary
\B	A nonword boundary
\d	A single digit character
\D	A single nondigit character
\n	The newline character
\r	The carriage return character
\s	A single whitespace character
\S	A single nonwhitespace character
\t	The tab character
\w	A single word character, alphanumeric and underscore
\W	A single nonword character

Character classes

A *character class* allows you to group several characters together and work with them in a regular expression as though they were one character. Use the square brackets ([]) to group the characters together. For example, to match any alpha character twice:

```
[a-zA-Z]{2}
```

You can also use a *negated character class*, which selects the opposite of the character class by adding a caret (^) character after the opening square bracket. Note that this is the only time that caret character doesn't represent an anchor. The following matches all nonalpha characters.

```
[^a-zA-Z]
```

Executing pattern matches in PHP

PHP uses a set of functions that start with `preg_` to perform regular expression operations on strings. These functions take a regular expression as a parameter in a string format. There are functions for doing a variety of operations on strings, including splitting them up and returning matching portions.

The regular expression string must be in Perl format, which specifies that the regular expression start with `'/` and end with `/'`. The regular expression goes between the single quote and slashes, as in `'/regular expression/'`. Forward slashes in the expression must be escaped with a backslash. For example, */home/example* becomes `'/\/home\/example/'`.

To specify regular expression options such as case insensitivity, add the parameter to the end of the regex string after the last slash. These most common parameters are listed in Table 15-2.

Table 15-2. Regular expression characters

Regex character	Meaning
s	Dot matches all characters
i	Case insensitive
m	Match start and end of line anchors at embedded new lines in the search string

For example, use `'/abc/i'` to do a case-insensitive search of abc.

preg_match

The function `preg_match` is used to return all matches based on the supplied regular expression and string. The function value returned is `true` if a match is found. Its syntax is:

```
preg_match (string pattern, string subject [, array groups])
```

In Example 15-3, we search the string example to see if it has words that start with `ple`. Since the string doesn't start with `ple`, no results are returned.

Example 15-3. Using preg_match to return an array of matches that start with ple

```php
<?php
$subject = "example";
$pattern = '/^ple/';
preg_match($pattern, $subject, $matches);
print_r($matches);
?>
```

Example 15-3 displays:

```
Array ( )
```

Redisplaying a Form After PHP Validation Fails

While you intend for JavaScript to catch errors up front, before the user has navigated away from the page through the form submission, there will be times when PHP catches an error. When this happens, an informative error message displays and the form is redisplayed that had a validation problem. When redisplaying the form, it's a much smoother user experience if the data the user submitted is pre-populated in the form. There's nothing worse than filling out a page-long form only to find out there's a missing checkbox, meaning you have to start over.

We'll modify our previous example to check whether a username is already present in the users table, as shown in Example 15-4.

Example 15-4. Displaying an error from PHP and redisplaying the form with submitted values

```
<html>
<head>
<title>Sample Form</title>
<script type="text/javascript" src="source.js"></script>
<script type="text/javascript">
function check_valid(form) {
var error = "";
error += verify_username(form.username.value);
error += verify_password(form.password.value);
error += verify_phone(form.phone.value);
error += verify_email(form.email.value);
if (error != "") {
alert(error);
return false;
}
return true;
}
</script>
</head>
<body>
<?php
// Check for form post submit
if ($_POST["submit"]){
require_once('db_login.php');
require_once('DB.php');
$connection = DB::connect("mysql://$db_username:$db_password@$db_host/$db_database");
if (DB::isError($connection)){
die ("Could not connect to the database: <br />". DB::errorMessage($connection));
}
// Remember to use htmlentities to prevent cross-site scripting vulerablities
$username = htmlentities($_POST["username"]);
$password = htmlentities($_POST["password"]);
```

Example 15-4. Displaying an error from PHP and redisplaying the form with submitted values (continued)

```php
$email = htmlentities($_POST["email"]);
$phone = htmlentities($_POST["phone"]);
$error = "";
if ($username == ""){
$error .= "Username must not be null.<br />";
}
if ($password == ""){
$error .= "Password must not be null.<br />";
}
if ($email == ""){
$error .= "Email must not be null.<br />";
}
if ($phone == ""){
$error .= "Phone must not be null.<br />";
}
// Query the posts with catagories and user information
$query = "SELECT * FROM `users` WHERE `username`='$username'";
// Execute the database query
$result = $connection->query($query);
if (DB::isError($result)){
die("Could not query the database: <br />".$query." ".DB::errorMessage($result));
}
$user_count = $result->numRows();
if ($user_count > 0) {
$error .= "Error: Username $username is taken already. Please select another.<br />";
}
if ($error){
echo $error;
}
else {
echo "User created successfully.";
exit;
}
}
?>
<form action="<?php echo $_SERVER["PHP_SELF"]; ?>" method="POST"
onsubmit="return check_valid(this);" id="test1" name="test1">
<table>
<tr>
<td width="30%" align="right">Username:</td>
<td><input type="text" name="username" value="<?php echo
htmlspecialchars(stripslashes($username)); ?>" /></td>
</tr>
<tr>
<td align="right">Password:</td>
<td><input type="password" name="password" value="<?php echo
htmlspecialchars(stripslashes($password)); ?>" /></td>
</tr>
<tr>
<td align="right">Phone:</td>
<td><input type="phone" name="phone" value="<?php echo
htmlspecialchars(stripslashes($phone)); ?>" /></td>
</tr>
```

Example 15-4. Displaying an error from PHP and redisplaying the form with submitted values (continued)

```
</tr>
<tr>
<td align="right">Email:</td>
<td><input type="email" name="email" value="<?php echo
htmlspecialchars(stripslashes($email)); ?>" /></td>
</tr>
<tr>
<td> </td>
<td><input type="submit" name="submit" value="Submit" /></td>
</tr>
</table>
</form>
</body>
</html>
```

If a user enters invalid data, as shown in Figure 15-3, she'll get the response shown in Figure 15-4. If the data is correct, she'll see the response in Figure 15-5.

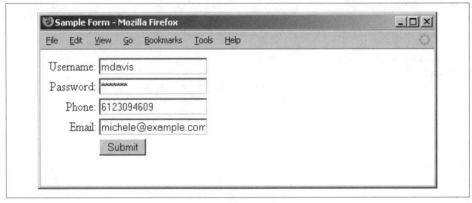

Figure 15-3. The form before submission with a conflicting username

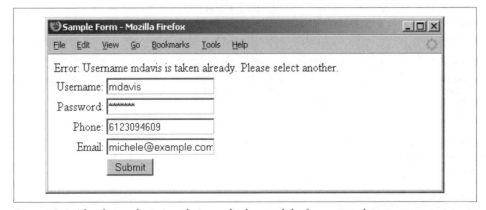

Figure 15-4. After form submission, the error displays and the form repopulates

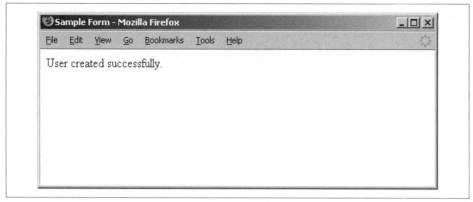

Figure 15-5. A successful submission

Chapter 15 Questions

Question 15-1. What are the pros and cons of using JavaScript to validate form input?

Question 15-2. Write the JavaScript code to display the warning "The username field must be at least six characters."

Question 15-3. Write a regular expression to validate a U.S. zip code, including the optional "zip plus four" style.

Question 15-4. Write the PHP code to test a variable called $zipcode using the regex expression from Question 15-3.

See the Appendix for the answers to these questions.

Sample Applications

You now know enough about PHP and MySQL to build full-featured web applications. These could be practically anything, from web-based mail clients to online stores with shopping carts and checkout capabilities. For our demonstration, we're going to work with *blogs*, as they're quite popular.

Building a Blog

A *blog* is short for weblog. It's an improvement on the simple guestbook/forums that started appearing on web sites years ago. They're now advanced enough to create mini-communities of people with similar interests or simply a place to post your rants about daily living. Blogs have been in the media as well. As Jeff Jarvis said in Buzz Machine, "...just as the raw voice of blogs makes newspeople uncomfortable. It's the sound of the future." Some blog examples are:

- *http://www.americablog.org/*
- *http://mark-watson.blogspot.com/2005/02/pushing-java-back-into-background-for.html*
- *http://www.doctorpundit.com*

As you can see from these three blog examples, one is political, one is about Mark Watson's life, and the third is a hodgepodge of RSS news feeds and personal podcasts. Of course, we've been given permission to use these blogs as examples, but go ahead and type in blogs in Google, and a million hits display. Weblogs are a huge trend; there are sites such as *http://www.blogclicker.com/* where you can register your blog and drive more traffic to it, or *http://www.blogarama.com/*, which is a blog search engine. The market is hot for these online diaries, or diatribes!

There are several things you need to do when you establish a blog:

- Register users
- View and post articles

- Categorize posts
- Make comments to existing posts
- Archive posts

All of these pages should be fairly configurable. If you decide to change the name of your blog, it won't be difficult to do.

Configuration File

We'll create a common configuration file called *config.php* to define where files are located, the name of the blog, and other basic configuration parameters. This is similar to the way you store your database connection information in the *db_login.php* file.

Example 16-1 shows what it looks like.

Example 16-1. The config.php script defines settings that are used throughout the site

```php
<?php
    // put full path to Smarty.class.php
    require('/usr/share/php/Smarty/Smarty.class.php');
    $smarty = new Smarty();

    $smarty->template_dir = '/home/www/htmlkb/smarty/templates';
    $smarty->compile_dir = '/home/www/htmlkb/smarty/templates_c';
    $smarty->cache_dir = '/home/www/htmlkb/smarty/cache';
    $smarty->config_dir = '/home/www/htmlkb/smarty/configs';

    $blog_title="Coffee Talk Blog";
?>
```

We use */home/www/htmlkb/smarty* as our path to the template engine files, but your path will be different based on where you installed Smarty. Note that all the template files go into the directory that $smart->template_dir points to. We also set the name of the blog to "Coffee Talk Blog."

Page Framework

We're going to use templates, which you learned about earlier, to help us build pages consistent in their appearance that are easy to modify. Let's start by setting up header and footer templates to include at the top and bottom of our pages using Smarty.

Again, these files must go into the directory defined in *config.php*, which isn't the same directory that the PHP files reside in. In our case, it's */home/www/htmlkb/ smarty/templates*, shown in Example 16-2.

Example 16-2. The header.tpl file

```
<html>
<head>
<title>{$blog_title}</title>
</head>
<body>
<h1>Welcome to the {$blog_title}</h1>
```

Example 16-2 uses the $blog_title variable that was set up in the *config.php* script. This way, the blog name appears on every page automatically.

The footer shown in Example 16-3 is very basic, providing a couple of navigation links, but we can add more to it later.

Example 16-3. The footer.tpl file

```
<hr>
<a href='posts.php'>Home</a> || <a href='logout.php'>Logout</a>
</head>
</body>
</html>
```

We'll add the code to include the header and footer shortly.

Our starting page provides the user with a way to log in. We'll use the PEAR Auth_ HTTP package to authenticate users. This package is configured to work directly with the users table. Don't worry if you don't have the users table in your database now; we'll go through the code to create it and the other tables that we'll use in the examples.

Example 16-4 shows you how to use Smarty and Auth_HTTP to build a flexible login page.

Example 16-4. The login script, called login.php

```
1 <?php
2 // Example of Auth_HTTP the also returns additional information about the user
3 require_once('config.php');
4 require_once('db_login.php');
5 require_once("Auth/HTTP.php");
6 // We use the same connection string as the pear DB functions
7 $AuthOptions = array(
8 'dsn'=>"mysql://$db_username:$db_password@$db_host/$db_database",
9 'table'=>"users", // your table name
10 'usernamecol'=>"username", // the table username column
11 'passwordcol'=>"password", // the table password column
12 'cryptType'=>"md5", // password encryption type in your db
13 'db_fields'=>"*" // enabling fetch for other db columns
14 );
15 $authenticate = new Auth_HTTP("DB", $AuthOptions);
16 // set the realm name
17 $authenticate->setRealm('Member Area');
```

Example 16-4. The login script, called login.php (continued)

```
18 // authentication failed error message
19 $authenticate->setCancelText('<h2>Access Denied</h2>');
20 // request authentication
21 $authenticate->start();
22 // compare username and password to stored values
23 if ($authenticate->getAuth()) {
24 session_start();
25 $smarty->assign('blog_title',$blog_title);
26 $smarty->display('header.tpl');
27 //setup session variable
28 $SESSION['username'] = $authenticate->username;
29 $SESSION['first_name'] = $authenticate->getAuthData('first_name');
30 $SESSION['last_name'] = $authenticate->getAuthData('last_name');
31 $SESSION['user_id'] = $authenticate->getAuthData('user_id');
32 echo "Login successful. Great to see you back ";
33 echo $authenticate->getAuthData('first_name');
34 echo " ";
35 echo $authenticate->getAuthData('last_name').".<br />";
36 $smarty->display('footer.tpl');
37 }
38 ?>
```

Since there are quite a few lines of code in this example, we'll discuss major points in the code by referencing their line numbers.

There are several lines devoted to including code and configuration details. Line 3 includes our blog configuration file. Line 4 includes the information required to log into the database. Line 5 includes the PEAR Auth_HTTP code.

To authenticate, we set up an array of options to tell Auth_HTTP how our database table stores the login information. Lines 7 through 14 set up that array. Lines 15 through 21 launch the authentication process. If it's successful, we start a session and store everything we know from the users table in the session so that it's available for easy access if we need it. Finally, we print out a message to welcome back the user with the user's full name.

If the user isn't logged in, she'll see a login prompt like the one in Figure 16-1.

After entering valid login credentials, the user will see Figure 16-2.

If the user cancels the authentication dialog, she'll get a page displaying "Access Denied." All subsequent pages in the examples check the $username from the session to make sure that a user is logged in. If the user isn't logged in, a message displays pointing her back to the login page defined in Example 16-4. That redirection page looks like Figure 16-3.

Now that we've taken care of logging in users, let's take another look at the database that supports our application.

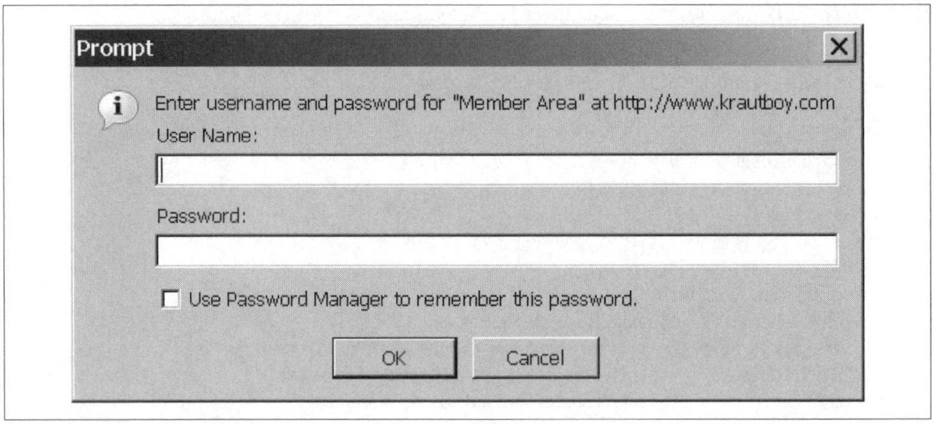

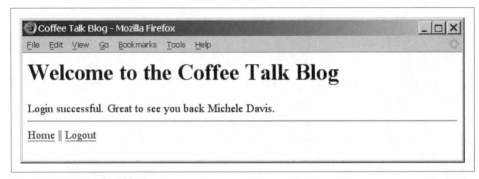

Figure 16-1. The login dialog

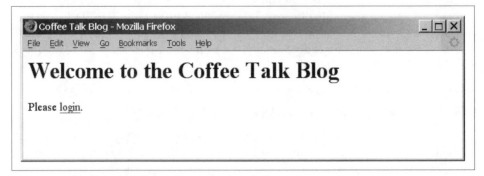

Figure 16-2. We're logged in now

Figure 16-3. The login link directs the user back to the login.php script

Database

We already created a users table for our bookstore examples. We'll add another user to that table to help us demonstrate ownership of postings and comments—specifically, how we can modify them. We'll then have three new tables for our blog: a table to store the categories, a table to store the posts, and a table to store the comments. We'll be using natural joins in our SELECT statements, since the key fields share the same names between related tables.

 You should be careful that you do your natural joins in the right order, since changing the order can cause unexpected results; most notably, there will be result sets that have extra sets of rows.

You can create these through the GUI web client, phpMyAdmin. We're including the scripts to create them from the mysql command-line tool in Example 16-5.

Example 16-5. SQL to create the posts table

```
CREATE TABLE `posts` (
  `post_id` int(11) NOT NULL auto_increment,
  `category_id` int(11) NOT NULL,
  `user_id` int(11) NOT NULL,
  `title` varchar(150) NOT NULL,
  `body` text NOT NULL,
  `posted` timestamp,
  PRIMARY KEY (`post_id`)
);
```

This returns the following information:

```
Query OK, 0 rows affected (0.02 sec)
```

This table holds the contents of the post in the body field. The other fields link to attributes such as the poster and category. Use the code in Example 16-6 to create the categories table.

Example 16-6. SQL to create the categories table

```
CREATE TABLE `categories` (
  `category_id` int(11) NOT NULL auto_increment,
  `category` varchar(150) NOT NULL,
  PRIMARY KEY (`category_id`)
);
```

Example 16-6 returns:

```
Query OK, 0 rows affected (0.01 sec)
```

The table created in Example 16-7 holds the categories that postings are posted to.

Example 16-7. SQL to create the comments table

```
CREATE TABLE `comments` (
  `comment_id` int(11) NOT NULL auto_increment,
  `user_id` int(11) NOT NULL,
  `post_id` int(11) NOT NULL,
  `title` varchar(150) NOT NULL,
  `body` text NOT NULL,
```

Example 16-7. SQL to create the comments table (continued)

```
 `posted` timestamp,
 PRIMARY KEY (`comment_id`)
);
```

This code returns the value that the query was OK:

```
    Query OK, 0 rows affected (0.02 sec)
```

The users table was created for our bookstore examples earlier, but we'll include it here, as Example 16-8, just in case you're starting fresh.

Example 16-8. SQL to create the users table (may have already been created)

```
CREATE TABLE `users` (
  `user_id` int(11) NOT NULL auto_increment,
  `first_name` varchar(100) NOT NULL,
  `last_name` varchar(100) NOT NULL,
  `username` varchar(45) NOT NULL,
  `password` varchar(32) NOT NULL,
  PRIMARY KEY (`user_id`));
```

SQL code returns, again, that the query value was OK:

```
    Query OK, 0 rows affected (0.02 sec)
```

Sample data

To keep thing simple, we're going to insert some test data, using Example 16-9. The test data lets us build pages to display posts and immediately see them displayed without having to build pages that add entries for them. Once we display posts, we'll code the pages to add posts and modify them. This same process is used for comments.

Example 16-9. Inserting sample data for the tables

```
INSERT INTO categories VALUES (1,'Press Releases');
INSERT INTO categories VALUES (2,'Feature Requests');

INSERT INTO posts VALUES (NULL,1,1,'PHP Version 12','PHP Version 12, to be
released third quarter 2006. Featuring the artificial inteligence engine that
writes the code for you.',NULL);
INSERT INTO posts VALUES (NULL,1,1,'MySQL Version 8','Returns winning lotto
number.',NULL);
INSERT INTO posts VALUES (NULL,2,2,'Money Conversion',' Please add functions
for converting between foreign currentcies. ',NULL);

INSERT INTO comments VALUES (NULL,1,1,'Correction','Release delayed till the
year 2099',NULL);

INSERT INTO users VALUES (NULL,'Michele','Davis','mdavis',md5('secret'));
INSERT INTO users VALUES (NULL,'Jon','Phillips','jphillips',md5('password'));
```

You should see a result similar to the one below for each of the INSERT SQL commands.

```
Query OK, 1 row affected, 1 warning (0.03 sec)
```

We now have some sample data loaded; therefore, we can start writing some pages that display data.

Displaying a Postings Summary

If you're not sure how to do something in the template beyond the objects we created, visit the online documentation for Smarty templates at *http://smarty.php.net*. The templates separate the look and feel of the pages from the code that populates their data. While using the templates requires a little more work to set up and figure out the syntax, it reduces the overall amount of code you need to write. Smarty knows how to automate mundane tasks such as generating drop-down lists when building forms.

We're going to go right ahead and jump into building the main display page that works in tandem with its template, shown in Example 16-10. Be sure to place the template files in the same directory that's established in your *config.php* file; the PHP files can go anywhere you like as long as they're web accessible.

Example 16-10. The posts.php script displays a listing of posts and their subjects

```
1 <?php
2 session_start();
3 require_once('config.php');
4 require_once('db_login.php');
5 require_once("DB.php");
6 // Display the page header
7 $smarty->assign('blog_title',$blog_title);
8 $smarty->display('header.tpl');
9 // Check for valid login
10 if (!isset($_SESSION['username'])) {
11 echo 'Please <a href="login.php">login</a>.';
12 exit;
13 }
14 // Connect to the database
15 $connection = DB::connect("mysql://$db_username:$db_password@$db_host/$db_database");
16
17 if (DB::isError($connection)){
18 die ("Could not connect to the database: <br />". DB::errorMessage($connection));
19 }
20 // Query the posts with catagories and user information
21 $query = "SELECT * FROM `users` NATURAL JOIN `posts` NATURAL JOIN `categories`
22 ORDER BY `posted` DESC";
23 // Execute the database query
24 $result = $connection->query($query);
25 if (DB::isError($result)){
26 die("Could not query the database: <br />".$query." ".DB::errorMessage($result));
```

```
27 }
28 // Place the query results into an array
29 while ($result_row = $result->fetchRow(DB_FETCHMODE_ASSOC)) {
30 $test[] = $result_row;
31 }
32 // Send the data to the template
33 $smarty->assign('posts', $test);
34 // Display the template with the data plugged in
35 $smarty->display('posts.tpl');
36 // Close the database connection
37 $connection->disconnect();
38 // Display the page footer
39 $smarty->display('footer.tpl');
40 ?>
```

Since Example 16-10 is a longer example, we'll break down what's happening line by line. Line 2 starts the session so we can check whether the user is logged in. Lines 7 and 8 display the header. Lines 10 through 13 check the $username_id session variable and display a login link if a user is not logged in. The rest of the page doesn't display because we use the exit command.

We're now ready to interact with the database. Lines 15 through 19 connect to the database and check for connection errors. Line 21 defines the query that we'll use to get all of the information about the postings. We have to be very careful with the order of the natural joins or we'll end up getting results that aren't properly linked together. The users table is referenced first. We also define an ORDER BY statement because we want the most recent postings displayed first. Lines 29 through 31 assign the query results to an array that we'll assign to the smarty template in line 33.

Now that we have all of the information from the database, we display the template in line 35. The template is defined below in Example 16-11. The last line of the template provides a link for users to add postings. Line 39 displays the footer.

Example 16-11. The posts.tpl template file defines how the postings appear on the page

```
{section name=mysec loop=$posts}
<a href="view_post.php?post_id={$posts[mysec].post_id}">{$posts[mysec].title}</a>
by <b>{$posts[mysec].first_name} {$posts[mysec].last_name}</b>
from the <b>{$posts[mysec].category}</b> category at <b>{$posts[mysec].posted}</b>.
<br />
{/section}
<br />
Click to <a href="modify_post.php?action=add">add</a> a posting.<br />
```

Because there may be numerous postings to display using the same format, we define a section in the template that'll go through the $posts array and substitute the values for the chunk of HTML enclosed in the section tags. To do the same thing outside of

Smarty, we'd have to use a `for` or a `while` loop to iterate through the posts in the array and display them one by one.

> Notice that the links that display the posting with its body on a separate page are generated with an embedded link in the template.

The *view_post.php* script uses the `post_id` value in the link to determine which posting to display. All of the pieces must work together for our pages to function correctly.

The sample data we loaded causes a page that looks like Figure 16-4 to display when we request the *posts.php* page, and then the template populates.

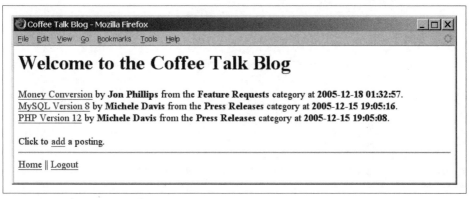

Figure 16-4. The summary of postings

As you can see in Figure 16-4, we've got a list of postings. We've also provided a couple of links. The link that is the title of a posting sends us to a posting detail and comments page. The link that displays after the list of postings points us to a page for adding posts. These two links are actually processed by the same script, since the process for adding a posting is similar to the process for updating a posting.

Displaying a Posting and Its Comments

To create the *view_post.php* script, we'll reuse some of the code and add a bit in Example 16-12. The script takes a `post_id` as a GET parameter and displays the posting, including its body. Comments for the posting are also listed. The user who creates the posting can delete or modify it. Likewise, users can delete or modify any comment entries they have made.

Example 16-12. The view_post.php script displays a summary of its comments

```php
<?php

session_start();

require_once('config.php');
require_once('db_login.php');
require_once("DB.php");

// Display the header
$smarty->assign('blog_title',$blog_title);
$smarty->display('header.tpl');

// Check for valid login
if (!isset($_SESSION["username"])) {
echo 'Please <a href="login.php">login</a>.';
exit;
}

// Connect to the database
$connection = DB::connect("mysql://$db_username:$db_password@$db_host/$db_database");

if (DB::isError($connection)){
die ("Could not connect to the database: <br />". DB::errorMessage($connection));
}

$post_id = $_GET["post_id"];

$query = "SELECT * FROM `users` NATURAL JOIN `posts` NATURAL JOIN `categories`
WHERE `post_id`=$post_id";
$result = $connection->query($query);

if (DB::isError($result)){
die("Could not query the database: <br />".$query." ".DB::errorMessage($result));
}

while ($result_row = $result->fetchRow(DB_FETCHMODE_ASSOC)) {
$test[]=$result_row;
}

$smarty->assign('posts',$test);
$smarty->assign('owner_id',$_SESSION["user_id"]);
$query = "SELECT * FROM `users` NATURAL JOIN `comments` WHERE `post_id`=$post_id";
$result = $connection->query($query);

if (DB::isError($result)){
die("Could not query the database: <br />".$query." ".DB::errorMessage($result));
}

$comment_count = $result->numRows();

while ($result_row = $result->fetchRow(DB_FETCHMODE_ASSOC)) {
$comments[] = $result_row;
}
```

```
$smarty->assign('posts',$test);
$smarty->assign('comments',$comments);
$smarty->assign('comment_count',$comment_count);

$smarty->display('view_post.tpl');

$connection->disconnect();

// Display the footer
$smarty->display('footer.tpl');

?>
```

The code in Example 16-12 starts out like the code in Example 16-10, since they both query and display postings. The difference is that the query string uses the post_id parameter in the WHERE clause to only retrieve information for one posting.

The second half of the code queries the comments table, also using the post_id in the WHERE clause to retrieve only comments for the posting that we're displaying. We run into two complications though. Any given posting may or may not have any comments associated with it, and we'd like to display a heading before we list the comments. However, if there are no comments, we don't want to display that heading.

To assign the variable $comment_count, we use:

```
$comment_count=$result->numRows();
```

The template will then be able to tell if there are any comments. The other problem is that we want to provide links for editing and deleting posts as well as comments, only if the logged-in user created the posting or comment. This means we need to send in the current user's ID to the template before calling it. We send in the user_id form to the session template like this:

```
$smarty->assign('owner_id',$_SESSION[user_id]);
```

When the template displays, it has the data from the posting, the comments, how many comments, and the currently logged-in user's ID.

Example 16-13 lists the contents of the *view_post.tpl* template used in the *view_posts. php* file.

Example 16-13. view_post.tpl

```
{section name=mysec loop=$posts}
<h2>{$posts[mysec].title}</h2>
{$posts[mysec].body}
<br />
Posted by <b>{$posts[mysec].first_name} {$posts[mysec].last_name}</b>
from the <b>{$posts[mysec].category}</b> category at
<b>{$posts[mysec].posted}</b>.<br />
{if $posts[mysec].user_id == $owner_id}
<a href="modify_post.php?post_id={$posts[mysec].post_id}&action=edit">Edit</a> ||
```

Example 16-13. view_post.tpl (continued)

```
<a href="modify_post.php?post_id={$posts[mysec].post_id}&action=delete">Delete</a> ||
<a href="modify_comment.php?post_id={$posts[mysec].post_id}&action=add"
>Add a comment</a>
<br />
{/if}
{/section}
{if $comment_count != "0"}
<h3>Comments</h3>
{section name=mysec2 loop=$comments}
<hr />
<b>{$comments[mysec2].title}</b>
<br />
{$comments[mysec2].body}
<br />
Posted by <b>{$comments[mysec2].first_name} {$comments[mysec2].last_name}</b>
at <b>{$comments[mysec2].posted}</b>.<br />
{if $comments[mysec2].user_id == $owner_id}
<a href="modify_comment.php?comment_id={$comments[mysec2].comment_id}&action=edit"
>Edit</a> ||
<a href="modify_comment.php?comment_id={$comments[mysec2].comment_id}&action=delete"
>Delete</a>
<br />
{/if}
{/section}
{/if}
```

This template builds on the template from Example 16-11 by forming another repeatable section for comments. We use the Smarty {if } evaluation to test for the presence of comments and to see whether the current user is also the creator of posts and comments. If the number of comments is 0, we don't display a heading for the comments. If the user's ID and the user_id from the posting or comment match, then we display the links for editing or modifying them, as shown in Figure 16-5.

Adding and deleting posts are handled, so we'll move on to doing the most advanced script yet, which can handle adding and changing posts.

Adding and Changing Posts

The adding and changing functionalities are grouped together, because they both build the same HTML form to add or modify the posting, as well as the validation steps before saving to the database. Again, we're building on the concept of using the same script to generate an HTML form and process its submission.

There are quite a few things going on in this script:

- In lines 26 through 31, we connect to the database, since most of the operations require interaction with the database.

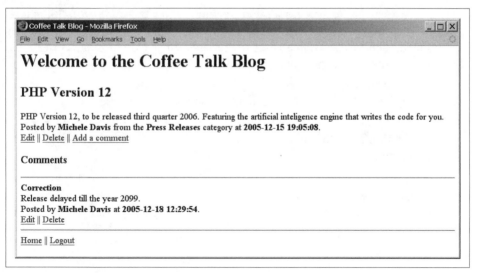

Figure 16-5. Our posting is displayed with its comments

- In lines 18 through 23, we grab variables from the environment, since the script might be taking a `post_id` to tell which posting we're editing, and we get other variables from the `POST` from submissions that must be processed.

- Lines 32 through 45 process a deletion if the `$action` variable is set to delete. The `WHERE` clause of the delete query includes both the `$post_id`, which was sent to the script and therefore may be forged. The `$user_id` validates that the logged-in user created the script. If someone sends in a `post_id` of a posting he doesn't own, he can't delete it. The `$stop` variable is set to stop any further processing, as this is an end point. Only the page footer is added.

- Lines 47 through 67 use the `$post_id` from the URL to grab post information from the database and prepopulate the form in the template with the existing data for the post. The `$action` variable is set to `edit` so `modify_posts.php` knows to process the data when the user submits the form after editing. The `$stop` variable is set to stop any further processing, as this is an end point. Only the page footer is added.

- Line 70 checks whether the script ran from a form submission. If it did, then we're processing data for an add operation or an update. Then this data must be validated.

- Lines 71 through 82 validate the data. If there's a problem, we tell the user exactly what the error is, and then redisplay the form using the code in lines 128 through 136 with the data the user sent in so that she don't have to start over. When the user resubmits her form, it checks again for correctness. Although the checks done here are just to make sure the fields aren't empty, they could be as complex as you desire and would go in the same place in the script.

- Lines 84 through 96 process an add operation after there is successful validation. The query is built using the data from the form submission, and then it is executed. The $stop variable is set to stop any further processing, as this is an end point. Only the page footer is added.

- Lines 97 through 112 process an update operation after successful validation. The query is built, and then executed. The $stop variable is set to stop any further processing, as this is an end point. Only the page footer will be added.

- Lines 114 through 126 display an empty form. This is the first step when adding a new posting.

Throughout the processing, we check that the value of the $stop variable skips processing remaining steps if an error is encountered or we simply have accomplished what needs to happen. All of the steps rely on the template to display the HTML form.

Example 16-14 lists the script.

Example 16-14. modify_posts.php

```
1  <?php
2    include('db_login.php');
3    require_once( 'DB.php' );
4    require_once( 'config.php' );
5
6    //check for valid login
7    session_start();
8
9    //display the header
10   $smarty->assign('blog_title',$blog_title);
11   $smarty->display('header.tpl');
12
13   if  (!isset($_SESSION['username'])) {
14     echo ("Please <a href='login.php'>login</a>.");
15     exit();
16   }
17   //grab submission variables
18   $post_id=$_POST[post_id];
19   $title=htmlentities($_POST['title']);
20   $body=htmlentities($_POST['body']);
21   $action=htmlentities($_POST['action']);
22   $category_id=htmlentities($_POST['category_id']);
23   $user_id=$_SESSION["user_id"];
24
25   //conected to database
26   $connection = DB::connect( "mysql://$db_username:$db_password@$db_
27 host/$db_database" );
28   if (!$connection)
29   {
30     die ("Could not connect to the database: <br>". DB::errorMessage());
31   };
32   if ($_GET['action']=="delete" and !$stop)
```

Example 16-14. modify_posts.php (continued)

```
33   {
34     $post_id=$_GET[post_id];
35     $query = "delete from posts where post_id='".$post_id."' and
36 user_id='".$user_id."'";
37     $result = $connection->query($query);
38     if (DB::isError($result))
39     {
40       die ("Could not query the database: <br>". $query. " ".
41 DB::errorMessage($result));
42     };
43     echo ("Deleted successfully.<br>");
44     $stop="TRUE";
45   }
46
47   //we're editing an entry, explicitly grab the id from the URL
48   if ($_GET[post_id] AND !$stop) {
49     $query = "SELECT * FROM users NATURAL JOIN posts NATURAL JOIN categories
50 where post_id = $_GET[post_id]";
51     $result = $connection->query($query);
52     if (DB::isError($result))
53     {
54       die ("Could not query the database: <br>". $query. " ".
55 DB::errorMessage($result));
56     };
57     while ($result_row = $result->fetchRow(DB_FETCHMODE_ASSOC)) {
58     $posts[]=$result_row;
59     }
60     $smarty->assign('action','edit');
61     $smarty->assign('posts',$posts);
62     //get those categories
63     $query = "SELECT category_id, category FROM categories";
64     $smarty->assign('categories',$connection->getAssoc($query));
65     $smarty->display('post_form.tpl');
66     $stop="TRUE";
67   }
68
69   //The form was submitted, was it an add or an edit?
70   if ($_POST['submit'] AND !$stop)
71   {
72     //validate fields
73     if ($title == ""){
74       echo ("Title must not be null.<br>");
75       $found_error=TRUE;
76       $stop="TRUE";
77     }
78     if ($body == ""){
79       echo ("Body must not be null.<br>");
80       $found_error=TRUE;
81       $stop="TRUE";
82     }
83     //validated OK lets hit the databae
84     if ( $_POST['action']=="add" AND !$stop)
```

Example 16-14. modify_posts.php (continued)

```
85     {
86         $query = "insert into posts values (NULL,
87 "."'".$category_id."'",'".$user_id."'",'".$title."'",'".$body."'", NULL)";
88         $result = $connection->query($query);
89         if (DB::isError($result))
90         {
91             die ("Could not query the database: <br>". $query. " ".
92 DB::errorMessage($result));
93         };
94         echo ("Posted successfully.<br>");
95         $stop="TRUE";
96     }
97     if ($_POST['action']=="edit" and !$stop)
98     {
99         //do nothing
100        $query = "update posts set category_id ='".$category_id."'",
101 title ='".$title."'",body='".$body."'" where post_id='".$post_id."'"
102 and user_id='".$user_id."'";
103        //echo $query;
104        $result = $connection->query($query);
105        if (DB::isError($result))
106        {
107            die ("Could not query the database: <br>". $query. " ".
108 DB::errorMessage($result));
109        };
110        echo ("Updated successfully.<br>");
111        $stop="TRUE";
112     }
113 }
114 if (!$stop)
115 {
116     //display blank form
117     //create an empty entry
118     $result_row=array('title'=>NULL,'body'=>NULL);
119     $posts[]=$result_row;
120     //get the categories
121     $query = "SELECT category_id, category FROM categories";
122     $smarty->assign('categories',$connection->getAssoc($query));
123     $smarty->assign('posts',$posts);
124     $smarty->assign('action','add');
125     $smarty->display('post_form.tpl');
126 }
127
128 if ($found_error) {
129     //assign old vals
130     //redisplay form
131     $result_row=array('title'=>"$title",'body'=>"$body",'post_id'=>"$post_id");
132     $posts[]=$result_row;
133     $smarty->assign('action',$action);
134     $smarty->assign('posts',$posts);
135     $smarty->display('post_form.tpl');
136 }
```

Example 16-14. modify_posts.php (continued)

```
137    //display the footer
138    $smarty->display('footer.tpl');
139
140 ?>
```

The good news is that the template isn't very complicated! Its job is simply to take information from the user and hang onto a couple of hidden fields, action and post_id. They help the *post_form.php* script keep track of whether we're adding, updating, or deleting. If we're editing, then the post_id tells the script which article is being edited.

This example highlights the advantage of using a template. If you want to make simple changes to the wording or layout of the form, then modifying the template is done by a user that just knows HTML.

 The Smarty tags shouldn't be altered.

If the HTML code is peppered into the PHP code, as in Example 16-14, users would probably break something when making modifications. You'll need the code for the templates, as shown in Example 16-15.

Example 16-15. post_form.tpl

```
<form action="modify_post.php" method="POST">
<label>
Title: <input type="text" name="title" value="{$posts[mysec].title}">
</label>
<br /><br />
<label>
Body: <textarea name="body" cols="40" rows="4">{$posts[mysec].body}</textarea>
</label>
<input type="hidden" name="action" value="{$action}">
<input type="hidden" name="post_id" value="{$posts[mysec].post_id}"><br>
<label>
Category:
{html_options name="category_id" options=$categories
selected=$posts[mysec].category_id}
</label>
<br />
<input type="submit" name="submit" value="Post" />
</form>
{/section}
```

The only thing new here is the {html_options} Smarty tag. This automates the generation of a drop-down selection list in the HTML form for the categories. Without Smarty, displaying a select element in a form requires using a for or while loop to display the elements; this can be very tedious, especially if you have a lot of selection lists.

Clicking on the Edit link for the first posting in Figure 16-5 causes a dialog to display, as in Figure 16-6.

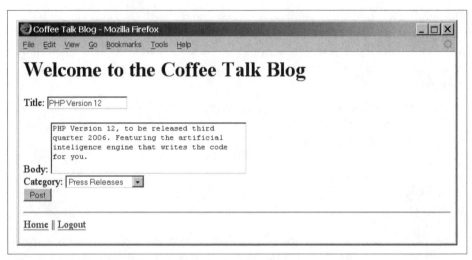

Figure 16-6. Editing the posting title PHP Version 12

Notice that the drop-down list defaults to the value we sent from the script. You can modify the entry, as shown in Figure 16-7.

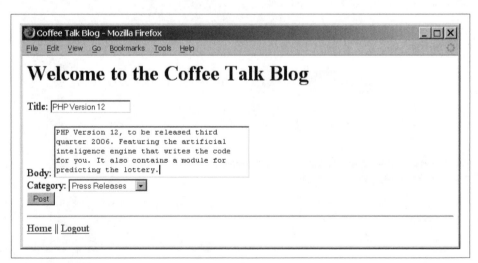

Figure 16-7. Adding text to a posting

After adding the text "It also contains a module for predicting the lottery," we click the Post button. Figure 16-8 indicates that the posting updated successfully.

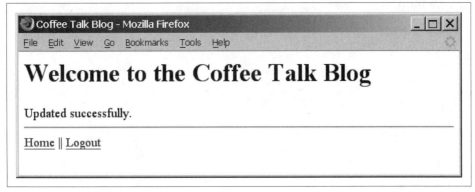

Figure 16-8. The update was successful

Now we can navigate back to the article, shown in Figure 16-9, by clicking on the Home link and selecting the PHP Version 12 posting.

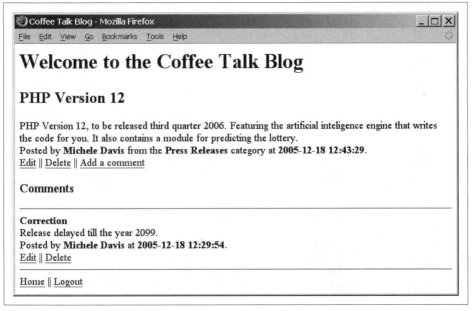

Figure 16-9. The new text appears in the post

You can go ahead and try sending in an empty field. The code alerts you that you can't do that and sends you back to the HTML form to fix the problem.

Adding and Changing Comments

The code for working with comments is nearly identical to the PHP code for modifying posts. The changes are emphasized in Example 16-16.

Example 16-16. modify_comment.php

```php
<?php

session_start();

require_once('config.php');
require_once('db_login.php');
require_once("DB.php");

// Display the header
$smarty->assign('blog_title',$blog_title);
$smarty->display('header.tpl');

// Check for valid login
if (!isset($_SESSION["username"])) {
echo 'Please <a href="login.php">login</a>.';
exit;
}

// Connect to the database
$connection = DB::connect("mysql://$db_username:$db_password@$db_host/$db_database");

if (DB::isError($connection)){
die ("Could not connect to the database: <br />". DB::errorMessage($connection));
}

$stop = false;

$post_id = $_REQUEST["post_id"];

$title = htmlentities($_POST['title']);
$body = htmlentities($_POST['body']);
$action = htmlentities($_POST['action']);
$category_id = htmlentities($_POST['category_id']);
$user_id = $_SESSION["user_id"];
$comment_id = htmlentities($_POST['comment_id']);

if ($_GET['action'] == "delete" and !$stop) {
$comment_id = $_GET["comment_id"];
$query = "DELETE FROM `comments` WHERE `comment_id`='".$comment_id."'
AND `user_id`='".$user_id."'";
$result = $connection->query($query);
if (DB::isError($result)){
die("Could not query the database: <br />".$query." ".DB::errorMessage($result));
}
echo "Deleted successfully.<br />";
$stop = true;
}

// We're editing an entry, explicitly grab the id from the URL
if ($_GET["comment_id"] and !$stop) {
$query = "SELECT * FROM `comments` NATURAL JOIN `users`
WHERE `comment_id`=".$_GET["comment_id"];
```

Example 16-16. modify_comment.php (continued)

```
$result = $connection->query($query);
if (DB::isError($result)){
die("Could not query the database: <br />".$query." ".DB::errorMessage($result));
}
while ($result_row = $result->fetchRow(DB_FETCHMODE_ASSOC)) {
$comments[] = $result_row;
}
$post_id = $_GET["post_id"];
$smarty->assign('action','edit');
$smarty->assign('comments',$comments);
$smarty->assign('post_id',$post_id);
$smarty->display('comment_form.tpl');
// Display the footer
$smarty->display('footer.tpl');
exit;
}

//The form was submitted, was it an add or an update?
if ($_POST['submit'] and !$stop) {
// Validate fields
if ($title == ""){
echo 'Title must not be null.<br />';
$found_error = true;
$stop = true;
}
if ($body == ""){
echo "Body must not be null.<br />";
$found_error = true;
$stop = true;
}
// Validated OK lets hit the database
if ($_POST['action'] == "add" AND !$stop) {
$query = "INSERT INTO `comments` VALUES (NULL,
'".$user_id."','".$post_id."','".$title."','".$body."', NULL)";
$result = $connection->query($query);
if (DB::isError($result)){
die("Could not query the database: <br />".$query." ".DB::errorMessage($result));
}
echo "Posted successfully.<br />";
$stop = true;
}
if ($_POST['action']=="edit" and !$stop){
$query = "UPDATE `comments` SET
`title`='".$title."',
`body`='".$body."'
WHERE `comment_id`='".$comment_id."' AND `user_id`='".$user_id."'";
$result = $connection->query($query);
if (DB::isError($result)){
die("Could not query the database: <br />".$query." ".DB::errorMessage($result));
}
echo 'Updated successfully.<br />';
$stop = true;
```

Example 16-16. modify_comment.php (continued)

```
}
}

if (!$stop){
// Display blank form
// Create an empty entry
$post_id = $_GET["post_id"];
$result_row = array('title'=>NULL,'body'=>NULL,'comment_id'=>NULL);
$comments[] = $result_row;
// Get the categories
$smarty->assign('post_id',$post_id);
$smarty->assign('comments',$comments);
$smarty->assign('action','add');
$smarty->display('comment_form.tpl');
}

if ($found_error) {
// Assign old vals
// Redisplay form
$post_id = $_POST["post_id"];
$result_row = array('title'=>"$title",'body'=>"$body",'comment_id'=>"$comment_id");
$comments[] = $result_row;
$smarty->assign('action',$action);
$smarty->assign('post_id',$post_id);
$smarty->assign('comments',$comments);
$smarty->display('comment_form.tpl');
}

// Display the footer
$smarty->display('footer.tpl');

?>
```

The changes revolved around working with a comment_id instead of a post_id as the key value, although you still track the posting_id for new comments. The name of the template is *comment_form.tpl* instead of *post_form.tpl*.

The template for building the comments form, shown in Example 16-17, is the same as the template for posts, except you no longer need the category selection drop-down list, and you've replaced posts with comments everywhere it appears in the template—except for the hidden form parameter post_id that is used for tracking, which is what posting a new comment is for.

Example 16-17. comment_form.tpl

```
{section name=mysec loop=$comments}
<form action="modify_comment.php" method="post">
<label>
Title:
<input type="text" name="title" value="{$comments[mysec].title}" />
</label>
```

Example 16-17. comment_form.tpl (continued)

```
<br />
<br />
<label>
Body:
<textarea name="body" cols="40" rows="4">{$comments[mysec].body}</textarea>
</label>
<input type="hidden" name="action" value="{$action}" />
<input type="hidden" name="post_id" value="{$post_id}" />
<input type="hidden" name="comment_id" value="{$comments[mysec].comment_id}" />
<br /><br />
<input type="submit" name="submit" value="Post" />
</form>
{/section}
```

Clicking on the edit link for the Correction comment displays Figure 16-10.

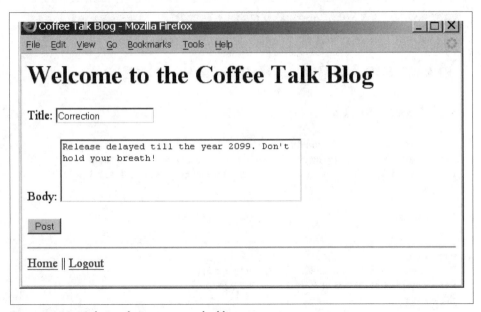

Figure 16-10. Updating the comment and adding some text

We add the text "Don't hold your breath!" and click Post, bringing us to the screen shown in Figure 16-11.

Finally, we navigate back to the post, in Figure 16-12.

We can see the comment has been updated in Figure 16-12. We can use the same format of PHP and template files to modify other entities in our database, such as categories or users. The possibilities are endless. You can embark on creating numerous dynamic web sites armed with your learning from this book.

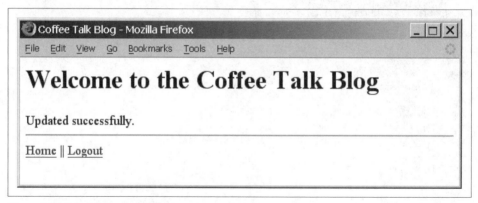

Figure 16-11. Confirmation of the comment update

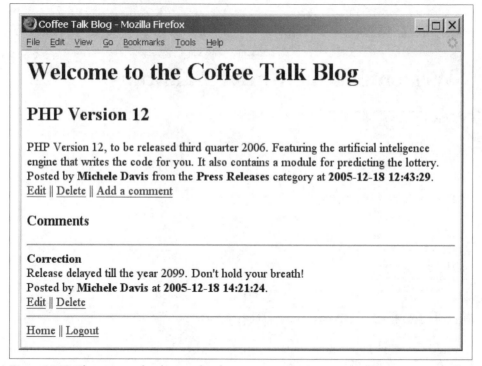

Figure 16-12. The comment has been updated

The next (and last) chapter discusses resources for PHP and MySQL questions. There is a plethora of information out there, and it's available right at your fingertips!

Chapter 16 Questions

Question 16-1. Change the blog name to "PHP and MySQL Zone."

Question 16-2. Add a new posting category called "Bugs."

Question 16-3. What's the advantage of using templates?

See the Appendix for the answers to these questions.

CHAPTER 17

Finishing Your Journey

You've created a blog. You've started out learning the ins and outs of dynamic web development and how the Internet world is changing rapidly. Dynamic web sites are what clients, your employer, and your volunteer organizations—or even just you— desire. While static pages have their place in web development, new tools such as Ajax and Ruby are stepping stones after learning PHP and MySQL.

This chapter will arm you with numerous resources that can help you during your PHP and MySQL journey.

Finding Help on the Web

The Web contains a plethora of information. Remember both PHP and MySQL are open source technologies, supported by a community of developers who share their work. That means that code is readily available on the Web for your use. There may be some code glitches, but there is help on the Web when you type your query into a search engine. We prefer Google, but you can use Yahoo! or even MSN to find useful links.

First of all, you should download the PHP manual available at *http://www.php.net/ docs*. The manual is pretty cool, since you can rapidly access any page of it if you're looking for a particular function by going to *http://www.php.net/function_name* (you'll fill in the italicized function name you're searching for). There is also a search utility for functions, so you don't need to always fill in the full function name.

One thing we haven't covered is the PHP Coding Standard. As you've probably guessed, this standard is a document that shows proper format and syntax for variable names, control structures, and much more. These format and syntax recommendations help you minimize coding errors. Currently, some sites that address this include:

- *http://srparish.net/writings/php_code_standards.html*
- *http://www.phpfreaks.com/tutorials/35/0.php*
- *http://www.phpcommunity.org/node/139*

We're going to do a minor recap of some of the important concepts covered through-out the book along with code examples. This is just a refresher to jog your brain into remembering a lot of the content you've already digested.

Comments

Some basic coding standards are comments that help you remember what your code is doing. You may need to go back and look at code you wrote several months ago. What seems straightforward now may take considerable time to discern later with-out leaving some meaningful explanations. Remember that PHP uses the same style for comments as C++, including /* */ and // for a single-line comment.

 Remember every file you create needs to start with a comment block.

The comment block should include the file's description, version, author, and per-haps a copyright. It can look like Example 17-1.

Example 17-1. File comments

```
/*
 *
 * this file is about furniture stores.
 * this file is about furniture stores in Minnesota, Wisconsin, Iowa and Illinois.
 *
 * Portions Copyright 2005-2006 (c) O'Reilly & Associates
 * The rest Copyright 2005 (c) from their respective authors
 *
 * @version    $Id: coding_standards.html,v 1.2 2005/12/19 24:49:50
 *
 */
```

Files should have comments, and every function should have a block comment speci-fying the name, parameters, return values, purpose, and last change date, as shown in Example 17-2.

Example 17-2. Function comments

```
/*
 * furniture stores locator.
 * Locate furniture stores in Minnesota, Wisconsin, Iowa and
 * Illinois based on their zip code.
 *
 * @author    michele davis mdavis@example.com
 * @param     zipcode  the zipcode to search for stores near
 * @return    store     the store id of the nearest store
 * @date      2005-12-21
 *
 */
```

The first line should be a short description, with the second line providing more details.

Formatting

While there are different acceptable styles for name and spacing, the most important thing is that you pick one and stick with it so that your code has consistent visual indicators to anyone who may work with it.

Indenting

Some people use tabs to indent, while others use spaces. If you do use spaces, make sure you use a consistent number of spaces; for example, two for each indent. You should indent any time you use a statement that contains a block of code, such as an `if` statement or a `for` loop. This will help you tell which block a statement belongs to and match it to closing brackets (}). Indenting isn't always necessary—it's pretty much a personal preference. As you may have noticed, not all our code in this book is indented. This is our preference, since indenting or not indenting doesn't change the code.

PHP tags

You should always use `<?php` and `?>` to delimit your PHP code. This is the most portable and supported format. Don't use the older `<?` and `?>` tags, as they're not fully supported and can confuse XML parsers.

Templating

We've used the Smarty templating system in many examples in this book. Smarty offers a nice mix between easy to use and flexible, but there are other templating systems you can use. Their use is highly recommended, as is placing the template files in a separate directory from the PHP code. Using PHP to gather and validate data, and then using a template system to display the results, maintains cleaner, easier-to-maintain code.

Expressions

Complex expressions can be difficult to decipher, but there are some guidelines to make them easier to understand:

- You can always use extra parentheses to make the order of evaluation clearer in expressions or to eliminate any gray areas.
- Keep it simple; if an evaluation is very complex, split it up into manageable chunks.
- The not (!) operator can make expressions difficult to read, so try to eliminate it.
- Use multiple `if else` statements instead of the ternary operator (x ? condition : condition), because it's more concise, but it's also harder to read.

Function calls

Add only one space after a comma in a parameter listing, as shown below:

```
$var = inventory($location, $category);
```

When assigning values, place one space before and one after the equals (=) sign. You can add more spaces when assigning multiple values to make them easier to read.

```
$count       = inventory("Minneapolis","home");
$count2      = inventory("Chicago","office");
```

Function definitions

Functions should be defined with an indent after the function line, and any included code blocks, such as the if statement, should be indented again.

```
function inventory($location, $category = 'office') {
    if (condition) {
        statement;
    }
    return $return_value;
}
```

If you have arguments with default values, place them at the end of the argument list. The return value from your function should indicate whether it was successful or whether there's a chance it may fail.

```
function inventory($location, $category = 'office') {
    if (!$location) {
        $return_value=false;
    }
    return $return_value;
```

Objects

Objects have general design rules to aid their design and use because of their complexity. Each object should only have attributes associated with it that are directly related to the object. Each object should have its own error handling defined so that errors don't need to propagate to higher level objects that likely don't know as much about the environment in which the error occurred. Likewise, all objects should have their own constructor methods.

Naming

Here are some guidelines for naming:

- Name your functions to indicate what they do; for example, `connectDatabase`, `deleteUser`.
- Name your variables to indicate what they store; for example, `DatabaseName`, `RowCount`.

- Name constants using uppercase descriptive words with underscores to separate words. If the constant belongs to an object, prefix the constant with the name of the package.
- Abbreviations are OK as long as they're used consistently and aren't too difficult to interpret.
- Global variables should use longer names than local variables do.

Control Structures

Control structures include `if`, `for`, `while`, and `switch`. You should indent a couple of spaces for the `if` statement. There should be one space between the statement and the opening parenthesis for the expression. This helps differentiate them visually from function calls. For example:

```
if ((expression1) || (expression2)) {
    do_something;
} elseif ((expression3) && (expression4)) {
    do_something_else;
} else {
    do_default;
}
```

Curly braces ({}) make reading your code easier and help reduce errors. Use them even if you have only one statement to execute in the block.

Here's an example for `switch` statements:

```
switch (expression) {
    case 1: {
        do_something_1;
        break;
    }
    case 2: {
        do_something_2;
        break;
    }
    default: {
        do_default;
        break;
    }
}
```

Including or requiring PHP files

When you use `include_once` and `require_once`, they guarantee that the code won't be included more than once. They're smart enough to keep track of which code has been included between them:

```
include_once('example.php');
require_once('example.php');
```

The above example won't include *example.php* more than once.

Be sure to use `require` when your code can't continue if the file to include is missing. Optional code can and should use `include`.

```
include('optional_functions.php');
```

Web Sites

There are numerous web sites available for your perusal. For PHP-specific information, the following web sites will help you:

- *http://www.php.net/*
- *http://codewalkers.com/*
- *http://www.phpfreaks.com/*
- *http://www.weberdev.com/*
- *http://www.w3schools.com/php/default.asp*
- *http://www.phpbuilder.com/*
- *http://www.htmlgoodies.com/beyond/php/*
- *http://www.zend.com/zend/tut/tutorial-yank.php*
- *http://www.sitepoint.com/article/php5-standard-library*

Chat and Listservs for PHP

Online help, chat, or listserv forums for PHP help are available at the following addresses:

- *http://www.codingforums.com/forumdisplay.php?s=b50928ffa8c7f97-cbe1f295975cdae4f&f=6*
- *http://www.devarticles.com/c/b/PHP/*
- *http://www.php-editors.com/forum/php_programming_help.php*
- *http://www.linuxcolumbus.com/*
- *http://www.php.net/*
- *http://php.resourceindex.com/*
- *http://www.hotscripts.com/*
- *http://www.phpbb.com/*

All these sites have code examples; some have question-and-answer sections and invaluable data.

PHP User Groups

Check out *http://www.phpusergroups.org/* if you wish to locate a group in your city or country. There are 348 PHP user groups in 69 countries. If you're in the U.S., there are numerous groups representing most major cities. The current U.S. groups are listed in Table 17-1.

Table 17-1. U.S. PHP groups

Group location	Group URL
Atlanta, GA	*http://atlphp.org/*
Austin, TX	*http://php.meetup.com/42/*
Cedar Lake, IN	*http://www.tjtechinc.com/nipug/*
Chicago, IL	*http://chiphpug.php.net/*
Dallas/Fort Worth, TX	*http://www.dallasphp.org/*
Denver, CO	*http://www.coloradophp.org/*
Des Moines, IA	*http://www.ciapug.org/*
Fort Lauderdale, FL	*http://www.browardphp.com/*
Libertyville, FL	*http://groups.yahoo.com/group/php4world/*
Minneapolis/St. Paul, MN	*http://www.tcphp.org/*
New York, NY	*http://www.nyphp.org/*
Provo, UT	*http://uphpu.org/*
San Diego, CA	*http://sdphp.net/*
San Francisco, CA	*http://www.phpgroup.org/*
Washington, DC	*http://groups.yahoo.com/group/washdcphp/*

Zend

PHP developers offer the Zend Certified Engineer (ZCE) Exam, which you can take after working with PHP for about a year. Having the certification helps you land jobs as a PHP developer, as more employers are looking for ZCEs.

> *http://www.zend.com/store/education/certification/zend-php-certification.php*

Zend also has shrink-wrapped software products to help you with your programming goals. Some of their programs are described here.

Zend Studio™ Professional is the premiere IDE to develop, debug, deploy, and manage PHP applications. Zend Encoder helps you with your intellectual property protection. The Zend Encoder allows an unlimited number of PHP applications to be distributed, all the while ensuring that your investment and source code are protected from copyright infringement.

The Zend Encoder compiles and converts plain-text PHP scripts into a platform-independent binary format known as a Zend Intermediate Code file. The binary files are distributed instead of the PHP code files. The user needs the free-of-cost Zend Optimizer, a runtime environment that allows end users to execute the binaries as if they were regular PHP scripts. The Optimizer provides more increased security against reverse engineering and still improves performance speed.

There is much more to Zend products, all of which you can evaluate and determine if you need them for the dynamic web site you're creating.

Lampshade

According to Aaron Greenspan, his company has been using its own PHP framework, called Lampshade, when building products for their clients. Now the framework is open source under a dual license: fee-based for commercial use, and free for noncommercial use. Just download it; even though it may have minimal bells and whistles, it's simple to use. You can take a look here: *http://www.thinkcomputer.com/corporate/news/pressreleases.html?id=24*.

Good luck with your journey involving PHP and MySQL. You've come a long way since you purchased this book. Keep in mind that O'Reilly Media, Inc. has numerous other programming titles to advance your skills beyond the scope of this book.

Chapter 17 Questions

Question 17-1. Why not use <? and ?> to start and end your PHP code blocks?

Question 17-2. What's the difference between using // comments and /* */ comments?

Question 17-3. What's the advantage of using the include_once() and require_once() directives instead of include() and require()?

Question 17-4. What's wrong with this code?

```
<? if ($_GET[user_id] == 'Admin') echo ('Welcome to the control panel.'); else
echo ('Welcome.'); ?>
```

See the Appendix for the answers to these questions.

Answers to Chapter Questions

Chapter 1

Solution to Question 1-1. A web server, a server-side programming language, and a database.

Solution to Question 1-2. Modules.

Solution to Question 1-3. 5.1.

Solution to Question 1-4. Structured Query Language.

Solution to Question 1-5. They enclose HTML markup.

Solution to Question 1-6. It processes the HTML and PHP files.

Chapter 2

Solution to Question 2-1. Apache, PHP, and MySQL.

Solution to Question 2-2. Mac OS X, and many Linux distributions.

Solution to Question 2-3. The desktop.

Solution to Question 2-4. It indicates lines that are commented out.

Solution to Question 2-5. By not working on your local drive and transferring your files to a server.

Solution to Question 2-6. You can use an FTP program.

Solution to Question 2-7. Through a web server.

Chapter 3

Solution to Question 3-1. Everything renders as text; there is no code.

Solution to Question 3-2. HTML markup.

Solution to Question 3-3. By using two slash (//) marks.

Solution to Question 3-4. Single-line comments, which are indicated by two slash (//) marks, and multiline comments, which are indicated by an asterisk and slash. Use (/*) to open a multiline comment and (*/) to close it.

Solution to Question 3-5. A semicolon (;) ends all statements in PHP.

Solution to Question 3-6. A value.

Solution to Question 3-7. By using the following form: `$variable_name = value;`

Solution to Question 3-8. Yes.

Solution to Question 3-9. They allow you to group code chunks together and execute them by their names.

Solution to Question 3-10. A super global.

Solution to Question 3-11. By using the backslash (\).

Solution to Question 3-12. It compares two strings, including case.

Solution to Question 3-13. Concatenation.

Solution to Question 3-14. A string.

Chapter 4

Solution to Question 4-1. Code that performs a task.

Solution to Question 4-2. An operator.

Solution to Question 4-3. An operator combines simple expressions into more complex expressions. It does so by creating relationships between the simple expressions that can then be evaluated.

Solution to Question 4-4. An operator.

Solution to Question 4-5. An operator that combines two expressions into a more complex single expression.

Solution to Question 4-6. An operator that takes three operands.

Solution to Question 4-7. No—they take only numbers.

Solution to Question 4-8. It's an array, integer, or string.

Solution to Question 4-9. Yes—you'll end up with the wrong operator.

Solution to Question 4-10. It checks whether or not a variable is set.

Solution to Question 4-11. The switch statement is written as follows:

```
switch ($action) {
  case "add":
    $x = $x+y;
    break;
  case "subtract":
    $x = $x-y;
    break;
  case "multiply":
    $x = $x*$y;
    break;
  case "divide":
    $x = $x/$y;
    break;
}
```

Solution to Question 4-12. It tells PHP not to execute cases other than the matching case.

Solution to Question 4-13. The loop is written as follows:

```
<?php
for ($num = 10; $num >= 1; $num--) {
    print "$num<br>";
}
?>
```

Chapter 5

Solution to Question 5-1. This isn't a valid function. It's missing the parentheses and furthermore, it's bad style to mix functions with your main code.

Solution to Question 5-2. To define the toast function with a parameter:

```php
<?php
function toast( $minutes )
{
  //do the toasting here
  echo ("done.");
}
?>
```

Solution to Question 5-3. To call toast with 5 as the minutes parameter:

```php
<?php
toast(5);
?>
```

Solution to Question 5-4. When you are using include() and a file can't be found, only a warning issues. However, when you are using require(), a missing file causes a fatal error that terminates the execution of the script.

Solution to Question 5-5. A method.

Chapter 6

Solution to Question 6-1. The first element is located in position 0 of the array.

Solution to Question 6-2. The $months array can be created as follows:

```php
<?php
$months[]='January';
$months[]='February';
$months[]='March';
$months[]='April';
$months[]='May';
$months[]='June';
$months[]='July';
$months[]='August';
$months[]='September';
$months[]='October';
$months[]='November';
$months[]='December';
?>
```

The array() function is also correct:

```
array('January,'February','March','April','May','June','July','August','September','O
ctober','November','December');
```

Solution to Question 6-3.   To create the array with the days in each month:

```php
<?php
$months= array('January' => 31,
               'February' => 28,
               'March' => 31,
               'April' => 30,
               'May' => 31,
               'June' => 30,
               'July' => 31,
               'August' => 31,
               'September' => 30,
               'October' => 31,
               'November' => 30,
               'December' => 31);
?>
```

Solution to Question 6-4.   To display the $months array:

```php
<?php
$months= array('January' => 31,
               'February' => 28,
               'March' => 31,
               'April' => 30,
               'May' => 31,
               'June' => 30,
               'July' => 31,
               'August' => 31,
               'September' => 30,
               'October' => 31,
               'November' => 30,
               'December' => 31);
echo var_dump($months);
?>
```

Chapter 7

Solution to Question 7-1.   Create the months table as follows:

```
CREATE TABLE months (
    month_id INT NOT NULL AUTO_INCREMENT,
    month VARCHAR (20),
    days INT,
    PRIMARY KEY (month_id));
```

Solution to Question 7-2. To add the months to the new table, specify:

```
INSERT INTO months VALUES (NULL,'January',31);
INSERT INTO months VALUES (NULL,'February',28);
INSERT INTO months VALUES (NULL,'March',31);
INSERT INTO months VALUES (NULL,'April',30);
INSERT INTO months VALUES (NULL,'May',31);
INSERT INTO months VALUES (NULL,'June',30);
INSERT INTO months VALUES (NULL,'July',31);
INSERT INTO months VALUES (NULL,'August',31);
INSERT INTO months VALUES (NULL,'September',30);
INSERT INTO months VALUES (NULL,'October',31);
INSERT INTO months VALUES (NULL,'November',30);
INSERT INTO months VALUES (NULL,'December',31);
```

Solution to Question 7-3. To display the months, use the query SELECT * FROM months;.

Solution to Question 7-4. To display only the months that have 28 days, use the query SELECT * FROM months WHERE days = 28;.

Solution to Question 7-5. To display only the months that end in "ber," use SELECT * FROM months WHERE months LIKE '%ber';.

Chapter 8

Solution to Question 8-1. The mysql command provides an interactive interface to MySQL.

Solution to Question 8-2. To back up a database called "blog" from the command line, execute:

```
mysqldump -u root -p blog > my_backup.sql
```

A password prompt appears before the backup begins.

Solution to Question 8-3. To restore the "blog" backup file from the command line, execute:

```
mysql -u root -p -D test < my_backup.sql
```

A password prompt appears before the restore begins.

Solution to Question 8-4. The advantages for creating an index are:

- Queries with where clauses that match the index columns are much faster.
- Verifying the uniqueness of an index value is much faster.

Some disadvantages are:

- Queries that insert or remove rows from an indexed table take longer for the index to update.
- Additional storage space is required to store the index.

Chapter 9

Solution to Question 9-1. The database connection string is formatted as follows:

mysql://*db_username*:*db_password*@*db_host*/*db_database*:
mysql://joe:my$ql@oreilly.com/survey

Solution to Question 9-2. The database connection requires two steps when you are not using PEAR. First, you must connect to the database. Once you have connected, the survey database is selected.

```php
<?php
//set the connection details
$db_host='localhost';
$db_database='test';
$db_username='test';
$db_password='yourpass';

//call mysql_connect to connect
$connection = mysql_connect($db_host, $db_username, $db_password);
if (!$connection){
die ("Could not connect to the database: <br />". mysql_error());
}

//select the database using mysql_select_db
$db_select = mysql_select_db($db_database);
if (!$db_select){
die ("Could not select the database: <br />". mysql_error());
}
?>
```

Solution to Question 9-3. Add the following to the end of the code from Solution 9-2:

```php
<?php
$query = "SELECT * FROM authors";
$result = mysql_query( $query );
if (!$result)
{
die ("Could not query the database: <br />". mysql_error());
}
while ($result_row = mysql_fetch_row(($result)))
{
        echo 'Author ID: '.$result_row[0] . '<br />';
        echo 'Title ID: '.$result_row[1] . '<br /> ';
        echo 'Author Name: '.$result_row[2] . '<br /><br />';
```

```
    }
    //Close the connection
    mysql_close($connection);
    ?>
```

Solution to Question 9-4. The PEAR functions are more compact, and they automate some of the manual work of connecting to and selecting from the database. Because PEAR code is used by many developers, it is less likely to have an error than to have code that's written from scratch.

Chapter 10

Solution to Question 10-1. The super global variable $_SERVER['PHP_SELF'] always returns the name of the running PHP script. You can rename a script containing the global variable, and your code automatically uses the new script name to process the results.

Solution to Question 10-2. The code to create a username and password form that processes the values is written as follows:

```
    <?php
    echo ('<form action="'.$_SERVER["PHP_SELF"].'" method="GET">');
    echo ('
    <label>Username:<input type="text" name="username" size="10" maxlength="30" /></
    label>
    <br>
    <label>Password:<input type="text" name="password" size="10" maxlength="30" /></
    label>
    <input type="submit" value="Submit">
    </form>');
    ?>
```

Solution to Question 10-3. In order to also display the username and password upon submission, specify:

```
    <?php
    //Get the username and passowrd from the GET global array
    $username = $_GET["username"];
    $password = $_GET["password"];
    //determine if this is after the form's been submitted
    if (!empty($username)){
      //display the values from the submission
      echo ("Username: $username<br>");
      echo ("Password: $password<br>");
    }
    else {
    //display the form
    echo ('<form action="'.$_SERVER["PHP_SELF"].'" method="GET">');
    echo ('
```

```
<label>Username:<input type="text" name="username" size="10" maxlength="30" /></
label>
<br>
<label>Password:<input type="text" name="password" size="10" maxlength="30" /></
label>
<input type="submit" value="Submit">
</form>');
}
?>
```

Solution to Question 10-4. To select only author names starting with an "A", use the following query:

```
SELECT * FROM authors WHERE author LIKE 'A%''
```

Chapter 11

Solution to Question 11-1. The `printf()` function prints to the output of your program, while `sprintf()` sends its output to a variable that you specify as one of its parameters.

Solution to Question 11-2. Check whether or not the date 1/31/2045 is valid as follows:

```
if (checkdate(1,31,2045)) {
   echo('Date is valid.');
 }
 else {
   echo ('Invalid date.');
 }
```

Solution to Question 11-3. To display the day of the week for 1/31/2045, you must first create a timestamp for that date. The 1 in the format string for `date()` indicates that the full day of the week displays.

```
<?php
$timestamp= mktime(1,31,2045);
echo date("l",$timestamp);
?>
```

Solution to Question 11-4. To rename the file *upload.tmp* to *sample.jpg*, specify:

```
<?php
$status=rename('upload.tmp','sample.jpg');
  if ($status) {
    echo ("Renamed file.");
  }
?>
```

Chapter 12

Solution to Question 12-1. To add the published_date column, use the connection and query code that are employed throughout the chapter, but modify the query string to create the new column:

```php
<?php
require_once('db_login.php');
//sets the values for the database connection
require_once('DB.php');
//connect to the database
$connection = DB::connect("mysql://$db_username:$db_password@$db_host/$db_database");
if (DB::isError($connection)){
die ("Could not connect to the database: <br />". DB::errorMessage($connection));
}
//modify the table
$query = "ALTER TABLE books ADD published_date date";
//check for an error
$result = $connection->query($query);
if (DB::isError($result)){
die("Could not query the database: <br />". $query." ".DB::errorMessage($result));
}
echo "Modified successfully!";
$connection->disconnect();
?>
```

Solution to Question 12-2. SQL Injection and Cross Site Scripting attacks. SQL Injection attacks attempt to insert special characters that change the meaning of an SQL query, while Cross Site Scripting attacks attempt to reveal private information from a session by inserting malicious HTML.

Solution to Question 12-3. The get_magic_quotes_gpc() function returns TRUE if magic quotes are enabled.

Solution to Question 12-4. The htmlentities() function escapes any HTML that might otherwise be exploited.

Chapter 13

Solution to Question 13-1. Cookies are stored on the web user's hard drive.

Solution to Question 13-2. The md5() function creates a one-way encoding of the password.

Solution to Question 13-3. To store the value 1 in the user_id session variable, specify:

```php
<?php
    session_start();
    $_SESSION['user_id'] = 1;
?>
```

Solution to Question 13-4. Display the value stored in the user_id session variable as follows:

```php
<?php
    session_start();
    echo $_SESSION['user_id'];
?>
```

Chapter 14

Solution to Question 14-1. The *.php* extension causes the PHP interpreter to process the file instead of displaying its contents. Displaying the contents might reveal useful information for breaching the security of your site, such as passwords or the inner workings of your code.

Solution to Question 14-2. The sh1() function creates a 160-bit key instead of md5()'s 128-bit string. It also uses a superior algorithm for making it difficult to determine the values that generate a particular encoding.

Solution to Question 14-3. If a malicious user knows that you're storing the logged-in user's ID in an automatic global variable, it's easy for him to send in his own value for the user ID as a URL parameter. He can then become any user.

Solution to Question 14-4. Untrustworthy data, or data that a user can easily manipulate before it is submitted to your program, includes:

- Data from the $GET global array
- Data from the $POST global array
- Cookie data
- Session data

Chapter 15

Solution to Question 15-1. JavaScript's pros are users get immediate feedback when entering data into fields about that data's validity, and the form doesn't need to be redisplayed by the PHP code.

One of JavaScript's cons is that the data must still be validated in your PHP code because it's possible for a user to turn off JavaScript in her browser or for a malicious user to directly submit data to your form-processing script. Additionally, the validation doesn't have access to any of the server data—for example, session information or database information.

Solution to Question 15-2. To display the warning "The username field must be at least six characters," execute:

```
alert("The username field must be at least six characters");
```

Solution to Question 15-3. Validate a U.S. zip code that may have the optional "plus four" style as follows:

```
'/^\d{5}(-\d{4})?$/'
```

Remember that the regex expression must be in Perl format, which starts with '/ and ends with /'.

Solution to Question 15-4. To test a variable called $zipcode using the regex from the last question, specify:

```php
<?php
$pattern = '/^\d{5}(-\d{4})?$/';
$matched=preg_match($pattern, $zipcode, $matches);
if ($matched) {
  echo ("Zipcode OK.");
}
?>
```

Chapter 16

Solution to Question 16-1. To change the blog name to "PHP and MySQL Zone," modify the *config.php* as follows:

```php
<?php
  // put full path to Smarty.class.php
  require('/usr/share/php/Smarty/Smarty.class.php');
  $smarty = new Smarty();

  $smarty->template_dir = '/home/www/htmlkb/smarty/templates';
  $smarty->compile_dir = '/home/www/htmlkb/smarty/templates_c';
  $smarty->cache_dir = '/home/www/htmlkb/smarty/cache';
  $smarty->config_dir = '/home/www/htmlkb/smarty/configs';

  $blog_title="PHP and MySQL Zone";
?>
```

Solution to Question 16-2. From the MySQL client, execute the SQL query:

```
insert into categories values (NULL, 'Bugs');
```

You can also add the row using phpMyAdmin. Because the drop-down category list is created dynamically, this is the only change required to add a new category.

Solution to Question 16-3. Templates make it easy to keep your site organized. Changes made to the header and footer automatically apply to all pages. Also, editing the HTML is easier because there isn't any PHP code mixed in with it.

Chapter 17

Solution to Question 17-1. Some PHP interpreters may not be configured to execute PHP code that starts with <?. It can also cause problems with XML parsing.

Solution to Question 17-2. The // comment style comments out the current line only, while /* comments out lines until a matching /* comment is encountered.

Solution to Question 17-3. If you are using include_once() and an include file is accidentally included more than once, a function redefinition error will not occur. This can easily happen when included files contain their own include lines.

Solution to Question 17-4. The code should follow the coding conventions to make it easy to read and portable:

```php
<?php
/*
 * this file welcomes the user.
 * this file welcomes the user and uses proper code styles.
 *
 * Copyright 2006 (c) O'Reilly & Associates
 *
 * @version   $Id: coding_standards_example.html,v 1.2 2006/1/19 24:49:50
 *
 */
//verify the user
if ($_GET[user_id] == 'Admin')
{
  //Welcome the admin user to the control panel.
  echo ('Welcome to the control panel.');
}
else
{
  //Welcome other user.
  echo ('Welcome.');
}
?>
```

Index

We'd like to hear your suggestions for improving our indexes. Send email to *index@oreilly.com*.

building forms, 181–199
  data validation, 192–193
  feet-to-meters conversion, 193–194
  querying database and, 196–198
  text, 185–189
  time zone conversion, 194–196
  values
    accessing, 183–184
    default, 184
    multiple, 189–191

C

calling functions, 79–81
CGI (Common Gateway Interface), 1
character classes, 296
chat forums, resources, 333
checkboxes, 186
class scope, 91
classes, 88
  creating, 88
  inheritance, 92
    extends operator, 92
    parent operator, 93
  instances, 88
    creating, 89
  variables, scope, 91
columns, databases
  adding, 139
  data types, 122–123, 138
  deleting, 139
command line, MySQL prompt, 135
commands
  create table, 124
  insert, 125
  MySQL, 136
  mysqldump, 143–146
  SELECT, 126
  touch, 222
comments, 329
  PHP, 35
compact function, 110
comparing strings, PHP, 46
comparison operators, 63
concatenation
  PHP, 47
  string functions, 150–151
conditional operators, 64
configuration file, blog, 303

connections
  close, PEAR, 179
  databases, 167
    closing, 170
constants, PHP, 48
  predefined, 49
constructors, 89–91
contact information, xii
continue statement, 75
control structures, 332
conventions used in book, xi
cookies, 252–255
  access, 254
  deleting, 255
  destroying, 255
  setting, 253–254
copying, files, databases, 143
create table command, 124
creating files, 222
cross-site scripting attacks, 243
CSS (Cascading Style Sheets), 9

D

data types, database columns, 122–123
data validation, 192–193
database engines, MySQL, 5
database normalization
  First Normal Form, 119
  Second Normal Form, 120
  Third Normal Form, 121
databases
  access
    blocking for external hosts, 286
    preventing, 285
  backups, 143–146
  blog, 306–309
  columns
    adding, 139
    data types, 122–123
    deleting, 139
  connections, 167
    closing, 170
  data
    deleting, 131
    modifying, 130–131
  date and time functions, 155–162
  fields, 113
  files, copying, 143

About the Authors

Michele E. Davis and **Jon A. Phillips** are the Krauts: Krautgrrl and Krautboy, respectively. Phillips has a background in computer science, having started programming in grade school. He's worked with numerous databases, including Oracle, SQL Server, and MySQL. Phillips is always looking for the best technologies, such as PHP, to solve real-world computing problems. He enjoys building computers, troubleshooting, designing custom web solutions for the Kraut clients, and his three rambunctious children. Davis has been a career writer since grade school and has focused on all forms of technology writing: from marcom to hardware or software user manuals. Davis has written (and coauthored) books for ibooks, Sybex, and Wiley & Sons. Her greatest skill is breaking down highly technical concepts into easy-to-digest information bites for her clients and readers. She is the creative edge of Kraut Companies, while Phillips handles the backend coding. Her hobbies are reading, writing, and pretending to be a soccer mom.

Krautgrrl and Krautboy would like to thank the Twin Cities PHP community for all their interesting comments on the listserv.

Colophon

The image on the cover of *Learning PHP and MySQL* is of Kookaburra birds (*Dacelo*). This "laughing" bird is indigenous to the eastern woodland parts of Australia, and it derives its name from its distinctive call. Similar to a loud, howling laugh, it sounds as if the bird is saying "koo koo koo ka ka ka." It typically makes this call at dawn and again in the early evening, to mark its territory. The call is also used as a greeting and can get quite loud if groups of the birds meet each other and begin engaging in "conversations."

A Kookaburra is also easily recognizable by its plumage. It has brown feathers on top and cream-colored feathers on the underside and a large, strong, black beak. There is a brown stripe through the eye area. Its wings are brown, tinged with a light shade of blue, and the tail feathers are black. Males also have a darker shade of blue streaked through their tail feathers. The Kookaburra is about 16–17 inches tall. Its diet varies and includes insects, lizards, snakes, and small birds. If the prey is small enough, the Kookaburra will snap it up quickly and eat it whole; if it's large, it kills the prey by dropping it to the ground from a high point or by beating it against a tree, rock, or the ground. Friendly and comfortable around humans, Kookaburras have been known to steal unattended BBQ or picnic fare, still choosing to beat it against a tree before eating.

Kookaburras are believed to mate for life. An interesting fact is the offspring stay with the family unit for extended periods, helping to raise the next generations of babies by assisting with such things as egg incubation and feeding.

The cover image is from *Cassell's Natural History*. The cover font is Adobe ITC Garamond. The text font is Linotype Birka; the heading font is Adobe Myriad Condensed; and the code font is LucasFont's TheSans Mono Condensed.

Related Titles from O'Reilly

Web Programming

ActionScript 3 Cookbook

ActionScript for Flash MX: The Definitive Guide, *2nd Edition*

Ajax Hacks

Dynamic HTML: The Definitive Reference, *2nd Edition*

Flash Hacks

Essential PHP Security

Google Advertising Tools

Google Hacks, *2nd Edition*

Google Map Hacks

Google Pocket Guide

Google: The Missing Manual, *2nd Edition*

Head First HTML with CSS & XHTML

Head Rush Ajax

HTTP: The Definitive Guide

JavaScript & DHTML Cookbook

JavaScript Pocket Reference, *2nd Edition*

JavaScript: The Definitive Guide, *4th Edition*

Learning PHP 5

Learning PHP and MySQL

PHP Cookbook

PHP Hacks

PHP in a Nutshell

PHP Pocket Reference, *2nd Edition*

PHPUnit Pocket Guide

Programming ColdFusion MX, *2nd Edition*

Programming PHP, *2nd Edition*

Upgrading to PHP 5

Web Database Applications with PHP and MySQL, *2nd Edition*

Web Site Cookbook

Webmaster in a Nutshell, *3rd Edition*

Web Administration

Apache Cookbook

Apache Pocket Reference

Apache: The Definitive Guide, *3rd Edition*

Perl for Web Site Management

Squid: The Definitive Guide

Web Performance Tuning, *2nd Edition*

O'REILLY®

Our books are available at most retail and online bookstores.

To order direct: 1-800-998-9938 • *order@oreilly.com* • *www.oreilly.com*

Online editions of most O'Reilly titles are available by subscription at *safari.oreilly.com*